SCHOLASTIC

100 MATHS ASSESSMENT

NS

YEAR 3

Scottish Primary 4

Minimum specification:
- PC or Mac with a CD-ROM drive and 512 Mb RAM (recommended)
- Windows 98SE or above/Mac OS X.4 or above
- Recommended minimum processor speed: 1 GHz

For all technical support queries, please phone Scholastic
Customer Services on 0845 603 9091.

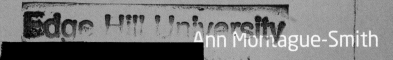
Ann Montague-Smith

CREDITS

Author
Ann Montague-Smith

Series Consultant
Ann Montague-Smith

Development Editor
Kate Baxter

Editor
Helen Kelly

Assistant Editor
Margaret Eaton

Series Designers
Joy Monkhouse, Micky Pledge
and Melissa Leeke

Designer
Melissa Leeke

Illustrations
Garry Davies

CD-ROM development
CD-ROM developed in
association with Vivid
Interactive

Additional material
Transitional tests written by
Lesley Fletcher

Mixed Sources
Product group from well-managed
forests and other controlled sources
www.fsc.org Cert no. TT-COC-002769
© 1996 Forest Stewardship Council
FSC

ACKNOWLEDGEMENTS

Extracts from the the Primary National Strategy's *Primary Framework for Mathematics* (2006) www.standards.dfes.gov.uk/primaryframework and the Interactive Teaching Programs originally developed for the National Numeracy Strategy © Crown copyright. Reproduced under the terms of the Click Use Licence.

Every effort has been made to trace copyright holders for the works reproduced in this book, and the publishers apologise for any inadvertent omissions.

Published by Scholastic Ltd
Villiers House
Clarendon Avenue
Leamington Spa
Warwickshire CV32 5PR

www.scholastic.co.uk

Designed using Adobe InDesign.

Printed by Bell and Bain Ltd, Glasgow

1 2 3 4 5 6 7 8 9   9 0 1 2 3 4 5 6 7 8 9

Text © 2009 Ann Montague-Smith

© 2009 Scholastic Ltd

British Library Cataloguing-in-Publication Data
A catalogue record for this book is available from the British Library.

ISBN 978-1407-10185-9

Contents

100 Maths Assessment Lessons

About the series

100 Maths Assessment Lessons is designed to provide assessment opportunities for all children. Linked to the renewed *Primary Framework for Mathematics*, it also supports the implementation of the new *Assessing Pupil's Progress* (APP) guidelines by linking the new APP assessment focuses to the PNS Framework objectives. Each title in the series also provides single-level tests that can be used at the end of a year, or at any point throughout the year, to provide a summary of where, in relation to national standards, learners are at a given point in time. By using the titles in this series, a teacher or school can be sure that they are covering the mathematics curriculum and obtaining relevant data about their children's achievements.

About assessment

100 Maths Assessment Lessons provides a wide range of opportunities for teachers and children to assess progress. There are three different types of assessment identified by the APP guidelines:

Day to day

Day-to-day assessment is an integral and essential part of effective learning and teaching. Teachers and children continually reflect on how learning is progressing, see where improvements can be made and identify the next steps to take. Strategies that should be part of everyday learning and teaching include:
- sharing and talking about learning objectives, learning outcomes and success criteria with children
- observing and listening to gather intelligence
- planning for group talk, peer assessment and self-assessment to help children develop as independent learners.

Periodic assessment

The purpose of periodic assessment is to give an overview of progress and provide diagnostic information about the progress of individual children, linked to national standards. It is intended to be used at regular (half-termly or termly) intervals to provide an overview of performance based on a wide range of evidence. Periodic assessment should be used to:
- make a periodic review of progress and attainment across a whole task
- identify gaps in experience and inform planning
- help learners know and recognise the standards they are aiming for
- involve both learner and teacher in reviewing and reflecting on evidence.

Transitional assessment

Transitional assessment should be used at points of transition which might be from year to year, school to school or level to level. The pupils' progress data from day-to-day assessment and periodic assessment will support the teacher in making decisions about how pupils are likely to perform in transitional assessments. The key characteristics of transitional assessment are:
- it brings together evidence, including tests, to reach a view of attainment

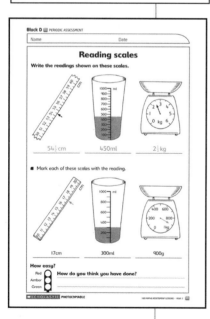

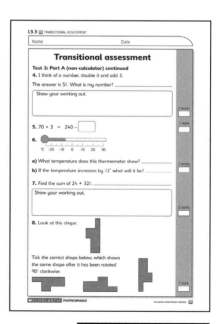

- it is externally validated and externally communicated
- it is set within the framework of national standards.

For a complete list of strategies for day-to-day assessment and further information about periodic and transitional assessment, visit the National Strategies website (**http://nationalstrategies.standards.dcsf.gov.uk**).

About this book

This book is set out in the five blocks that form the renewed *Primary Framework for Mathematics*. Each block consists of three units, with each unit containing:
- an overview of the work covered in the unit, including the objectives, assessment focuses and learning outcomes for each activity (end-of-year objectives are denoted in bold text)
- day-to-day assessment activities based upon the assessment for learning and children's learning outcomes for each objective within a unit (note that the using and applying objectives are either incorporated into other assessments, or assessed on their own, depending upon the content and context of the unit)
- periodic assessment activities based on the end-of-year objectives within each unit.

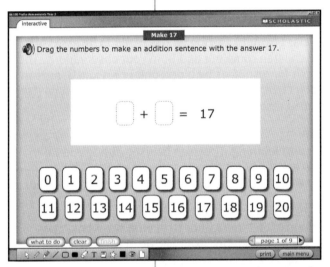

Assessment activities

Each activity contains:
- details of children's expected prior learning before the activity is used
- the relevant objective(s) and vocabulary that children are expected to know
- description of the activity for the teacher or learning support assistant
- group, paired or individual work for the children. Where adult intervention is required, this is explained. Most of the activities include the use of a worksheet or interactive activity from the CD-ROM
- clear differentiation, to support less confident learners in the group or to extend the learning for the more confident learners
- common misconceptions and how to remediate these
- probing questions to ask the children
- next steps: these are differentiated to help teachers decide how to help children who need further support. Suggestions for further work and references to related Framework units or blocks are given to support or extend the children.

What's on the CD-ROM?

Each CD-ROM contains a wealth of resources. These include:
- **worksheets** with answers, where appropriate, that can be toggled by clicking on the 'show' or 'hide' buttons at the bottom of the screen
- **transitional assessments:** year-appropriate single-level tests, oral tests, mark schemes and instructions
- **general resource sheets** (for example, number grids) designed to support a number of lessons
- **interactive activities:** for individuals or small groups, with in-built marking to assess specific objectives
- **Interactive Teaching Programs:** specific ITPs, originally developed for the National Numeracy Strategy
- **whiteboard tools:** a set of tools (including a pen, highlighter and eraser) that can be used to annotate activity sheets for whole-class lessons. These tools will work on any interactive whiteboard
- **display pages:** some activities require a problem or investigation to be shown to the whole class on an interactive whiteboard. The whiteboard tools can also be used with these images to annotate them as necessary
- **editable planning grids** (in Word format) are available to help teachers integrate the lessons into their planning.

How to use the CD-ROM

System requirements
Minimum specification:
- PC or Mac with a CD-ROM drive and 512 Mb RAM (recommended)
- Windows 98SE or above/Mac OS X.4 or above
- Recommended minimum processor speed: 1 GHz

Getting started
The *100 Maths Assessment Lessons* CD-ROM should auto run when inserted into your CD drive. If it does not, browse to your CD drive to view the contents of the CD-ROM and click on the *100 Maths Assessment Lessons* icon.

From the start-up screen you will find four options: select **Credits** to view a list of acknowledgements. Click on **Register** to register the product in order to receive product updates and special offers. Click on **How to use this CD-ROM** to access support notes for using the CD-ROM. Finally, if you agree to the terms and conditions, select **Start** to move to the main menu.

For all technical support queries, contact Scholastic Customer Services help desk on 0845 6039091.

How to use the materials
The materials contained in the book and on the CD-ROM can be used with one child, a group, or in a whole-class activity. Decide who is ready to be assessed from the daily work that the children complete and from your observations. The CD-ROM allows users to search for resources by block, unit or lesson. Users can also search by Framework objective, assessment focus or by resource type (for example, worksheet, interactive resource, display page or ITP).

Day-to-day assessments
These should be used to support learning. They can be used during a lesson, when you judge that children are ready for an assessment activity. The materials can also be used weekly or after a unit of work has been completed.

Periodic assessments
These can be used with a group of children rather than with the whole class. This could be at the end of a unit of work (for example, at the end of a half-term or term). Decide who is ready to be assessed using the outcomes of the day-to-day assessment activities and your observations of children's performance.

Self-assessment
A self-assessment sheet is provided for you and the children to complete. It can be used where there is no activity sheet, so that there is evidence of the children's confidence in what they have learned and how well they can use that learning. There are 'traffic lights' at the bottom of the sheet that children can shade to show their confidence: red for 'need help'; orange for 'having some understanding'; green for 'go!' (ie the child feels confident with his/her learning).

All the activity sheets also have the traffic light system for the children to record their level of confidence, along with a space for them to write about how easy/hard they found the activity.

Transitional tests
These tests provide evidence of where, in relation to national standards, children are at a given point in time. Photocopiable tests (both written and oral), mark schemes and answer sheets are all available on the CD-ROM.

Class PET
A whole-school version of *100 Maths Assessment Lessons* is available with an expanded range of digital assessment activities, as well as the facility to report, record and track pupil's work. For further information visit the Class PET website, **www.scholastic.co.uk/classpet**.

BLOCK A
Counting, partitioning and calculating

Expected prior learning
Check that children can already:
- talk about their methods and solutions to one-step problems, identifying and recording the number sentences involved
- read, write, partition and order two-digit numbers, explaining what each digit represents
- recall all addition and subtraction facts for each number to at least 10, all pairs with totals to 20 and all pairs of multiples of 10 with totals up to 100
- add or subtract mentally pairs of one-digit numbers
- recall multiplication and division facts for the 2-, 5- and 10-times tables.

Objectives overview
The text in this diagram identifies the focus of mathematics learning within the block.

Key aspects of learning
- Social skills
- Problem solving
- Communication
- Reasoning

Solving one- and two-step word problems involving numbers, money or measures

Reading, writing, ordering, partitioning and rounding two- and three-digit numbers

Explaining methods and reasoning, orally and on paper

BLOCK A: Counting, partitioning and calculating

Addition and subtraction

Mental methods: one- and two-digit numbers

Written methods: one- and two-digit numbers

Multiplication and division

Multiplying one- and two-digit numbers by 10 or 100

Informal written methods: multiplying and dividing TU by U; rounding remainders

Unit 1 ▢ Counting, partitioning and calculating

Introduction

In this unit, children demonstrate how they solved a problem and explain the mathematics and methods that they chose. They show how systematic they are in recording their work so that it is clear to both themselves and others how they went about solving the problem. They are encouraged to explain to others the process that they used and to present information in a clearly sequenced way, showing the relevant details. They use numbers to at least 1000, demonstrating their understanding of place value and their knowledge of addition and subtraction to solve problems.

Framework objectives	Assessment focuses		Success criteria for Year 3	Learning outcomes
	Level 3	Level 2		
① Counting ② Number order				
Read, write and order whole numbers to at least 1000 and position them on a number line; count on from and back to zero in single-digit steps or multiples of 10	• understand place value in numbers to 1000, e.g. • represent/compare numbers using number lines, 100-squares, base 10 materials, etc. • recognise sequences	• count sets of objects reliably, e.g. • group objects in tens, twos or fives to count them • begin to understand the place value of each digit; use this to order numbers up to 100, e.g. • know the relative size of numbers to 100 • use 0 as a placeholder • demonstrate knowledge using a range of models/images • recognise sequences of numbers, including odd and even numbers, e.g. • continue a sequence increasing/decreasing in regular steps	• Recognises all numbers to at least 100 • Writes numbers accurately, taking account of place value • Orders numbers and can place them onto a number line • Can count from and to zero in single steps and in multiples of 10	*I can read and write numbers to 1000 and put them in order.*
③ Hundreds, tens and units				
Partition three-digit numbers into multiples of 100, 10 and 1 in different ways	• understand place value in numbers to 1000, e.g. • represent/compare numbers using number lines, 100-squares, base 10 materials, etc. • recognise that some numbers can be represented as different arrays • use understanding of place value to multiply/divide whole numbers by 10 (whole number answers)	• begin to understand the place value of each digit; use this to order numbers up to 100, e.g. • know the relative size of numbers to 100 • use 0 as a placeholder • demonstrate knowledge using a range of models/images	• Can partition three-digit numbers into hundreds, tens and ones • Can do this in different ways	*I can split a number into hundreds, tens and ones.* *I can explain how the digits in a number change when I count in tens or hundreds.*

Unit 1 Counting, partitioning and calculating

Framework objectives	Assessment focuses		Success criteria for Year 3	Learning outcomes
	Level 3	Level 2		
④ Make 17 ⑤ Tens				
Describe and explain methods, choices and solutions to puzzles and problems, orally and in writing, using pictures and diagrams	• begin to organise their work and check results, e.g. • begin to develop own ways of recording • develop an organised approach as they get into recording their work on a problem • discuss their mathematical work and begin to explain their thinking, e.g. • use appropriate mathematical vocabulary • talk about their findings by referring to their written work	• discuss their work using mathematical language, e.g. with support • describe the strategies and methods they use in their work • listen to others' explanations, try to make sense of them, compare… evaluate… • begin to represent their work using symbols and simple diagrams, e.g. with support • use pictures, diagrams and symbols to communicate their thinking, or demonstrate a solution or process • begin to appreciate the need to record and develop their own methods of recording	• Explains orally methods chosen and why these choice were made • Can use writing, pictures and diagrams to record evidence	*I can explain how I solve problems.*
Derive and recall all addition and subtraction facts for each number to 20, sums and differences of multiples of 10 and number pairs that total 100	• add and subtract two-digit numbers mentally, e.g. • calculate 36 + 19, 63 − 26, and complements to 100 such as 100 − 24	• use mental recall of addition and subtraction facts to 10, e.g. • use addition/subtraction facts to 10 and place value to add or subtract multiples of 10, e.g. know 3 + 7 = 10 and use place value to derive 30 + 70 = 100	• Has quick recall of addition and subtraction facts to 20 • Has quick recall of sums and differences of multiples of 10 • Has mental methods for finding pairs that total 100	*I know and use addition and subtraction facts for all numbers to 20. I can add and subtract multiples of 10 in my head.*
⑥ Add and subtract				
Add or subtract mentally combinations of one-digit and two-digit numbers Describe and explain methods, choices and solutions to puzzles and problems, orally and in writing, using pictures and diagrams	• add and subtract two-digit numbers mentally, e.g. • calculate 36 + 19, 63 - 26, and complements to 100 such as 100 - 24	• use mental recall of addition and subtraction facts to 10, e.g. • use addition/subtraction facts to 10 and place value to add or subtract multiples of 10, e.g. know 3 + 7 = 10 and use place value to derive 30 + 70 = 100	• Adds or subtracts mentally combinations of one-digit and two-digit numbers	*I can add and subtract one-digit and two-digit numbers in my head (e.g. 62 + 7, 7 + 45, 48 - 6, 60 - 8).*

BLOCK A

Activities

Prior learning
Children can read, write and order numbers to at least 1000.

Framework objective
Read, write and order whole numbers to at least 1000 and position them on a number line; count on from and back to zero in single-digit steps or multiples of 10

Vocabulary
place value, partition, digit, ones, tens, hundreds, one-digit number, two-digit number, three-digit number, compare, order

Resources
Interactive activity: Bricks
Worksheet: Counting
Resource sheet: Self-assessment
Classroom resources: individual whiteboards and pens

① Counting

Provide the children with the worksheet 'Counting'. Explain that you will give a start number, then ask them to write that number on the sheet in the first space. Ask them to continue counting on seven more numbers and write these on the sheet. Repeat four times. Repeat for counting *back* from five different start numbers. Differentiate by adjusting the size of the start number. Record these start numbers.

Teacher support
Less confident learners: Decide whether to work as a group and whether to use just two-digit start numbers.
More confident learners: If children are confident with numbers to 1000, consider asking them to use start numbers greater than 1000. Ask them to work in pairs, giving each other a start number.

Common misconceptions
Children do not understand place value and write the digits in the wrong order.
Provide further experiences of counting and writing the number patterns.

Probing questions
● What number comes before ___ / after ___?
● How did you work that out?
● Count on/back from ___ for ___ numbers. What was the last number?

Next steps
Support: Continue to ask the children to write a number that they hear, then to count on or back in ones from that number. Begin with two-digit numbers and move on to three-digit numbers as their confidence grows. Refer back to Year 2 Block A Unit 1.
Extension: Provide further examples of counting on or back from larger numbers and writing down the number sequences. Refer to Year 4 Block A Unit 1.

② Number order

Reveal the interactive activity 'Bricks'. Press 'Go' to generate five numbers on bricks between 0 and 1000. Explain that the bricks must be placed in number order. Ask the children to give the number order, then drag/drop the bricks onto the wall in ascending order. If this activity is carried out with the whole class,

SCHOLASTIC

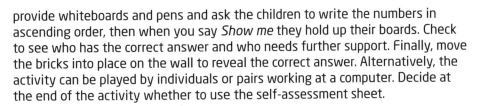

provide whiteboards and pens and ask the children to write the numbers in ascending order, then when you say *Show me* they hold up their boards. Check to see who has the correct answer and who needs further support. Finally, move the bricks into place on the wall to reveal the correct answer. Alternatively, the activity can be played by individuals or pairs working at a computer. Decide at the end of the activity whether to use the self-assessment sheet.

Teacher support
Less confident learners: Work with these children as a group. Ask them to say each number and explain how they know that it is larger/smaller than ___ .
More confident learners: Write some numbers that have the same hundreds or tens, or hundreds and tens digits. Ask children to order these and to explain the ordering.

Common misconceptions
Children do not recognise the place value of individual digits so that they are unsure of how to order the numbers.
Work with two-digit numbers and ask questions such as: *Which is the tens/units digit? How can you tell? Which one is worth more? What does the tens/units digit represent?*

Probing questions
● Tell me what each number represents.
● Which is the tens/hundreds/units/thousands digit in this number?
● Look at this number. Swap over the hundreds and units digits. What is the new number?

Next steps
Support: Repeat the activity, this time using smaller numbers, until the children are confident with those. Refer back to Year 2 Block A Unit 1.
Extension: Provide further examples of numbers to order, extending the size of the numbers. Refer to Year 4 Block A Unit 1.

Activity ③

| **Prior learning** Children can partition three-digit numbers and explain how the digits in a number change when they count in tens or hundreds. | **Framework objective** **Partition three-digit numbers into multiples of 100, 10 and 1 in different ways**

 Vocabulary ones, tens, hundreds, place value, partition, digit, number, one-digit number, two-digit number, three-digit number, compare, order

 Resources **Interactive activity:** Hundreds, tens and units
 Resource sheet: Self-assessment |

③ Hundreds, tens and units

Write three numbers on the board (for example, 5, 3 and 8). Invite the children to make a three-digit number from the cards. For example, for 5, 3, 8 they might make 853. Next, challenge them to make as many numbers as they can from these digits and to arrange them in ascending order of value (358, 385, 538, 583, 835, 853). Now ask the children to write 403 as an addition sentence of hundreds + tens + units (400 + 0 + 3). Ask: *What does the zero mean?* Repeat this for another number. Finally, open the interactive activity 'Hundreds, tens and units' and ask the children to complete the on-screen questions, making six three-digit numbers (in ascending order) using the same digits shown each time on the screen. Decide whether to use the self-assessment sheet for the children to record their achievements and what they need to do next.

Teacher support
Less confident learners: Decide whether to work with these children as a group, using two-digit numbers to begin with. Discuss how the placing of the digit affects its value (for example, 62 is greater than 26).
More confident learners: Challenge the children to repeat the activity, on this occasion using four digits drawn randomly from a set of 0–9 numeral cards.

Common misconceptions
Children do not understand that the value of a number depends upon the placing of the digits.
Provide further examples of making two-digit numbers and discuss the value of each digit. For example, 2 and 5 can make 25 or 52.

Probing questions
● A number is partitioned as 200 + 30 + 5. What is the number? How did you work that out?
● How many different three-digit numbers can you make from the digits 2, 3 and 4? What will the largest number be? How do you know?

Next steps
Support: Provide further practice in making two-digit then three-digit numbers from the digits 0 to 9. Refer back to Year 2 Block A Unit 3.
Extension: Challenge the children to make as many four-digit numbers as they can from 0, 1, 2 and 3. Discuss how the zero can be placed and what it means if placed in the units, tens, hundreds or thousands place. Refer to Year 3 Block A Unit 3.

Activities

Prior learning
Children can add and subtract subtraction facts for all numbers to 20. They can add and subtract multiples of 10 mentally. They can explain how they solve problems.

Framework objectives
● **Derive and recall all addition and subtraction facts for each number to 20, sums and differences of multiples of 10 and number pairs that total 100**
● Describe and explain methods, choices and solutions to puzzles and problems, orally and in writing, using pictures and diagrams

Vocabulary
problem, solution, calculate, answer, method, explain, reasoning, pattern, predict, count on, count back, add, subtract, sum, total, difference, plus, minus

Resources
Interactive activity: Make 17
Worksheet: Make 17
Resource sheet: Self-assessment
Classroom resources: individual whiteboards and pens

④ Make 17

Explain the challenge: find ten different ways to add or subtract two numbers to 20 to give the answer 17 (for example, 9 + 8 = 17). Demonstrate this using the interactive activity 'Make 17'. Provide the children with copies of the worksheet

'Make 17', on which they can record their answers. Decide whether to use the self-assessment sheet for the children to record their achievements and what they need to do next.

Teacher support

Less confident learners: Decide whether to ask the children to just make addition sentences. Encourage them to explain how they found the answers.
More confident learners: Challenge the children to find as many ways as they can to make 17.

Common misconceptions

Children do not use number facts that they already know to derive others. For example, if 1 + 6 = 7 then 11 + 6 = 17 can be derived.
Provide further practice of quick recall of number facts to 10. Then help the children to build patterns of other facts based on these.

Probing questions

● Are there any more number facts which make 17? How do you know if you have them all?
● Now try the same with the answer of 4. What sort of number sentence will produce more answers?
● How did you solve this problem?
● Suppose the problem had the number 16 as the answer. Would that change the way in which you solved the problem?

Next steps

Support: Gradually extend the children's knowledge of number facts for all numbers to 20. Provide experience of recall, especially in starter activities. Refer back to Year 2 Block A Unit 3.
Extension: Challenge the children to use number sentences such as □ + □ − □ = □. Refer to Year 3 Block A Unit 2.

⑤ Tens

Explain that you will say two tens numbers. Ask the children to total them mentally, then to write the answer on their whiteboards. When you say *Show me*, they hold up their whiteboards. Check who has the correct answer and who needs more support. Say, for example: *What is 20 + 30? 90 − 40? 60 + 50?* Decide whether to use the self-assessment sheet for children to record their achievements and what they need to do next.

Teacher support

Less confident learners: Decide whether to just ask addition questions. Discuss how children can use what they know for addition with numbers to 10 in order to find the answer.
More confident learners: Challenge the children to explain how they find the answers.

Common misconceptions

Children do not see a link between addition and subtraction for numbers to 10 and addition and subtraction of multiples of 10.
Discuss how if the children know 3 + 4 they can find 30 + 40, and so on.

Probing questions

● What is 30 + 90? How did you work that out?
● What is 80 − 40? How did you work that out?

Next steps

Support: Link the addition and subtraction of multiples of 10 to addition and subtraction of the digits 1 to 9, so that the children see the pattern. Refer back to Year 2 Block A Unit 3.

BLOCK A

▷
◌

Extension: Challenge the children to write addition and subtraction of hundreds, for example 300 + 900. Ask them to explain their answers. Refer to Year 3 Block A Unit 2.

Activity ⑥

Prior learning
Children can add and subtract one-digit and two-digit numbers mentally. They can explain how they solve problems.

Framework objectives
● **Add or subtract mentally combinations of one-digit and two-digit numbers**
● Describe and explain methods, choices and solutions to puzzles and problems, orally and in writing, using pictures and diagrams

Vocabulary
problem, solution, calculate, calculation, answer, method, explain, reasoning, pattern, predict, count on, count back, add, subtract, sum, total, difference, plus, minus, pound (£), pence (p), note, coin

Resources
Worksheet: Add and subtract (1)

⑥ Add and subtract

Hand out copies of the worksheet 'Add and subtract (1)'. Working in pairs, ask the children to take turns to choose a two-digit number then a one-digit number, add them, write the answer and explain their mental calculation strategies to their partner, who checks the calculation. After five turns each, they repeat the activity, this time choosing the two numbers and finding the difference.

Teacher support
Less confident learners: Decide whether to simplify the two-digit numbers, perhaps choosing numbers between 20 and 30. Listen to the explanations of how the children calculated. Intervene when necessary to suggest more efficient strategies.
More confident learners: Encourage the children to write a sentence to explain the strategy that they chose. Ask them to compare their strategies with others in their group. Discuss with them which strategy is most efficient and why.

Common misconceptions
Children do not cross the tens barrier when adding or subtracting.
Give further experience, such as using an empty number line to model number sentences. Try: 26 + 7; 32 − 8 (and so on).

Probing questions
● Look at this calculation: ☐6 + 8 = ☐☐. Write a digit in each box so that the calculation is correct.
● Are there other ways to do this?
● What patterns do you notice?

Next steps
Support: Provide more experience using smaller two-digit numbers, then extend the number range. Refer back to Year 2 Block A Unit 3.
Extension: Ask the children to complete this calculation: ☐3 − 4 = ☐☐. Challenge them to find as many different solutions as they can and to explain the patterns that they observe. Refer to Year 3 Block A Unit 2.

Unit 2 ◻ Counting, partitioning and calculating

Introduction
In this ten-lesson unit, the children listen carefully to other children's points of view and find helpful ways to respond in whole-class discussions, especially when they have an alternative point of view. They should explain how they solved problems and use number lines, 100-squares and mental methods to solve problems. They partition three-digit numbers; round two- or three-digit numbers to the nearest 10 or 100, learning the rules for such roundings. They extend the range of mental calculation or recall for addition and subtraction and for multiplication and division. They continue to learn multiplication and division table facts.

Framework objectives	Assessment focuses		Success criteria for Year 3	Learning outcomes
	Level 3	Level 2		
(1) Hundreds				
Partition three-digit numbers into multiples of 100, 10 and 1 in different ways	• understand place value in numbers to 1000, e.g. • represent/compare numbers using number lines, 100-squares, base 10 materials, etc. • recognise that some numbers can be represented as different arrays • use understanding of place value to multiply/divide whole numbers by 10 (whole number answers)	• begin to understand the place value of each digit; use this to order numbers up to 100, e.g. • know the relative size of numbers to 100 • use 0 as a placeholder • demonstrate knowledge using a range of models/images	• Can partition three-digit numbers into hundreds, tens and ones • Can do this in different ways	*I can split a number into hundreds, tens and ones.* *I can explain how the digits in a number change when I count in tens or hundreds.*
(2) Rounding and estimating				
Round two-digit or three-digit numbers to the nearest 10 or 100 and give estimates for their sums and differences	• use place value to make approximations	• begin to understand the place value of each digit; use this to order numbers up to 100, e.g. • know the relative size of numbers to 100 • use 0 as a placeholder • demonstrate knowledge using a range of models/images	• Can round two-digit or three-digit numbers to the nearest 10 or 100 • Can give estimates for sums and differences	*I can round numbers to the nearest 10 or 100 and estimate a sum or difference.*

Unit 2 Counting, partitioning and calculating

Framework objectives	Assessment focuses		Success criteria for Year 3	Learning outcomes
	Level 3	Level 2		
(3) What do you know? (4) Sums and differences (5) Make 100				
Derive and recall all addition and subtraction facts for each number to 20, sums and differences of multiples of 10 and number pairs that total 100	• add and subtract two-digit numbers mentally, e.g. • calculate 36 + 19, 63 - 26, and complements to 100 such as 100 - 24	• use mental recall of addition and subtraction facts to 10, e.g. • use addition/subtraction facts to 10 and place value to add or subtract multiples of 10, e.g. know 3 + 7 = 10 and use place value to derive 30 + 70 = 100	• Has quick recall of addition and subtraction facts to 20 • Has quick recall of sums and differences of multiples of 10 • Has mental methods for finding pairs that total 100	*I know the sum and difference of any pair of numbers to 20. I can add or subtract multiples of 10 or 100 in my head. I know number pairs that sum to 100.*
(6) Add or subtract				
Add or subtract mentally combinations of one-digit and two-digit numbers	• add and subtract two-digit numbers mentally, e.g. • calculate 36 + 19, 63 - 26, and complements to 100 such as 100 - 24	• use mental recall of addition and subtraction facts to 10, e.g. • use addition/subtraction facts to 10 and place value to add or subtract multiples of 10, e.g. know 3 + 7 = 10 and use place value to derive 30 + 70 = 100	• Adds and subtracts mentally combinations of one-digit and two-digit numbers	*I can add and subtract one-digit and two-digit numbers in my head (e.g. 62+7, 7+45, 4-6, 60-8).*
(7) Spin 10 or 100				
Multiply one-digit and two-digit numbers by 10 or 100, and describe the effect	• understand place value in numbers to 1000, e.g. • use understanding of place value to multiply/divide whole numbers by 10 (whole number answers)	• recognise sequences of numbers, including odd and even numbers, e.g. • recognise numbers from counting in tens or twos	• Multiplies one-digit and two-digit numbers by 10 • Multiplies one-digit and two-digit numbers by 100 • Explains what happens and understands the place value effect	*I can multiply by 10 or 100 and say what happens to the number I multiply.*
(8) Bingo				
Derive and recall multiplication facts for the 2-, 3-, 4-, 5-, 6- and 10-times tables and the corresponding division facts; recognise multiples of 2, 5 or 10 up to 1000	• derive associated division facts from known multiplication facts	• understand halving as a way of 'undoing' doubling and vice versa	• Knows the 2-, 5- and 10-times tables • Is beginning to know the 3-, 4- and 6-times tables	*I know my tables for 2, 3, 4, 5, 6 and 10.*

Activity ①

Prior learning
Children can split a number into hundreds, tens and ones and explain how the digits in a number change when counting in tens or hundreds.

Framework objective
Partition three-digit numbers into multiples of 100, 10 and 1 in different ways

Vocabulary
problem, solution, calculate, calculation, answer, method, explain, reasoning, pattern, predict, place value, partition, digit, ones, tens, hundreds, one-digit number, two-digit number, three-digit number, compare, order, equals (=), count on, count back

Resources
Interactive activity: Hundreds
Worksheet: Hundreds
Resource sheet: Self-assessment

① Hundreds

Reveal the interactive activity 'Hundreds' and ask the children to think about the pattern if they count back in tens from 98. *Which is the smallest number that you will reach? Will 65 be in your pattern? Why not?* Point to the pattern on the screen as the children say the counting-back sequence and pull out the numbers from the number square as they are identified. Now provide each child with the worksheet 'Hundreds'. Ask them to work with a partner to complete this, saying the counting patterns together as they answer the questions. Decide whether to use the self-assessment sheet for children to record their achievements and what they need to do next.

Teacher support
Less confident learners: Decide whether to work with this group, counting forwards and backwards in tens within 100. Extend to counting beyond 100 in tens, then in hundreds.
More confident learners: Ask the children to explain the changes in digits as they count forwards and backwards.

Common misconceptions
Children do not understand how to cross the tens or hundreds barrier.
Provide more practice in counting in tens where they cross the hundreds barrier.

Probing questions
● Start at 64. Count back in tens. What is the smallest number that you would reach on the 100-square?
● What do you look for when finding a number a hundred less/hundred more than a number?
● Why do the units and tens not change?
● Which digits change when you count in tens?

Next steps
Support: Provide further experience of counting in tens and hundreds. Encourage the children to explain what happens when you cross the tens or hundreds barrier. Refer back to Year 3 Block A Unit 1.
Extension: Where children are confident, ask them to make up more counting patterns for a partner, such as: *Start on 457. Count on for three hundreds; back for six hundreds; on for three tens. What number are you on now?* (187) Refer to Year 3 Block A Unit 3.

Activity ②

Prior learning
Children can round numbers to the nearest 10 or 100 and estimate a sum or difference.

Framework objective
Round two-digit or three-digit numbers to the nearest 10 or 100 and give estimates for their sums and differences

Vocabulary
problem, solution, calculate, calculation, answer, method, explain, reasoning, pattern, predict, estimate, round up, round down, place value, partition, digit, ones, tens, hundreds, one-digit number, two-digit number, three-digit number, compare, order, equals (=), count on, count back, add, subtract, total, difference, plus, minus

Resources
Worksheet: Rounding and estimating

② Rounding and estimating

Provide the worksheet 'Rounding and estimating'. Ask the children to work individually to complete the activity.

Teacher support
Less confident learners: Decide whether to work as a group to find the answers. Discuss how the children found the answers, especially whether a specific number will round up or down and why.
More confident learners: Invite the children to explain why specific numbers rounded up or down.

Common misconceptions
Children may round a number such as 84 up to 90 because it is a larger two-digit number.
Remind children of the rounding rules. For rounding to the nearest 10: 1 to 4 round down; 5 to 9 round up. For rounding to the nearest 100: 1 to 49 round down; 50 to 99 round up. Discuss which are the significant digits in the numbers that are to be rounded.

Probing questions
● Choose two of your rounded numbers. What do you estimate would be their total?
● How did you work that out?
● Now find the difference between them. How did you do that?

Next steps
Support: Provide further experience of rounding to the nearest 10 before rounding to the nearest 100. Refer back to Year 2 Block A Unit 3.
Extension: Challenge the children to write their own estimation word problems, similar to the last question on the worksheet. Refer to Year 3 Block A Unit 3.

Activities

Prior learning
Children know the sum and difference of any pair of numbers to 20. They can add and subtract multiples of 10 or 100 mentally and know number pairs that sum to 100.

Framework objectives
● **Derive and recall all addition and subtraction facts for each number to 20, sums and differences of multiples of 10 and number pairs that total 100**
● Describe and explain methods, choices and solutions to puzzles and problems, orally and in writing, using pictures and diagrams

Vocabulary
problem, solution, calculate, calculation, answer, method, explain, reasoning, pattern, predict, place value, partition, digit, ones, tens, hundreds, one-digit number, two-digit number, three-digit number, compare, order, equals (=), count on, count back, add, subtract, sum, total, difference, plus, minus

Resources
Worksheet: Make 100
Resource sheets: Self-assessment, 0–20 numeral cards (two sets for each pair of children), 100-square
Classroom resources: five small cubes (per pair of children), individual whiteboards and pens

③ What do you know?

Provide each pair of children with two sets of 0–20 numeral cards and five small cubes. Ask them to shuffle the cards together, then take turns to draw two cards. Their partner says the addition and the subtraction sentences, including the answer. If their partner agrees with their response, they take a cube. They repeat this until one of them has three cubes. The game can be extended by the winner requiring more than three cubes to end the game. Decide whether to use the self-assessment sheet for the children to record their achievements and what they need to do next.

Teacher support
Less confident learners: Decide whether to simplify the activity by concentrating on addition sentences only.
More confident learners: Encourage the children to work quickly to encourage rapid recall of the facts.

Common misconceptions
Children do not make use of the facts that they already know to help them to build the new ones, such as if 1 + 3 = 4; then 11 + 3 = 14.
Work with the children to make lists of number facts, in order, so that they can make the connections. Start with the pair 0 + 1 = 1 and 10 + 1 = 11, and so on.

Probing questions
● Two numbers add up to 20. They have a difference of 2. What are the numbers? (9 and 11.)
● The difference of two numbers is 3. Their total is 13. What are the numbers? (8 and 5.)

Next steps
Support: Give opportunities for children to recall these number facts, such as during a starter activity. Concentrate on addition, then subtraction, and then ask mixed addition and subtraction questions. Refer back to Year 3 Block A Unit 1.
Extension: Provide opportunities for the children to work against the clock. They can repeat the activity and check how many correct answers they can give in, say, five minutes. Refer to Year 3 Block B Unit 3.

④ Sums and differences

Ask the children to have their whiteboards and pens ready. Explain that you will say an addition or subtraction using multiples of 10. Ask them to write the answer on their whiteboards. When you say *Show me,* they must hold up their whiteboards. Keep the pace sharp so that children show whether or not they can derive or recall these facts with ease. Ask, for example: *What is 30 + 50? 90 − 40? 30 + 30?* Observe who answers with ease and who needs further support. Decide whether to use the self-assessment sheet. Repeat the activity for multiples of 100. Ask: *What is 500 + 400? 900 − 300?*

Teacher support

Less confident learners: Decide whether to have these children work as a group. Concentrate on addition first, then subtraction, then a combination of these. Remind the children of the link between 6 + 3, 60 + 30 and 600 + 300.
More confident learners: Decide whether to offer another opportunity to demonstrate rapid recall of these facts. Work orally and more quickly than previously so that children have very little thinking time.

Common misconceptions

Children do not make the link between addition and subtraction of units and addition and subtraction of multiples of 10 and multiples of 100.
Draw up a table like this with the children:

Adding units	Adding tens	Adding hundreds
1 + 1 = 2	10 + 10 = 20	100 + 100 = 200
1 + 2 = 3	10 + 20 = 30	100 + 200 = 300

Continue the table, then repeat for subtraction facts. Remind the children that they can use what they know in order to derive new facts.

Probing questions

● What is 9 − 6? 90 − 60? 900 − 600? How do you know this?
● Can you explain how knowing addition and subtraction facts for adding units helps you with adding multiples of 10 and multiples of100?

Next steps

Support: Continue to give opportunities for children to practise recall of these facts, such as in oral starters, until they have developed rapid recall. Refer back to Year 3 Block B Unit 1.
Extension: Ask the children to write word problems for each other that utilise these facts, such as: *There are 60 children in Year 3 and 20 children in Year 4. How many children are there altogether?* Refer to Year 3 Block B Unit 3.

⑤ Make 100

Provide the children with the worksheet 'Make 100'. The children choose pairs of numbers from the grid to make totals of 100. Then they answer some word problems based on these facts.

Teacher support

Less confident learners: Work with the children. Provide the resource sheet '100-square' so that they can count on to find the solutions if necessary.
More confident learners: Ask the children to explain to their partner how they found the answers in the grid and solved the problems.

Common misconceptions

Children fail to use what they know to derive totals for 100.
With the children's help, list some useful strategies, such as: looking at the unit

■SCHOLASTIC

digit and asking themselves what digit is needed to total 10 (for example, 36 needs a two-digit number with a 4 in the units position); if the number they are looking at is odd then they need to find the odd number that will total with theirs to 100; if their number is even, then it needs an even partner number.

Probing questions
- I spend 54p. What change will I get from £1? How did you work that out?
- How did you solve the grid numbers problem?
- What clues can you use to help you to find number partners to total 100?

Next steps
Support: Provide further opportunities for children to find partner numbers that total 100. Using a 100-square to begin with can help them to spot patterns. Refer back to Year 3 Block B Unit 1.
Extension: Ask the children to work in pairs to invent word problems for each other using number pairs that total 100. They can share these in the plenary session for other children to solve. Discuss how the problems were solved. Refer to Year 3 Block B Unit 3.

Activity ⑥

Prior learning Children can add or subtract one-digit and two-digit numbers mentally. They can explain how they solved problems.	**Framework objectives** • **Add or subtract mentally combinations of one-digit and two-digit numbers** • Describe and explain methods, choices and solutions to puzzles and problems, orally and in writing, using pictures and diagrams **Vocabulary** problem, solution, calculate, calculation, answer, method, explain, reasoning, pattern, predict, place value, partition, digit, ones, tens, hundreds, one-digit number, two-digit number, three-digit number, compare, order, equals (=), count on, count back, add, subtract, sum, total, difference, plus, minus **Resources** **Interactive activity:** Add or subtract **Resource sheet:** Self-assessment **Classroom resources:** individual whiteboards and pens

⑥ Add or subtract

Reveal the interactive activity 'Add or subtract'. Explain that you would like the children to help you to complete the first problem: 3 ☐ + ☐ = 41. Ask them to work mentally to find the answer. *How did you work that out? Did anyone use a different method?* Discuss the children's methods for finding solutions. Demonstrate the solution to the problem by dragging and dropping the correct numbers into the blank spaces to show 36 + 5 = 41. Now ask the children to follow the same procedure to complete the remaining on-screen questions (these involve either addition or subtraction). Invite feedback on how they solved the problems. Decide whether to use the self-assessment sheet.

Teacher support
Less confident learners: Have these children work as a group and provide the two-digit and one-digit numbers for the left-hand side of the equation. Ask the children to explain how they solved the problems.
More confident learners: Ask these children to be ready to explain their solutions to the rest of the class.

BLOCK A

Common misconceptions
Children do not use their knowledge of addition and subtraction to 10, then 20, to help them to find solutions.
Discuss how problems could be solved. For example, with 64 + 9, discuss what will happen to the 4 units when 9 is added to them.

Probing questions
- What is 46 + 8? Explain how you did it.
- How would you add 18 to 46?
- What is 73 − 7? Explain how you did it.
- How would you subtract 17 from 73?
- Think of two numbers that have a difference of 9. Write a number sentence to show this. Now find and record some more pairs of numbers with a difference of 9.
- What is 58 + 30? What is 58 + 29? How do you know? What is 58 − 30? What is 58 − 29? How did you work these out? Show me on an empty number line.

Next steps
Support: Give simpler examples at first, so that children add single digits to two-digit numbers up to 30. Then include subtraction. At all times discuss the mental method that the children could use. Use an empty number line to demonstrate, and encourage the children to use this when calculating. Refer back to Year 3 Block D Unit 1.
Extension: Ask the children to invent some number problems involving addition or subtraction of two-digit and one-digit numbers. These can be used during the plenary session for other children to solve. Ask about the mental methods that children used to solve the problems and discuss whether there are more efficient methods. Refer to Year 3 Block D Unit 2.

Activity ⑦

Prior learning
Children can multiply by 10 or 100 and say what happens to the number they multiply. They can explain how they solved problems.

Framework objectives
- Multiply one-digit and two-digit numbers by 10 or 100, and describe the effect
- Describe and explain methods, choices and solutions to puzzles and problems, orally and in writing, using pictures and diagrams

Vocabulary
problem, solution, calculate, calculation, answer, method, explain, reasoning, pattern, predict, place value, partition, digit, ones, tens, hundreds, one-digit number, two-digit number, three-digit number, multiply, times

Resources
Worksheet: Spin 10 or 100
Resource sheet: Spin 10 or 100 grid
Classroom resources: counters

⑦ Spin 10 or 100

Provide the worksheet 'Spin 10 or 100' with the accompanying resource sheet 'Spin 10 or 100 grid'. Ask the children to work in pairs. Explain that they must take turns to choose a number from the 'Spin 10 or 100 grid' by dropping a counter onto it and then dropping another counter onto the spinner below the grid. They multiply their two results and write a number sentence to show what they have done. Ask them to explain to their partner what has happened to the number that they multiplied by 10 or 100.

SCHOLASTIC

Unit 2 📖 Counting, partitioning and calculating

Teacher support

Less confident learners: Decide whether to limit this to ×10 to begin with and listen to the children's explanations of what has happened to the number that is multiplied by 10.

More confident learners: Listen to the children's explanations of what happens when a number is multiplied by 10 or 100. Ask them to write their explanations as sentences.

Common misconceptions

Children do not understand that the place value of the digits is changed by multiplying by 10 or 100.

Write a number sentence on the board, such as 5 × 10 = 50. Ask: *What digit is in the tens column in the answer? What is in the units column? So what happens to the number when we multiply by 10?*

Probing questions

- Multiply 7 by 10. What has happened to the value of the digit 7?
- Now multiply 8 by 10. And multiply the answer by 10. What happens to the 8 when we multiply it by 100?
- What number is 10 times larger than 90?
- What is 10 times larger than 34?

Next steps

Support: Provide further experience of multiplying by 10 using one-digit numbers, then two-digit numbers. When children are confident with that, move on to multiplying by 100. Ask the children to explain what happens to their start number each time. Refer back to Year 2 Block E Unit 2.

Extension: Refer to Year 3 Block E Unit 2.

Activity ⑧

Prior learning
Children know their 2-, 3-, 4-, 5-, 6- and 10-times tables.

Framework objective
Derive and recall multiplication facts for the 2-, 3-, 4-, 5-, 6- and 10-times tables and the corresponding division facts; recognise multiples of 2, 5 or 10 up to 1000

Vocabulary
multiply, times, equals

Resources
Interactive activity: Bingo multiplication
Resource sheets: Bingo cards, Self-assessment
Classroom resources: counters

⑧ Bingo

On blank bingo cards taken from the 'Bingo cards' resource sheet, write a range of numbers that appear in the 2-, 3-, 4-, 5-, 6- and 10-times tables. Provide each child with one bingo card, then reveal the interactive activity 'Bingo multiplication'. Explain that the children must read the multiplication table number sentence displayed on the screen, work out the answer, and if they have that answer on their bingo card they cover it with a counter. When someone has covered all the answers on their card they call *Bingo!* and then the answers can be checked. Decide whether to use the self-assessment sheet for the children to record their achievements and what they need to do next.

SCHOLASTIC

Unit 2 ▢ Counting, partitioning and calculating

▶ **Teacher support**

Less confident learners: Work with these children as a group. Ask them to say the multiplication sentence and its answer each time.

More confident learners: Use a timer so that the pace is quicker. This will challenge the children to recall the table facts quickly.

Common misconceptions

Children do not know their table facts.

Provide more experience of building tables, then of chanting the facts. Provide activities that utilise the table facts so that children can build up their ability to recall them. Concentrate on one table at a time.

Probing questions

● How can you work out the 4-times table from the 2-times table?
● How can you work out the 6-times table from the 3-times table?

Next steps

Support: Encourage the children to become confident in one set of table facts at a time. Keep those that have been learned fresh in children's minds by providing experience of recalling facts through oral starters. Refer back to Year 3 Block E Unit 1.

Extension: Ask the children to work out the 7- and 8-times table facts from those that they already know. Challenge them to explain how this can be done. Refer to Year 3 Block E Unit 2.

Unit 3 ▢ Counting, partitioning and calculating

Introduction
In this ten-lesson unit children solve problems for addition, subtraction, multiplication and division. They work in groups, pairs and individually. Where they work in groups or pairs, the children are encouraged to listen to the others and to give positive comments about their work. This will help them to develop ways of responding without hurting others' feelings, even when they disagree. They round numbers to the nearest 10 or 100, add and subtract mentally and develop written methods for addition and subtraction. Children begin to recognise and use vertical methods for computation. They continue to develop their rapid recall of multiplication table facts and to derive division ones. They find remainders after division and decide whether to round up or down. They continue to develop their written methods for multiplication and division.

Framework objectives	Assessment focuses		Success criteria for Year 3	Learning outcomes
	Level 3	Level 2		
① Round up or down				
Round two-digit or three-digit numbers to the nearest 10 or 100 and give estimates for their sums and differences	• use place value to make approximations	There is no assessment focus for this level.	• Rounds two-digit numbers to the nearest 10 • Rounds three-digit numbers to the nearest 10 or 100 • Gives estimates for sums and differences, using rounding	*I can use rounding to estimate a sum or difference.*
② Adding one-digit numbers ③ Add and subtract ⑦ Rounding				
Solve one-step and two-step problems involving numbers, money or measures, including time, choosing and carrying out appropriate calculations	• select the mathematics they use in a wider range of classroom activities, e.g. • use classroom discussions to break into a problem, recognising similarities to previous work • put the problem into their own words • use mathematical content from Levels 2 and 3 • choose their own equipment appropriate to the task, including calculators • use mental recall of addition and subtraction facts to 20 in solving problems involving larger numbers, e.g. • choose to calculate mentally, on paper or with apparatus • solve one-step whole number problems appropriately • solve two-step problems that involve addition and subtraction	• select the mathematics they use in some classroom activities • choose the appropriate operation when solving addition and subtraction problems, e.g. • use repeated addition to solve multiplication problems • begin to use repeated subtraction or sharing equally to solve division problems • solve number problems involving money and measures, e.g. • add/subtract two-digit and one-digit numbers, bridging tens where necessary in contexts using units such as pence, pounds, centimetres	• Recognises which mathematics to use • Uses mental methods where appropriate • Uses paper and pencil and/or resources for larger number calculations • Identifies the steps to take to solve the problem • Checks answer using a different calculation	*I can solve a problem by writing down what calculation I should do.*

Unit 3 ⬜ Counting, partitioning and calculating

Framework objectives	Assessment focuses		Success criteria for Year 3	Learning outcomes
	Level 3	Level 2		
② Adding one-digit numbers ③ Add or subtract				
Add or subtract mentally combinations of one-digit and two-digit numbers	• add and subtract two-digit numbers mentally, e.g. • calculate 36 + 19, 63 - 26, and complements to 100 such as 100 - 24	• use mental recall of addition and subtraction facts to 10, e.g. • use addition/subtraction facts to 10 and place value to add or subtract multiples of 10, e.g. know 3 + 7 = 10 and use place value to derive 30 + 70 = 100	• Adds and subtracts mentally combinations of one-digit and two-digit numbers	*I can find the sum of or difference between one-digit and two-digit numbers in my head (e.g. 7 + 45, 45 - 7).* *I can add several one-digit numbers in my head.*
④ Number line - add and subtract ⑤ Partitioning				
Develop and use written methods to record, support or explain addition and subtraction of two-digit and three-digit numbers	• add and subtract three-digit numbers using a written method, e.g. • use written methods that involve bridging 10 or 100 • add and subtract decimals in the context of money, where bridging is not required	• record their work in writing, e.g. • record their mental calculations as number sentences	• Uses a written method for addition and subtraction of two-digit and three-digit numbers • Uses the written method to explain how the problem was solved	*I can add and subtract numbers using an empty number line.* *I can add and subtract numbers by writing one number under the other and using partitioning.*
⑥ Division function machine				
Derive and recall multiplication facts for the 2-, 3-, 4-, 5-, 6- and 10-times tables and the corresponding division facts; recognise multiples of 2, 5 or 10 up to 1000	• recognise a wider range of sequences, e.g. • recognise sequences of multiples of 2, 5 and 10 • derive associated division facts from known multiplication facts, e.g. • given a number sentence, use understanding of operations to create related sentences • use mental recall of the 2, 3, 4, 5 and 10 multiplication tables • multiply and divide two-digit numbers by 2, 3, 4 or 5 as well as 10 with whole number answers and remainders	• recognise sequences of numbers, including odd and even numbers, e.g. • recognise numbers from counting in tens or twos • use mental calculation strategies to solve number problems including those involving money and measures, e.g. • recall doubles to 10 + 10 and other significant doubles, e.g. double 50p is 100p or £1 • use knowledge of doubles to 10 + 10 to derive corresponding halves	• Knows the 2-, 5- and 10-times tables • Is beginning to know the 3-, 4- and 6-times tables	*I can use my tables for 2, 3, 4, 5, 6 and 10 to work out division facts.*
⑦ Rounding				
Use practical and informal written methods to multiply and divide two-digit numbers (e.g. 13 × 3, 50 ÷ 4); round remainders up or down, depending on the context	• solve whole number problems including those involving multiplication or division that may give rise to remainders, e.g. • identify appropriate operations to use • round up or down after simple division, depending on context	• choose the appropriate operation when solving addition and subtraction problems, e.g. • use repeated addition to solve multiplication problems • begin to use repeated subtraction or sharing equally to solve division problems	• Uses a practical and informal method to multiply and divide two-digit numbers • Can round remainders up or down • Uses the context to decide on how to round	*I can use the tables facts that I know to work out division facts.* *I can multiply or divide a two-digit number by a one-digit number.* *If there is a remainder when I divide, I can work out whether to round the answer up or down.*

Activity ①

Prior learning
Children can use rounding to estimate a sum or difference.

Framework objective
Round two-digit or three-digit numbers to the nearest 10 or 100 and give estimates for their sums and differences

Vocabulary
round, rounding, guess, how many, estimate, nearly, roughly, close to, approximate, approximately, about the same as, just over, just under, exact, exactly, problem, solution, calculate, calculation, answer, method, explain, reasoning, pattern, predict, place value, partition, digit, ones, tens, hundreds, one-digit number, two-digit number, three-digit number, compare, order, equals (=), count on, count back, add, subtract, sum, total, difference, plus, minus

Resources
Worksheet: Round up or down
Resource sheet: 0-9 numeral cards (three sets per pair)

① Round up or down

Ask the children to work in pairs with the worksheet 'Round up or down'. They must take turns to pick three 0-9 numeral cards and make a HTU number. Their partner then rounds the number up or down to the nearest 10, depending upon the rounding rule (1-4 round down, 5-9 round up). When they have a pair of rounded numbers, they must add the rounded numbers then find the difference between them, recording each calculation in the table on the worksheet.

Teacher support
Less confident learners: Decide whether to limit the number range to TU, choosing just two cards each time.
More confident learners: Ask the children to calculate the 'real' answer to the addition and difference for the two original numbers and to compare this with their rounded answers.

Common misconceptions
Children round all numbers up.
Remind the children of the rule: 0-4 round down, 5-9 round up. Provide some simple examples such as 72, 68 and 85 to round up or down.

Probing questions
● Look at your first answer. How close to the real answer do you think this is? How do you know that?
● Is your answer a bit too much or just less than the real answer?
● Round 345 and 543. Add, then subtract, the rounded numbers. Is the answer a bit too much or just less than the real answer?

Next steps
Support: Continue with examples using two-digit numbers until the children are confident with this. Refer back to Year 3 Block A Unit 2.
Extension: Challenge the children to repeat the activity, this time adding three numbers and estimating how close to the 'real' answer their estimate is. Refer to Year 4 Block A Unit 1.

BLOCK A

Activities

Prior learning
Children can find the sum of or difference between one-digit and two-digit numbers and add several one-digit numbers, using mental calculations. They can solve a problem by writing down the calculation.

Framework objectives
● **Add or subtract mentally combinations of one-digit and two-digit numbers**
● Solve one-step and two-step problems involving numbers, money or measures, including time, choosing and carrying out appropriate calculations

Vocabulary
problem, solution, calculate, answer, method, explain, reasoning, pattern, equals, count on, count back, add, subtract, sum, total, difference, plus, minus

Resources
Display page: Adding one-digit numbers
Worksheet: Add and subtract (2)
Resource sheets: Empty number lines, Self-assessment

② Adding one-digit numbers

Reveal the first screen of the display page 'Adding one-digit numbers'. Ask the children to choose three of the numbers and to total them. Discuss the methods that they chose. Use the pen and highlighter tools in the teacher's toolbox to highlight different combinations of numbers. Now reveal the second screen. Ask the children to write number sentences to show how they solved the problem. Decide whether to use the self-assessment sheet for the children to record their achievements and what they need to do next.

Teacher support
Less confident learners: Decide whether to limit this activity to totalling just two of the numbers until the children demonstrate confidence. Then extend it to totalling three numbers each time.
More confident learners: When the children have demonstrated that they are confident with this, ask them to work mentally to total four or five of the numbers.

Common misconceptions
Children are unsure of how to cross the tens barrier.
Provide examples with just two one-digit numbers, such as 9 + 8; 7 + 6. Ask: *How did you work that out?* Discuss their method and, if necessary, introduce a more efficient one. Then extend to totalling three one-digit numbers.

Probing questions
● Do this calculation in your head: 9 + 5 + 4. How did you work that out?
● Write down another calculation that you could work out in this way.

Next steps
Support: Check that the children are confident with totalling two one-digit numbers. Then extend to totalling three. Refer back to Year 3 Block D Unit 2.
Extension: Check that the children are confident with totalling three or more one-digit numbers. Refer to Year 4 Block A Unit 1.

③ Add and subtract

Provide the resource sheet 'Empty number lines'. Explain that you would like the children to calculate the answers to addition and subtractions of two two-digit numbers. Explain that they can use the empty number lines if this would help them with their calculations. Give out the worksheet 'Add and subtract (2)' for the children to work through.

Teacher support
Less confident learners: Decide whether to limit this to addition and subtraction of a two-digit and a one-digit number.
More confident learners: Challenge the children to complete the task mentally, without using empty number lines.

Common misconceptions
Children do not use appropriate calculation strategies.
Read the problem together. Ask: *Which words tell you what sort of problem this is?* Using an empty number line, explore ways of finding the answer, such as counting on to the higher number or dealing with the tens digits first.

Probing questions
- Tell me how to start to solve this problem.
- Show me how to solve this problem using an empty number line.
- How could you check that your answer is correct?
- Write down another calculation that you could work out quickly in this way.

Next steps
Support: Provide further experience of adding and subtracting two-digit numbers. Refer back to Year 3 Block D Unit 2.
Extension: Challenge the children to invent their own problems for others to solve. Refer to Year 4 Block A Unit 1.

Activities

Prior learning
Children can add and subtract numbers using an empty number line. They can add and subtract numbers by writing one number under the other and using partitioning.

Framework objective
Develop and use written methods to record, support or explain addition and subtraction of two-digit and three-digit numbers

Vocabulary
problem, solution, calculate, calculation, answer, method, explain, reasoning, pattern, predict, place value, partition, digit, ones, tens, hundreds, one-digit number, two-digit number, three-digit number, compare, order, equals (=), count on, count back, add, subtract, sum, total, difference, plus, minus

Resources
Display page: Number line – add and subtract
Worksheet: Partitioning (1)
Resource sheets: Empty number lines, Self-assessment

④ Number line – add and subtract

Provide the resource sheet 'Empty number lines'. Reveal the display page 'Number line – add and subtract'. Give the children a couple of minutes to complete the example on the first screen. Ask: *How did you work that out?* Using the pen and arrow tools from the teacher's toolbox, write in the suggestions on the on-screen number line. Repeat for the further examples on the following screens. Decide whether to use the self-assessment sheet for the children to record their achievements and what they need to do next.

Teacher support
Less confident learners: Decide whether to continue with the addition and

Unit 3 ☐ Counting, partitioning and calculating

difference of a two-digit and one-digit number.
More confident learners: Provide further examples where the addition of two two-digit numbers crosses the hundreds barrier.

Common misconceptions
Children do not use appropriate calculation strategies.
Work together to solve the problems. Discuss, and demonstrate using a number line, how counting up can be very helpful for both addition and subtraction problems.

Probing questions
● Show me how you use counting up on an empty number line to work out 236 + 75 and 236 – 75.
● Which number did you start with?
● What are the important landmark numbers to use? (Multiples of 10 or 100.)

Next steps
Support: Provide simple examples of adding and subtracting two two-digit numbers where crossing the tens or hundreds barrier is not required. Extend to those that do cross the tens or hundreds barrier. Refer back to Year 2 Block A Unit 3.
Extension: Provide problems that include three-digit numbers. Refer to Year 3 Block E Unit 3.

⑤ Partitioning

Ask the children to work in pairs. They must choose two numbers from the grid on the 'Partitioning (1)' worksheet. They must show their workings for how they partitioned to add the numbers and then write the answer. They repeat this for finding the difference between the two numbers and then do one more example of each.

Teacher support
Less confident learners: Decide whether to limit this to addition and subtraction of low-value two-digit numbers.
More confident learners: Check that the children are confident with the task and can explain how they calculated and recorded.

Common misconceptions
Children do not use appropriate calculation strategies.
Work together to solve the problems. Discuss how partitioning allows the children to deal with each part of the numbers individually so they can be re-combined to find the answer.

Probing questions
● Here are two numbers to add: 654 and 148. Partition 148. What is the answer when you add 8 units to 654? Now add the 40. Now add the 100. How will you record this? What is the answer? Show me this method for two other numbers.
● Here are two numbers, 514 and 136. Partition 136. What is the answer when you subtract the 6 units from 514? How will you record this? Now subtract the 30. Now subtract the 100. What is the difference? Can you use this method to subtract 263 from 514?

Next steps
Support: Continue with smaller two two-digit numbers until the children are confident with the method. Extend to higher value two-digit numbers. Refer back to Year 2 Block A Unit 3.
Extension: Provide two three-digit numbers and ask the children to find the total and difference. Refer to Year 3 Block E Unit 3.

Activity ⑥

Prior learning
Children can use table facts for 2-, 3-, 4-, 5-, 6- and 10-times tables to work out division facts.

Framework objective
Derive and recall multiplication facts for the 2-, 3-, 4-, 5-, 6- and 10-times tables and the corresponding division facts; recognise multiples of 2, 5 or 10 up to 1000

Vocabulary
problem, solution, calculate, calculation, answer, method, explain, reasoning, pattern, predict, multiply, times, divide, share, group

Resources
Interactive activity: Division function machine
Resource sheet: Self-assessment

⑥ Division function machine

Open the interactive activity 'Division function machine'. Decide which two windows on the function machine to reveal to the children each time. Challenge them to calculate the solution mentally before the machine gives the answer. This activity can be used for practice of division by one divisor at a time (such as ÷ 3, ÷ 4) and then by a range of divisors. Decide whether to use the self-assessment sheet for the children to record their achievements and what they need to do next.

Teacher support
Less confident learners: Decide whether to limit the work to division for a specific table.
More confident learners: Decide whether to use all or some of the divisors to challenge the children's recall of table facts for division.

Common misconceptions
Children cannot recall table facts in order to find the division fact.
Provide plenty of practice at recalling table facts and then ask the children to find the four facts, multiplication and division, for a set of numbers, such as 3, 4 and 12: 3 × 4 = 12; 4 × 3 = 12; 12 ÷ 3 = 4; 12 ÷ 4 = 3.

Probing questions
● Count back in fours from 32 to 0. How many fours did you count? Show me hops of four back from 32 on the number line.
● What is the missing number in this statement: ☐ × 5 = 35? How do you know?
● Can you tell me some numbers that will divide exactly by 2? By 5? By 10? How do you know?

Next steps
Support: Provide more opportunities for children to practise recalling table facts and deriving the related division facts. This could be done as a simple game, such as setting the table and asking the children to choose a number from 1 to 10. They must say the relevant multiplication fact and the related division fact. Refer back to Year 3 Block E Unit 2.
Extension: Encourage rapid recall. Use the division function machine again and work quickly so that children demonstrate their rapid recall. Refer to Year 3 Block E Unit 3.

Activity ⑦

Prior learning

Children can use the tables facts that they know to work out division facts. They can multiply or divide a two-digit number by a one-digit number. If there is a remainder after division, they know whether to round the answer up or down. They can solve a problem by writing down what calculation they should do.

Framework objectives

● Use practical and informal written methods to multiply and divide two-digit numbers (for example, 13 × 3, 50 ÷ 4); round remainders up or down, depending on the context
● Solve one-step and two-step problems involving numbers, money or measures, including time, choosing and carrying out appropriate calculations

Vocabulary

problem, solution, calculate, calculation, answer, method, explain, reasoning, pattern, predict, remainder, round up, round down, divide, share, group

Resources

Worksheet: Rounding

⑦ Rounding

Provide the children with the worksheet 'Rounding'. Tell them that they should show their workings (they can use extra paper if necessary). Remind them that the answers may need rounding.

Teacher support

Less confident learners: Decide whether to provide simplified problems. Work together on problems such as: *There are 12 eggs to go into two trays. How many eggs will there be in each tray?*
More confident learners: Challenge the children to invent their own problems, work out the answer, and be ready to explain solutions to the rest of the class.

Common misconceptions

Children do not understand how to deal with a remainder.
Discuss the word problem. Ask the children to explain the problem in their own words. Discuss whether they will need to round up or down, and why. Ask them if the remainder is important to the question or not, and why they think that.

Probing questions

● There are 72 cubes. Put them into groups of five. How many groups have you made? How many cubes are left over?
● If you put the 72 cubes into boxes that hold five cubes, how many boxes would you need? Explain why.
● If you put the 72 cubes in rows of five, how many rows could you make? Why?
● Do you need to round up or down for this problem? Why do you think that? How did you solve this problem? Why did you decide to do it this way?

Next steps

Support: Provide problems using table facts with which the children are confident. For example: *There are 16 pencils on the table. How many pencils can five children have each? What do you do with the remainder? Why?* Refer to Year 3 Block E Unit 2.
Extension: Challenge the children to invent problems from pairs of numbers that you give them. For example: *Using the numbers 6 and 84, invent a division problem and find the solution.* Refer to Year 3 Block E Unit 3.

Units 1, 2 & 3 ▢ Periodic assessment

These activities can be used at any time during the teaching of this block to assess those children that you think have achieved the objective. A grid highlighting the related assessment focuses and expected learning outcomes for each activity can be found on the CD-ROM.

Number split

Framework objective
Partition three-digit numbers into multiples of 100, 10 and 1 in different ways

Learning outcomes
● I can split a number into hundreds, tens and ones.
● I can explain how the digits in a number change when I count in tens or hundreds.

Provide the worksheet 'Number split'. Ask the children to work individually to answer the questions. They must split three-digit numbers into hundreds, tens and units in different ways. Discuss how they split the numbers, and how they know that their split number is the same as the start number.

Add and subtract

Framework objective
Derive and recall all addition and subtraction facts for each number to 20, sums and differences of multiples of 10 and number pairs that total 100

Learning outcomes
● I know the sum and difference of any pair of numbers to 20.
● I can add and subtract multiples of 10 or 100 in my head.
● I know number pairs that sum to 100.

Provide the worksheet 'Add and subtract (3)'. Children work examples of addition and subtraction facts for numbers to 20, sums and differences of multiples of 10, and number pairs that total 100. Invite the children to explain how they calculated their answers. Discuss the various mental strategies that they used.

One-digit and two-digit add and subtract

Framework objective
Add or subtract mentally combinations of one-digit and two-digit numbers

Learning outcomes
● I can find the sum of or difference between one-digit and two-digit numbers in my head (for example, 7 + 45, 45 – 7).
● I can add several one-digit numbers in my head.

Provide the worksheet 'One-digit and two-digit add and subtract'. This contains examples of adding and subtracting one-digit and two-digit numbers, and adding several one-digit numbers. Ask questions such as: *What is the largest multiple of 10 that you can add to 46 where the answer is smaller than 100?*

BLOCK A

Name	Date

Number split

- Read each number.
- Find two different ways to split it into hundreds, tens and units.
- Here is an example.

465 = $\underline{200 + 200 + 60 + 5}$

465 = $\underline{300 + 100 + 50 + 10 + 5}$

357 = _____

357 = _____

492 = _____

492 = _____

884 = _____

884 = _____

951 = _____

951 = _____

- Write these numbers as HTU numbers.

300 + 200 + 40 + 6 = _____

600 + 200 + 80 + 15 = _____

100 + 400 + 0 + 7 = _____

90 + 80 + 3 = _____

500 + 200 + 46 + 5 = _____

How easy?

Red
Amber
Green

How do you think you have done?

_____

_____

Name	Date

Add and subtract (3)

Write the answers to these addition and subtraction number sentences.

1	8 + 9	
2	16 + 14	
3	20 − 13	
4	16 − 9	
5	13 + 19	

6	19 − 11	
7	18 − 4	
8	17 + 19	
9	11 − 5	
10	4 + 13	

Complete this table.

■ The first one is done for you.

9 − 4 = 5	90 − 40 = 50	900 − 400 = 500
6 − 2 =	60 − 20 =	600 − 200 =
3 + 6 =	30 + 60 =	300 + 600 =
4 + 7 =	40 + 70 =	400 + 700 =

Choose pairs of numbers from the grid that total 100.

■ Cross out the numbers that you choose.

■ Write a number sentence for each one.

13	34	74	9	11
58	67	63	72	42
89	91	55	87	33
45	26	28	37	66

_____ _____

_____ _____

_____ _____

_____ _____

How easy?

Red
Amber
Green

How do you think you have done?

_____

_____

Name   Date

One-digit and two-digit add and subtract

Write the answers to these addition and subtraction sentences.

1	53 – 8		6	6 + 78	
2	74 + 7		7	77 – 8	
3	92 – 8		8	45 + 7	
4	36 + 7		9	36 + 4	
5	7 + 68		10	93 – 8	

Choose three digits each time.

◼ Total them mentally, then write an addition sentence.

◼ Do this three times.

3   9   4   6   8

_____

_____

_____

Now add four of the digits.

◼ Write an addition sentence.

◼ Do this twice.

_____

_____

How easy?

Red
Amber
Green

How do you think you have done?

_____

_____

BLOCK B
Securing number facts, understanding shape

Expected prior learning

Check that children can already:
- solve one-step problems in the context of numbers, measures or money
- check solutions make sense in the context of the problem
- recognise patterns in numbers or shapes and predict and test with examples
- recall addition and subtraction facts for each number to at least 10, all pairs with totals to 20 and all pairs of multiples of 10 with totals up to 100
- recall multiplication facts for the 2-, 5- and 10-times tables and the related division facts
- recognise multiples of 2, 5 and 10 up to 100
- describe the properties of and sort common 2D and 3D shapes and recognise them in pictures
- identify and draw lines of symmetry
- identify right angles in shapes and as quarter turns.

Objectives overview

The text in this diagram identifies the focus of mathematics learning within the block.

Key aspects of learning
- Problem solving
- Reasoning
- Social skills
- Communication
- Enquiry

Solving one- and two-step problems involving numbers, money or measures

Dividing and recalling number facts for all operations

Estimating and checking

Identifying and using patterns and relationships to solve problems

BLOCK B: Securing number facts, understanding shape

Recognising, using and drawing right angles

Drawing and comparing angles

Interpreting drawings of shapes and using reflective symmetry to draw and complete shapes

Unit 1 ◼ Securing number facts, understanding shape

Introduction

In this unit, children solve problems in the context of money. They use empty number lines to help them to solve problems. They are encouraged throughout the unit to explain their thinking and to give reasons for their views or mathematical choices. During lessons encourage the children, when working in pairs or groups, to hold sustained conversations so that they develop the skills of mathematical speaking and listening.

Framework objectives	Assessment focuses		Success criteria for Year 3	Learning outcomes
	Level 3	Level 2		
① Money problems				
Represent the information in a puzzle or problem using numbers, images or diagrams; use these to find a solution and present it in context, where appropriate using £.p notation or units of measure	● begin to organise their work and check results, e.g. ● begin to develop own ways of recording ● develop an organised approach as they get into recording their work on a problem ● discuss their mathematical work and begin to explain their thinking, e.g. ● use appropriate mathematical vocabulary ● talk about their findings by referring to their written work ● use and interpret mathematical symbols and diagrams	● discuss their work using mathematical language, e.g. with support ● describe the strategies and methods they use in their work ● listen to others' explanations, try to make sense of them, compare... evaluate... ● begin to represent their work using symbols and simple diagrams, e.g. with support ● use pictures, diagrams and symbols to communicate their thinking, or demonstrate a solution or process ● begin to appreciate the need to record and develop their own methods of recording	● Begins to develop ways of recording ● Demonstrates an organised approach to the task and recording outcomes ● Uses mathematical vocabulary appropriately when discussing their work ● Uses mathematical symbols and diagrams to demonstrate their findings	*I can solve problems using numbers, pictures and diagrams.*
① Money problems ⑥ Shape match ⑦ Shape sort				
Identify patterns and relationships involving numbers or shapes, and use these to solve problems	● understand a general statement by finding particular examples that match it, e.g. ● make a generalisation with the assistance of probing questions and prompts	● predict what comes next in a simple number, shape or spatial pattern or sequence and give reasons for their opinions	● Predicts what comes next in a number sequence, shape or spatial pattern ● Begins to make a generalisation with help (e.g. can explain that the 4-times table can be extended by adding 4 each time)	*I can describe patterns when I solve problems.*

Unit 1 ▢ Securing number facts, understanding shape

BLOCK B

Framework objectives	Assessment focuses		Success criteria for Year 3	Learning outcomes
	Level 3	Level 2		
② Quick add and subtract				
Derive and recall all addition and subtraction facts for each number to 20, sums and differences of multiples of 10 and number pairs that total 100	● add and subtract two-digit numbers mentally, e.g. ● calculate 36 + 19, 63 – 26, and complements to 100 such as 100 – 24	● use mental recall of addition and subtraction facts to 10, e.g. ● use addition/subtraction facts to 10 and place value to add or subtract multiples of 10, e.g. know 3 + 7 = 10 and use place value to derive 30 + 70 = 100	● Has quick recall of addition and subtraction facts to 20 ● Has quick recall of sums and differences of multiples of 10 ● Has mental methods for finding pairs that total 100	*I know and use addition and subtraction facts for all numbers to 20.*
③ Quick multiplication facts ④ Quick division facts				
Derive and recall multiplication facts for the 2-, 3-, 4-, 5-, 6- and 10-times tables and the corresponding division facts; recognise multiples of 2, 5 or 10 up to 1000	● recognise a wider range of sequences, e.g. ● recognise sequences of multiples of 2, 5 and 10 ● derive associated division facts from known multiplication facts, e.g. ● given a number sentence, use understanding of operations to create related sentences, e.g. given 14 × 5 = 70, create 5 × 14 = 70, 70 ÷ 5 = 14, 70 ÷ 14 = 5, 14 × 5 = 10 × 5 add 4 × 5 ● use mental recall of the 2, 3, 4, 5 and 10 multiplication tables, e.g. ● multiply a two-digit number by 2, 3, 4 or 5 ● understand finding a quarter of a number of objects as halving the number and halving again ● begin to know multiplication facts for the 6-, 8-, 9- and 7-times tables	● recognise sequences of numbers, including odd and even numbers, e.g. ● recognise numbers from counting in tens or twos ● use mental calculation strategies to solve number problems including those involving money and measures, e.g. ● recall doubles to 10 + 10 and other significant doubles, e.g. double 50p is 100p or £1 ● use knowledge of doubles to 10 + 10 to derive corresponding halves	● Has quick recall of 2-, 3-, 4-, 5-, 6- and 10-times tables ● Recognises, for example, that if 6 × 4 = 24 then 24 ÷ 4 = 6 and uses this to derive division facts ● Recognises the patterns in the 2-, 5- and 10-times tables and can extend these to find multiples of 2, 5 or 10 to 1000.	*I know the 2-, 3-, 4-, 5-, 6- and 10-times tables and use them for division facts.* *I recognise multiples of 2, 5 and 10.*
⑤ Estimate and check				
Use knowledge of number operations and corresponding inverses, including doubling and halving, to estimate and check calculations	● derive associated division facts from known multiplication facts, e.g. ● use inverses to find missing whole numbers in problems such as 'I think of a number, double it and add 5. The answer is 35. What was my number?'	● use the knowledge that subtraction is the inverse of addition, e.g. ● given 14, 6 and 8, make related number sentences 6 + 8 = 14, 14 – 8 = 6, 8 + 6 = 14, 14 – 6 = 8 ● understand halving as a way of 'undoing' doubling and vice versa	● Estimates answers using rounding, doubling and halving ● Checks calculations using inverses, knowledge of number operations and doubling and halving	*I can estimate and check my calculations.*

Unit 1 Securing number facts, understanding shape

Framework objectives	Assessment focuses		Success criteria for Year 3	Learning outcomes
	Level 3	Level 2		
(6) Shape match (7) Shape sort				
Relate 2D shapes and 3D solids to drawings of them; describe, visualise, classify, draw and make the shapes	• classify 3D and 2D shapes in various ways using mathematical properties such as reflective symmetry for 2D shapes, e.g. • sort objects and shapes using more than one criterion, e.g. pentagon/not pentagon and all edges the same length/ not the same length • sort the shapes which have all edges the same length and all angles the same size from a set of mixed shapes and begin to understand the terms 'regular' and 'irregular' • recognise right angles in shapes in different orientations • recognise angles which are bigger/smaller than 90° and begin to know the terms 'obtuse' and 'acute' • recognise right-angled and equilateral triangles • demonstrate that a shape has reflection symmetry by folding and recognise when a shape does not have a line of symmetry • recognise common 3D shapes, e.g. triangular prism, square-based pyramid • relate 3D shapes to drawings and photographs of them, including from different viewpoints • begin to recognise nets of familiar 3D shapes, e.g. cube, cuboid, triangular prism, square-based pyramid	• use mathematical names for common 3D and 2D shapes, e.g. • identify 2D and 3D shapes from pictures of them in different orientations, e.g. square, triangle, hexagon, pentagon, octagon, cube, cylinder, sphere, cuboid, pyramid • describe their properties, including numbers of sides and corners, e.g. • make and talk about shapes referring to properties and features such as edge, face, corner • sort 2D and 3D shapes according to a single criterion, e.g. shapes that are pentagons or shapes with a right angle • visualise frequently used 2D and 3D shapes • begin to understand the difference between shapes with two dimensions and those with three • recognise properties that are the same even when a shape is enlarged, e.g. comparing different size squares, circles, similar triangles, cubes or spheres	• Names drawings of 2D and 3D shapes • Sorts shapes by various criteria, including symmetry in 2D shapes • Draws shapes with some accuracy • Makes shapes from modelling materials and makes recognisable models	*I can recognise shapes from drawings.*

Activity ①

Prior learning
Children can solve problems using numbers, pictures and diagrams. They can describe patterns when they solve problems.

Framework objectives
● Represent the information in a puzzle or problem using numbers, images or diagrams; use these to find a solution and present it in context, where appropriate using £.p notation or units of measure
● Identify patterns and relationships involving numbers or shapes, and use these to solve problems

Vocabulary
problem, solution, calculate, calculation, operation, answer, method, explain, reasoning, pattern, predict, add, subtract, sum, total, difference, plus, minus, pound (£), pence (p), note, coin

Resources
Worksheet: Money problems
Classroom resources: coins

① Money problems

Explain that the children will be working in pairs to solve some money problems. Provide each child with the worksheet 'Money problems'. Ask them to work together to find three different ways of making the total of £1, using the coins on the sheet. They record their number sentence and their working out. Remind them that they can, if they find it helpful, draw an empty number line as a means to help them to calculate.

Teacher support
Less confident learners: Decide whether to provide real coins for the children to use as an aid.
More confident learners: Ask the children to see if they can find another way of making £1 using the coins shown.

Common misconceptions
Children may not recognise the value of the coins and count each silver coin, for example, as '10p'.
Provide further experience of handling coins and making totals with them.

Probing questions
● What counting patterns did you use when you totalled the coins?
● What can you tell me about counting in fives… tens…?
● How did you record your working out? How did this help you?
● What addition calculations did you make?
● How could you use subtraction to solve the problem? (For example, start at £1, then subtract coins until zero is reached.)

Next steps
Support: Provide further experience of using patterns to help with addition and subtraction. For example, ask the children to find coins that total to £1 choosing from five 5p coins, three 10p coins, four 20p coins and a 50p piece. They could draw an empty number line, for example, to demonstrate how they calculated. Refer back to Year 2 Block B Unit 3.
Extension: Provide further challenges, such as increasing the coins available and the amounts to be made. Refer to Year 3 Block B Unit 2.

BLOCK B

Activity ②

BLOCK B

Prior learning
Children know and use addition and subtraction facts for all numbers to 20.

Framework objective
Derive and recall all addition and subtraction facts for each number to 20, sums and differences of multiples of 10 and number pairs that total 100

Vocabulary
problem, solution, calculate, calculation, operation, answer, method, explain, reasoning, pattern, predict, add, subtract, sum, total, difference, plus, minus

Resources
Resource sheet: Self-assessment

② Quick add and subtract

Explain that you would like the children to work in two teams, each with a team leader. You will ask an addition or subtraction question for numbers to 20 and the teams take turns to find the answer. The team leaders decide who will answer. However, every child must have a turn. If the answer is correct, the team wins a point. If it is incorrect, the other team can answer. Keep score, by writing the points won onto the board. Note mentally which children are secure in these number facts and which will need further help to acquire them. Decide whether to use the self-assessment sheet for the children to record their achievements and what they need to do next.

Teacher support
Less confident learners: If possible, provide adult support. The children can give their answers to the adult, and the adult give points for correct answers.
More confident learners: Challenge the children to answer more quickly - perhaps using a timer - so that they demonstrate their ability to recall and derive the number facts.

Common misconceptions
Children fail to use what they know to derive an unknown fact.
Write down some facts such as 3 + 7 and ask for the answer. Now write 13 + 7 and ask the children what they can use to help them to find the answer. Discuss the patterns that they see and how these can help them.

Probing questions
● Tell me two numbers that sum to 17. And another pair?
● What would you add to 7 to make a total of 16?
● Give me three pairs of numbers that total 19. Now tell me some of the subtraction facts that use these numbers.
● What two numbers could I subtract to make 13? What is 15 − 2? What is 15 − 4? What is 15 − 6?

Next steps
Support: Provide further opportunities for the children to practise recall of facts. If children are unsure, give them suggestions for how they can find the fact, such as counting on or using a fact they already know to find a new fact (for example, 7 − 4 and 17 − 4). Refer back to Year 3 Block A Unit 1.
Extension: Encourage the children to recall these facts as quickly as they can. Give them opportunities to use these facts to find new ones - for example, if they know 17 − 4, can they find 47 − 24? Refer to Year 3 Block B Unit 3.

Activities

Prior learning
Children know the 2-, 3-, 4-, 5-, 6- and 10-times tables and use them for division facts.
They can recognise multiples of 2, 5 and 10.

Framework objective
Derive and recall multiplication facts for the 2-, 3-, 4-, 5-, 6- and 10-times tables and the corresponding division facts; recognise multiples of 2, 5 or 10 up to 1000

Vocabulary
problem, solution, calculate, calculation, operation, answer, method, explain, reasoning, pattern, predict, multiply, divide, group, sum, double, halve, multiple

Resources
Worksheets: Quick multiplication facts, Quick division facts
Classroom resources: small counters

③ Quick multiplication facts

Ask the children to work in pairs with the worksheet 'Quick multiplication facts'. They must take turns to drop one counter onto the 1–9 grid and then another counter onto the grid which gives the times table. Their partner must say the multiplication fact and the answer. Encourage them to work quickly so that they can demonstrate that they know these facts. Observe the children as they work and note those who give confident answers.

Teacher support
Less confident learners: Decide whether to limit this to recall of one multiplication table at a time, until the children are more confident with finding the answers.
More confident learners: Encourage the children to work quickly to determine for which tables they have rapid recall and for which they need more experience.

Common misconceptions
Children fail to find an answer to a multiplication table question.
Discuss strategies the children could use, such as (for the 4-times table) doubling the 2-times table facts.

Probing questions
● What is 8 × 4? How did you find the answer?
● What are the multiplication facts each side of 8 × 4?
● What is 7 × 3? What is the table fact just before this? And just after this?
● You know that 6 × 3 is 18. Tell me a division fact using these numbers.
● Tell me how you know that a number is in the 2/5/10-times table.

Next steps
Support: Gradually extend the range of multiplication facts that the children practise until they are confident with them all. Refer back to Year 2 Block B Unit 3.
Extension: Challenge the children to give their answers to multiplication facts as quickly as possible, so that they demonstrate that they have rapid recall. Refer to Year 3 Block E Unit 1.

BLOCK B

④ Quick division facts

Ask the children to work in pairs on the worksheet 'Quick division facts'. They take turns to choose a number from the number grid, then a divisor, and say the division fact. For example, if they choose 14 and ÷2, they say *14 divided by 2 is 7*. Encourage them to work quickly so that they can demonstrate that they know these facts. Observe the children as they work and note those who give confident answers.

Teacher support

Less confident learners: Decide whether to limit the children to deriving the division facts for one times table at a time, so that they build their confidence and ability to derive more quickly.

More confident learners: Encourage the children to work quickly to determine for which facts they can derive the answers quickly and for which they need more experience.

Common misconceptions

Children do not make the links between a table fact and the corresponding division fact.

Choose one table and ask the children to give a multiplication fact, such as 7 × 2 = 14. Now ask them to give the corresponding division fact. If they are unclear about the link between the two, ask them to make a 7 × 2 array with counters and then to divide their counters into two piles. Repeat this for other multiplication facts and the corresponding division facts until the children have grasped the connection between the two sets of facts and can use one to derive the other.

Probing questions

● What is 6 × 4? What two division facts can you find from this?
● What multiplication facts give the answer of 24? What are the corresponding division facts?
● Tell me a multiple of 10. Say a multiple of 10 that has three digits.
● Do this again for a multiple of 5, then multiples of 2.

Next steps

Support: Repeat the activity, gradually covering all the table facts to be practised, until the children demonstrate confidence. Refer back to Year 2 Block B Unit 3.

Extension: Challenge the children to give their answers to division facts as quickly as possible, so that they demonstrate that they can derive rapidly. Refer to Year 3 Block E Unit 1.

Activity ⑤

Prior learning
Children can estimate and check their calculations.

Framework objective
Use knowledge of number operations and corresponding inverses, including doubling and halving, to estimate and check calculations

Vocabulary
problem, solution, calculate, calculation, operation, answer, method, explain, reasoning, pattern, predict, multiply, divide, group, sum, double, halve, multiple

Resources
Interactive activity: Estimate and check
Resource sheet: Self-assessment

⑤ Estimate and check

Reveal the first screen of the interactive activity 'Estimate and check'. This gives a multiplication fact for which the children find the corresponding division fact. Ask the children to say the answer and to drag and drop the correct digits into the boxes. Repeat this for screen 2. Screens 3 and 4 each give a division fact for which the children find the corresponding multiplication fact. Screen 5 asks children to find doubling facts while screen 6 asks them to find halving facts. Decide whether to use the self-assessment sheet for the children to record their achievements and what they need to do next.

Teacher support
Less confident learners: Decide whether to simplify the numbers for the children to make their estimates.
More confident learners: Encourage the children to write some estimates of their own and to explain how their estimate would help them.

Common misconceptions
Children do not understand how to use an estimate to help them with a calculation.
Provide an example, such as 40 + 30 and 43 + 27. Discuss how these numbers are linked. Use an empty number line to demonstrate the addition of 40 and 30; then 43 and 27.

Probing questions
● What is 50 + 30? If we know that 50 + 30 = 80, how can this help us to estimate 53 + 27? Give me an estimate for 83 − 28, 81 − 52.
● What is 24 ÷ 6? Can we check this with a multiplication fact?
● If half of 30 is 15, what is double 15? Give me the doubling facts for these halving facts: half of 32 is 16; half of 34 is 17.

Next steps
Support: Provide further experience of adding multiples of 10 to ensure that children are confident with this. Then ask the children to use this to estimate other additions. Encourage them to find doubles and halves and use this in oral starters. Similarly, provide experience of checking division with multiplication (and vice versa) using table facts. Refer back to Year 2 Block B Unit 3.
Extension: Ask the children to estimate addition and subtraction of HTU numbers, such as 460 + 380. Refer to Year 3 Block B Unit 3.

Activities

Prior learning
Children can recognise shapes from drawings and describe patterns when they solve problems.

Framework objectives
● Relate 2D shapes and 3D solids to drawings of them; describe, visualise, classify, draw and make the shapes
● Identify patterns and relationships involving numbers or shapes, and use these to solve problems

Vocabulary
triangle, square, rectangle, quadrilateral, pentagon, hexagon, octagon, cube, cuboid, pyramid, sphere, hemisphere, cone, cylinder, prism, face, edge, vertex, surface, solid, side, flat, straight, curved, two-dimensional (2D), three-dimensional (3D), right-angled

Resources
Display page: 2D and 3D shapes
Worksheets: Shape match, Shape sort (1) and (2)

⑥ Shape match

Provide the children with the worksheet 'Shape match'. Explain that you will reveal a shape on the screen using the display pages '2D and 3D shapes'. Ask the children to identify each shape as it is revealed and write its name on their worksheet. Repeat this for the other shapes. Ask the children to explain how they recognised a specific shape and to describe its properties.

Teacher support
Less confident learners: Decide whether to ask an adult to work with the group. Instead of writing the name of the shape, the children can tell the adult what shape they see and how they know what shape it is by describing its properties.
More confident learners: Challenge the children to find up to four different properties for each shape, then to describe these to the other children.

Common misconceptions
Children do not discriminate between 3D and 2D shapes, so that any shape with, say, a rectangular face must be a rectangle.
Provide further experience of exploring the properties of 3D shapes. Discuss how some shapes can have at least two differently shaped faces, such as a pyramid (triangular faces and a square base).

Probing questions
● Here is a drawing of a shape. What is its name?
● How can you tell that it is that shape? What are its properties?
● How do you know that that shape is not a ___?

Next steps
Support: Provide children with further opportunities to recognise shapes from pictures. Ask them to say the properties they saw in the shape which helped them to decide what the shape was. Refer back to Year 2 Block B Unit 3.
Extension: Extend the range of shapes for children to explore and give opportunities for children to recognise shapes in drawings. Refer to Year 3 Block B Unit 2.

⑦ Shape sort

Provide the children with the worksheets 'Shape sort (1)' and 'Shape sort (2)'. Ask them to sketch some shapes that fit given criteria, then set their own criteria and enter shapes into a Carroll diagram. Ask them to explain why they have chosen the shapes and to confirm that these do have the given properties. Invite individual children to explain their completed Carroll diagram. Ask other children to check that they agree with the chosen criteria and where the shapes are placed.

Teacher support
Less confident learners: Decide whether to have the children work as a group for this activity. Children may at this stage be more confident with a two-region Carroll diagram and the 'has'/'does not have' statements for just one criterion.
More confident learners: Challenge the children to sketch more shapes that fit the criteria. Suggest that they consider, for example, line symmetry as one of the criteria for their Carroll diagram.

Common misconceptions
Children may not identify the common properties of a particular shape, such as what makes a triangle a triangle.
Ask the children to identify a shape from your description, such as: *My shape has four sides and all of them are the same length. It has four right angles.* Repeat this for other shapes.

Probing questions
● All the shapes on this table except one are prisms. Which shape does not belong?
● How did you recognise the odd one out?
● Describe this shape. What are its properties?

Next steps
Support: Provide more experience of recognising the properties of a shape. Children should understand that more than one shape can have the same properties, but that there will be another property that identifies it. For example: *My shape has three sides. Yes, it is a triangle. It has a right angle. So it is a right-angled triangle.* Refer back to Year 2 Block B Unit 1.
Extension: Ask the children to investigate, with geostrips, using a computer program or by cutting paper, what combinations of shapes they can make. They should describe the properties of the new shapes. Refer to Year 3 Block B Unit 2.

BLOCK B

Unit 2 ▢ Securing number facts, understanding shape

Introduction
In this unit, using and applying and speaking and listening apply to every lesson. Children are encouraged to discuss with each other, give their reasons and listen to others' points of view. They solve problems, discussing the methods that they chose and identifying patterns and relationships. They make 2D shapes and investigate lines of symmetry. They sketch shapes and compare their sketches, discussing differences and similarities. They identify simple fractions, make these fractions from shapes and find equivalent fractions.

Framework objectives	Assessment focuses		Success criteria for Year 3	Learning outcomes
	Level 3	**Level 2**		
① Motor sports problems ② Fruity problems				
Solve one-step and two-step problems involving numbers, money or measures, including time, choosing and carrying out appropriate calculations	• use mental recall of addition and subtraction facts to 20 in solving problems involving larger numbers, e.g. • choose to calculate mentally, on paper or with apparatus • solve one-step whole number problems appropriately • solve two-step problems that involve addition and subtraction	• choose the appropriate operation when solving addition and subtraction problems, e.g. • use repeated addition to solve multiplication problems • begin to use repeated subtraction or sharing equally to solve division problems • solve number problems involving money and measures	• Recognises which mathematics to use • Uses mental methods where appropriate • Uses paper and pencil and/or resources for larger number calculations • Identifies the steps to take to solve the problem • Checks answer using a different calculation	*I can explain how I solve problems.*
③ Multiplication by 2, 5 and 10				
Derive and recall multiplication facts for the 2-, 3-, 4-, 5-, 6- and 10-times tables and the corresponding division facts; recognise multiples of 2, 5 or 10 up to 1000	• recognise a wider range of sequences, e.g. • recognise sequences of multiples of 2, 5 and 10 • derive associated division facts from known multiplication facts, e.g. • given a number sentence, use understanding of operations to create related sentences, e.g. given 14 × 5 = 70, create 5 × 14 = 70, 70 ÷ 5 = 14, 70 ÷ 14 = 5, 14 × 5 = 10 × 5 add 4 × 5 • use mental recall of the 2, 3, 4, 5 and 10 multiplication tables	• recognise sequences of numbers, including odd and even numbers, e.g. • recognise numbers from counting in tens or twos • use mental calculation strategies to solve number problems including those involving money and measures, e.g. • recall doubles to 10 + 10 and other significant doubles, e.g. double 50p is 100p or £1 • use knowledge of doubles to 10 + 10 to derive corresponding halves	• Has quick recall of 2, 3-, 4-, 5-, 6- and 10-times tables • Recognises, for example, that if 6 × 4 = 24 then 24 ÷ 4 = 6 and uses this to derive division facts • Recognises the patterns in the 2-, 5- and 10-times tables and can extend these to find multiples of 2, 5 or 10 to 1000	*I know the 2-, 3-, 4-, 5-, 6- and 10-times tables and use them for division facts. I recognise multiples of 2, 5 and 10.*

Unit 2 Securing number facts, understanding shape

Framework objectives	Assessment focuses		Success criteria for Year 3	Learning outcomes
	Level 3	Level 2		
④ The baker's shop				
Represent the information in a puzzle or problem using numbers, images or diagrams; use these to find a solution and present it in context, where appropriate using £.p notation or units of measure	• begin to organise their work and check results, e.g. • begin to develop own ways of recording • develop an organised approach as they get into recording their work on a problem • discuss their mathematical work and begin to explain their thinking, e.g. • use appropriate mathematical vocabulary • talk about their findings by referring to their written work • use and interpret mathematical symbols and diagrams	• discuss their work using mathematical language, e.g. with support • describe the strategies and methods they use in their work • listen to others' explanations, try to make sense of them, compare... evaluate... • begin to represent their work using symbols and simple diagrams, e.g. with support • use pictures, diagrams and symbols to communicate their thinking, or demonstrate a solution or process • begin to appreciate the need to record and develop their own methods of recording	• Begins to develop ways of recording • Demonstrates an organised approach to the task and recording outcomes • Uses mathematical vocabulary appropriately when discussing their work • Uses mathematical symbols and diagrams to demonstrate their findings	*I can draw pictures and make notes to help me solve a problem.*
⑤ Add and subtract to 20 ⑥ Pirates				
Derive and recall all addition and subtraction facts for each number to 20, sums and differences of multiples of 10 and number pairs that total 100	• add and subtract two-digit numbers mentally, e.g. • calculate 36 + 19, 63 – 6, and complements to 100 such as 100 – 24	• use mental recall of addition and subtraction facts to 10, e.g. • use addition/subtraction facts to 10 and place value to add or subtract multiples of 10, e.g. know 3 + 7 = 10 and use place value to derive 30 + 70 = 100	• Has quick recall of addition and subtraction facts to 20 • Has quick recall of sums and differences of multiples of 10 • Has mental methods for finding pairs that total 100	*I know and use addition and subtraction facts for all numbers to 20. I can add and subtract multiples of 10 in my head.*
⑦ Odd and even differences				
Identify patterns and relationships involving numbers or shapes, and use these to solve problems	• understand a general statement by finding particular examples that match it, e.g. • make a generalisation with the assistance of probing questions and prompts	• predict what comes next in a simple number, shape or spatial pattern or sequence and give reasons for their opinions	• Predicts what comes next in a number sequence, shape or spatial pattern • Begins to make a generalisation with help (e.g. can explain that the 4-times table can be extended by adding 4 each time)	*I can describe and continue patterns.*

Unit 2 ◻ Securing number facts, understanding shape

Framework objectives	Assessment focuses		Success criteria for Year 3	Learning outcomes
	Level 3	Level 2		
⑧ Shape sort ⑨ Drawing shapes				
Relate 2D shapes and 3D solids to drawings of them; describe, visualise, classify, draw and make the shapes	• classify 3D and 2D shapes in various ways using mathematical properties such as reflective symmetry for 2D shapes • begin to recognise nets of familiar 3D shapes, e.g. cube, cuboid, triangular prism, square-based pyramid	• use mathematical names for common 3D and 2D shapes, e.g. ○ identify 2D and 3D shapes from pictures of them in different orientations, e.g. square, triangle, hexagon, pentagon, octagon, cube, cylinder, sphere, cuboid, pyramid • describe their properties, including numbers of sides and corners	• Names drawings of 2D and 3D shapes • Sorts shapes by various criteria, including symmetry in 2D shapes • Draws shapes with some accuracy • Makes shapes from modelling materials and makes recognisable models	*I can name and describe shapes.* *I can sort shapes into sets, saying what is the same about each of the shapes.* *I can recognise whether a 2D shape is symmetrical or not and describe how I know.*
⑩ Shapes and mirrors				
Draw and complete shapes with reflective symmetry; draw the reflection of a shape in a mirror line along one side	• recognise shapes in different orientations • reflect shapes, presented on a grid, in a vertical or horizontal mirror line	• describe the position of objects, e.g. ○ recognise and explain that a shape stays the same even when it is held up in different orientations	• Recognises reflective symmetry in 2D shapes • Can draw the reflection of a shape in a mirror line when the mirror line is along one side of the shape	*I can draw a symmetrical shape.* *I can reflect a shape when the mirror line is one of its sides.*
⑪ Cube fractions ⑫ Fractions of shapes				
Read and write proper fractions (e.g. $^3/_7$, $^9/_{10}$), interpreting the denominator as the parts of a whole and the numerator as the number of parts; identify and estimate fractions of shapes; use diagrams to compare fractions and establish equivalents	• use simple fractions that are several parts of a whole and recognise when two simple fractions are equivalent • begin to use decimal notation in contexts such as money, e.g. ○ order decimals with one dp, or two dp in context of money	• begin to use halves and quarters, e.g. ○ use the concept of a fraction of a number in practical contexts such as sharing sweets between two to get ½ each , among four to get ¼ each ○ work out halves of numbers up to 20 and begin to recall them • relate the concept of half of a small quantity to the concept of half of a shape, e.g. ○ shade one half or one quarter of a given shape including those divided into equal regions	• Understands what each of the numbers in a fraction, i.e. denominator and numerator • Can demonstrate that two fractions are equivalent by, for example, shading squares on a diagram	*I can find ½ and ¼ of different shapes.*

◾ S C H O L A S T I C

BLOCK B

Activities

Prior learning
Check children can use mental strategies to solve problems and respond to questions about the methods that they chose.

Framework objective
Solve one-step and two-step problems involving numbers, money or measures, including time, choosing and carrying out appropriate calculations

Vocabulary
problem, solution, predict, calculate, calculation, operation, inverse, answer, method, explain, reasoning, pattern, predict, estimate, approximate

Resources
Worksheets: Motor sports problems, Fruity problems
Resource sheet: Word problem frame

① Motor sports problems

Provide each child with a copy of the worksheet 'Motor sports problems', which offers a range of one-step problems. Ask them to write a number sentence with the answer for each problem.

Teacher support
Less confident learners: Read the problems to the children and invite individuals to explain their methods. Once children are confident with one-step problems, move on to Activity 2, which involves two-step problems.
More confident learners: Check the children's methods. If they are secure with one-step problems, provide Activity 2 which involves two-step problems.

Common misconceptions
Children do not recognise the type of calculation needed to find the answer. Read the questions through together and ask the children to look for words that give a clue as to the type of number sentence needed.

Probing questions
- What type of number sentence do you need for this question?
- Which words give a clue?

Next steps
Support: Provide additional one-step problems. Each time ask the children to find the words in the problem that give a clue as to the type of number sentence needed to solve it. Alternatively, refer back to Year 3 Block D Unit 1.
Extension: Provide a range of two-step problems. Refer also to Year 3 Block E Unit 2.

② Fruity problems

Provide each child with a copy of the resource sheet 'Word problem frame'. Reveal the first problem from the worksheet 'Fruity problems' on the whiteboard: *There are 16 apples, 12 oranges and 8 bananas in a box. How many pieces of fruit are there altogether?* Ask the children to use the 'Word problem frame' to solve this and the other problems.

Teacher support
Less confident learners: Have these children work as a group with an adult to assist. Encourage children to explain how they will solve the problems.
More confident learners: Challenge these children to compare their mental calculation methods and to discuss which method was the most efficient.

BLOCK B

BLOCK B

Common misconceptions
Children complete only the first part of the question in a two-step problem.
Discuss the question and invite the child to explain what they have to find out.

Probing questions
● How did you work out the answer?
● What is the answer to 15 + 19 − 12? Make up a problem to match this calculation.

Next steps
Support: Provide further experience of one-step problems until children are secure with these. Then reintroduce simple two-step problems and ask the children to discuss their solutions and methods. Alternatively, refer back to Year 3 Block D Unit 1.
Extension: Give some more complex problems. Include some that involve multiple steps. Refer also to Year 3 Block E Unit 2.

Activity ③

Prior learning
Children can quickly recall multiplication facts from the 2-, 3-, 4-, 5-, 6- and 10-times tables.

Framework objective
Derive and recall multiplication facts for the 2-, 3-, 4-, 5-, 6- and 10-times tables and the corresponding division facts; recognise multiples of 2, 5 or 10 up to 1000

Vocabulary
Multiplication, division, multiple

Resources
Interactive activity: Bingo – multiples of 2, 5 and 10
Resource sheets: Bingo cards (×2), Bingo cards (×5), Bingo cards (×10), Bingo cards (×2, ×5 and ×10), Self-assessment

③ Multiplication by 2, 5 and 10

Play the bingo game from the CD-ROM ('Bingo – multiples of 2, 5 and 10'). Choose from the 2-, 5- or 10-times tables (or a mixture of all three). Provide each child with an appropriate bingo card (available on the CD-ROM) and display the first screen. Children cross through any answer that they have on their card. The first player to cover all numbers on their card and call *Bingo!* wins. Invite them to click on 'Check grid' to check their card, and then click on the 'Winner' button to hear the fanfare. Decide whether to use the self-assessment sheet for the children to record their achievements and what they need to do next.

Teacher support
Less confident learners: Have these children work as a group. Ask them to say the multiplication table fact as they cross through their answer.
More confident learners: Challenge these children to say the answers to a time limit in order to demonstrate rapid recall of these facts.

Common misconceptions
Children fail to demonstrate rapid recall of the facts.
Use a range of strategies to help, including chanting the tables, building the table facts with repeated addition, and playing simple multiplication games.

Probing questions
● What is 5 multiplied by 2? So what is 2 multiplied by 5?

- What do you notice about these two facts?
- What is 3 multiplied by 2? So what do you think 2 multiplied by 3 will be?

Next steps

Support: Provide further experience of multiplication tables through chanting the tables and games for recall of facts. Refer back to Year 3 Block B Unit 1.

Extension: Extend children's knowledge of table facts by including the 3-, 4- and 6-times tables and playing the alternative bingo game 'Bingo: multiplication'. Refer to Year 3 Block A Unit 3.

Activity ④

Prior learning
Children can solve problems and record the information that they gather. They can use money notation.

Framework objective
Represent the information in a puzzle or problem using numbers, images or diagrams; use these to find a solution and present it in context, where appropriate using £.p notation or units of measure

Vocabulary
problem, solution, predict, calculate, calculation, operation, inverse, answer, method, explain, reasoning, pattern, predict, estimate, approximate

Resources
Worksheet: The baker's shop

④ The baker's shop

Ask the children to solve the problem on the worksheet 'The baker's shop'. Encourage them to use the space on the sheet to record the information they have gathered, then to write their solutions, showing their working.

Teacher support
Less confident learners: Discuss how to find the cheapest way. If necessary, give a hint, such as ordering the prices to find the three cheapest, then three most expensive.

More confident learners: Invite children to explain their thinking. They should compare their recording with a partner and discuss the merits of each method.

Common misconceptions
Children do not recognise the key information in the problem.
Read the problem through together and identify the words that identify the information the children need.

Probing questions
- How did you solve this problem?
- Did you make any notes to help you? Tell me what you did.
- Suppose there was another cake priced at 17p. Would this have changed your solutions? Why not?

Next steps
Support: Give further experience of solving problems like this one. Read the problem together and check that the children understand what is key information, and why. Also refer to Year 3 Block B Unit 1.

Extension: Encourage the children to invent their own problems for a partner to solve. Refer to Year 3 Block D Unit 2.

BLOCK B

Activities

BLOCK B

Prior learning
Children can use their knowledge of addition and subtraction facts for each number to 20, and can quickly recall these facts. They can quickly find the sums and differences of multiples of 10 and number pairs that total 100.

Framework objective
Derive and recall all addition and subtraction facts for each number to 20, sums and differences of multiples of 10 and number pairs that total 100

Vocabulary
add, addition, more, plus, make, sum, total, altogether, subtract, take (away), minus, leave, (how many are) left/left over?, difference between

Resources
Interactive activity: Pirates!
Resource sheets: Numeral cards 0–10, Numeral cards 11–20, Self-assessment
Classroom resources: cubes or counters, individual whiteboards and pens

⑤ Add and subtract to 20

Provide each child with two sets of 0–10 numeral cards, and have two sets of 11–20 teaching cards. Show two cards and ask the children to add the two numbers. They make the answer with their numeral cards, and when you say *Show me,* they hold up their cards. If they are correct, they place a cube or counter in front of them. Repeat for the difference between the two numbers. After 20 questions, the child with the most correct answers (cubes or counters) wins. Observe who is responding well and who needs more experience of these additions and subtractions. Decide whether to use the self-assessment sheet.

Teacher support
Less confident learners: Decide whether to play the game as a group. Where children are unsure of the answer, remind them of strategies for finding the answer, such as adding the tens digits first.
More confident learners: Suggest that the children play the game in small groups. One child draw two cards from two sets of 0–20 cards to make an addition or subtraction sentence for the others to answer.

Common misconceptions
Children may not have the strategies for deriving answers.
Give further practice of addition and subtraction strategies, especially where it is necessary to cross the tens barrier.

Probing questions
● How do you know that that is the correct answer?
● If 20 − 17 is 3, what is 3 + 17?

Next steps
Support: Provide further experience of these additions and subtractions until children are confident with them. Refer back to Year 3 Block E Unit 1.
Extension: Encourage the children to use their knowledge of these facts in solving problems such as: *There are 17 apples in the tray and 15 in the box. How many apples are there in total?* Alternatively, refer to Year 3 Block B Unit 3.

⑥ Pirates!

Using the 'Pirates!' interactive activity, choose from the tabs on the left-hand side of the screen whether to add or subtract in multiples of 10 (or a combination of both operations). Reveal the screen and explain that an addition or subtraction of multiples of 10 will appear when you click 'New'. The children should work mentally to find the solution, write their answers on their whiteboards and hold them up when you say *Show me.* Then click on the crow's nest to move it to the correct answer on the screen. Observe who is responding well and who needs more experience of adding and subtracting in multiples of 10. Decide whether to use the self-assessment sheet.

Teacher support
Less confident learners: Decide which set of questions would be most appropriate. Compare the addition and subtraction of multiples of 10 to addition and subtraction of pairs of numbers to 10 and discuss what the children observe. For example: 5 + 4 = 9; 50 + 40 = 90.
More confident learners: Invite the children to explain their methods.

Common misconceptions
Children may not make the connection between 0-9 numbers and multiples of 10.
Encourage the children to write number sentences such as: *If I know that 4 + 3 = 7, then I can work out that 40 + 30 = 70. If I know that 9 − 5 = 4, then I can work out that 90 − 50 = 40.*

Probing questions
- Which pairs of multiples of 10 add to make 80?
- Which pairs of multiples of 10 have a difference of 20?
- How did you work those out?

Next steps
Support: Provide further experience of addition, then finding the difference, through playing simple games. Refer back to Year 3 Block E Unit 1.
Extension: Encourage the children to use these number facts when solving problems. Refer to Year 3 Block B Unit 3.

Activity ⑦

Prior learning
Children can find examples to satisfy general statements about numbers.

Framework objective
Identify patterns and relationships involving numbers or shapes, and use these to solve problems

Vocabulary
problem, solution, predict, calculate, calculation, operation, inverse, answer, method, explain, reasoning, pattern, predict

Resources
Worksheet: Odd and even differences

⑦ Odd and even differences

Reveal the worksheet 'Odd and even differences' on the whiteboard. Ask the children to consider the statement displayed on the board and decide whether it is true or false. Now ask them to write six number sentences to support what they believe.

Teacher support
Less confident learners: Encourage the children to choose smaller number pairs in order to show that the statement is true.

More confident learners: Encourage the children to try a range of number pairs, from small numbers to much larger ones. Ask them to check whether it matters if the even or odd number comes first in their pair and to explain why it does not matter.

Common misconceptions
Children may think that because they have begun their number pair with an odd or even number, that that will affect the outcome of finding the difference. Ask these children to find the difference between pairs of numbers such as 5 and 3, 8 and 7 (and so on) and to see that it makes no difference.

Probing questions
● Does it matter if the number pair has an odd or an even number first? Why not?
● Why is the statement true? Explain in your own words.

Next steps
Support: Ask an adult to work with the children to decide whether the statement 'An even number plus an even number is always even' is true. Ask the adult to encourage the children to give examples and to explain in their own words why the statement is true. Refer back to Year 3 Block E Unit 1.
Extension: Provide other general statements for the children to try such as: 'The difference between two even numbers is always even.' Challenge the children to demonstrate their response with at least six examples and to explain why this statement is true. Refer to Year 3 Block B Unit 3.

Activities

Prior learning	**Framework objective**
Children can explore the properties of 3D solids, recognise the shapes from drawings of them and draw the shapes themselves.	Relate 2D shapes and 3D solids to drawings of them; describe, visualise, classify, draw and make the shapes

Framework objective
Relate 2D shapes and 3D solids to drawings of them; describe, visualise, classify, draw and make the shapes

Vocabulary
triangle, square, rectangle, quadrilateral, pentagon, hexagon, octagon, cube, cuboid, pyramid, cone, cylinder, prism, face, edge, vertex, surface, solid, side, straight, curved, diagram, right-angled, line of symmetry, mirror line, reflection, symmetrical, 2D, 3D

Resources
Interactive activity: Venn diagram
Worksheets: Venn diagram (1), Drawing shapes
Classroom resources: a selection of 3D solids including cube, cuboid, pyramid, cone, cylinder

⑧ Shape sort

Ask the children to work in pairs. Provide each pair with a copy of the worksheet 'Venn diagram (1)' and ask them to sort the solids according to their chosen criteria, either by drawing a line from each solid to the correct area or by drawing the solids in their correct area. Ask the children to label each of the circles and to decide whether any of their solids should be placed in the intersection. Next, display the interactive activity 'Venn diagram'. Ask the children to drag and drop the shapes provided at the foot of the screen into the correct areas of the Venn diagram. Discuss, as a class, what shape(s) might go into the intersecting area of the two labels. The second screen of this activity allows children to choose their own labels to sort the shapes.

Teacher support
Less confident learners: Decide whether to work as a group to undertake this task, with an adult asking them questions about the properties of the solids.
More confident learners: Ask the children to write some sentences to explain their sorting of the solids. Encourage them to explain why specific shapes fit in the intersection of the diagram.

Common misconceptions
Children may still confuse 'cuboid' and 'cube'.
If this occurs, ask the children to compare the two shapes and to describe the similarities and differences so that they can then differentiate between the two.

Probing questions
- What criteria could you choose?
- So which solid goes in this section?
- What fits in the intersection? (Point to the overlap on the diagram.) Why does that fit there?

Next steps
Support: If children are unsure about sorting with two criteria, revert to sorting with one criterion until they are more confident. Refer back to Year 3 Block B Unit 1.
Extension: Provide more examples of prisms and ask the children to find ways to sort these, using two criteria. Refer to Year 3 Block B Unit 3.

⑨ Drawing shapes

Show the children a 3D solid such as a cube, cuboid, pyramid, cone or cylinder. Ask them to look at the shape and to write its name on the worksheet 'Drawing shapes'. Repeat for three more solids. Now provide each child (or group of children) with some solids. Ask them to choose a solid, and to draw it as carefully and accurately as they can in the space on their worksheet.

Teacher support
Less confident learners: Check that the children recognise the solids that you show them and can name them. Then check that they are observing carefully the solid that they have chosen to draw.
More confident learners: Ask the children to draw their chosen solid in different orientations. Ask them to describe how it looks the same and in what ways it looks different when looked at from different angles.

Common misconceptions
Children may not draw with sufficient accuracy and may confuse, for example, a rectangular face with a square face of a shape.
Ask the children to look again at the solid and to describe what they can see, then to compare this with their drawing. Invite them to say how they can change their drawing so that it is more accurate.

Probing questions
- What solid is this? How can you tell?
- Tell me three properties of this solid.
- How many faces does this solid have? If I placed it on the table like this [demonstrate], which face would be hidden by the table?
- What if I turned the solid like this? Which face would be hidden now?

Next steps
Support: Provide further experience in naming the solids from drawings, recognising their properties and sketching them with increasing accuracy. Refer back to Year 3 Block B Unit 1.
Extension: Challenge the children to combine two or more 3D solids, then to sketch them as accurately as they can. Refer to Year 3 Block B Unit 3.

Activity ⑩

BLOCK B

Prior learning
Children can understand line symmetry, recognising examples of shapes with and without symmetry. They can complete shapes where half is already drawn and draw their own shapes with line symmetry and with no line symmetry.

Framework objective
Draw and complete shapes with reflective symmetry; draw the reflection of a shape in a mirror line along one side

Vocabulary
line of symmetry, mirror line, reflection, symmetrical

Resources
Interactive activity: Reflection square
Worksheet: Shapes and mirrors
Classroom resources: centimetre-squared paper, coloured pencils, safety mirrors

⑩ Shapes and mirrors

Show some simple shapes with a mirror line using the interactive activity 'Reflection square'. Invite the children to describe each shape that they see and to say what they think the reflected shape will look like. The children may find it helpful to first sketch the shape, the mirror line and the reflection on the worksheet 'Shapes and mirrors' (alternatively, they may prefer to use centimetre-squared paper).

Teacher support
Less confident learners: Work as a group with an adult to assist. Encourage children to explain where the lines of symmetry are and how they know that.
More confident learners: Challenge these children to find shapes with line symmetry. Use the probing questions below to check their understanding.

Common misconceptions
Child draws a diagonal line on a rectangle and says that this is the line of symmetry.
Provide a mirror. Ask the child to place the mirror along the diagonal line and to describe the shape that the reflection makes. Invite them to place the mirror onto another rectangle in order to find a line of symmetry.

Probing questions
● How do you find the line of symmetry in a shape?
● How would you use a mirror to help you to find the line of symmetry?
● What do you look for when trying to find the line of symmetry in a shape?

Next steps
Support: Ask the children to fold some paper then cut a pattern in the paper without cutting the fold line. They open up the paper and identify the centre line, or fold. Discuss the fact that the shape they have made is symmetrical. This can be repeated several times to ensure that the children understand the vocabulary of symmetry. Alternatively, refer back to Year 2 Block B Unit 2 for earlier work on symmetry.
Extension: Ask the children to work in pairs with some centimetre-squared paper. They should draw a mirror line, then take turns to colour squares each side of the mirror line so that the pattern is symmetrical. Alternatively, refer to Year 3 Block D Unit 2 for further activities.

■ S C H O L A S T I C

Activities

Prior learning
Children can read and write proper fractions and know the meaning of the denominator and numerator. They can find fractions of shapes and compare these to find equivalents such as $^1/_2$ and $^2/_4$.

Framework objective
Read and write proper fractions (for example, $^3/_7$, $^9/_{10}$), interpreting the denominator as the parts of a whole and the numerator as the number of parts; identify and estimate fractions of shapes; use diagrams to compare fractions and establish equivalents

Vocabulary
problem, solution, calculate, calculation, operation, inverse, answer, method, explain, reasoning, pattern, predict, estimate, approximate, add, subtract, multiply, divide, group, sum, total, difference, plus, minus, double, halve, multiple, part, fraction, one whole, one half, two halves, one quarter, two/three/four quarters

Resources
Interactive activity: Fractions of shapes
Resource sheet: Self-assessment
Classroom resources: centimetre-squared paper, cubes

⑪ Cube fractions

Provide pairs of children with 24 cubes. Ask them to find $^1/_2$, $^1/_3$, $^1/_4$, $^1/_6$ and $^1/_8$. Ask them to record their work, deciding for themselves how to do this. Have squared paper ready for those who decide to make a visual recording. Decide whether to use the self-assessment sheet for the children to record their achievements and what they need to do next.

Teacher support
Less confident learners: Decide whether to use, say, 12 cubes, so that the children have fewer cubes to share out.
More confident learners: Challenge children to find all of the fractions parts (ie $^1/_6$, $^2/_6$, $^3/_6$, $^4/_6$, $^5/_6$) and to record the fractions and to write what they notice. For example, they may note that all of the fractions apart from $^1/_6$ and $^5/_6$ are equivalents (for example, $^2/_6$ and $^1/_3$).

Common misconceptions
Children do not understand the meaning of the denominator.
Explain that the denominator represents the number of parts into which the whole amount has been divided. Give simple examples using small numbers of cubes.

Probing questions
- What is $^1/_2$ of 16? How did you work that out?
- What is $^1/_4$ of 16?
- What would $^2/_4$ be?
- What would $^4/_4$ be?

Next steps
Support: Provide further examples, using larger quantities of cubes until the children are confident with finding unitary fractions. Then move on to finding simple fractions such as $^3/_4$. Refer back to Year 3 Block D Unit 1.
Extension: Provide a similar activity, but this time challenge the children to use the facts that they know in order to work mentally. Refer to Year 3 Block D Unit 2.

⑫ Fractions of shapes

Provide pairs of children with centimetre-squared paper. Explain that you would like them to draw four 5 × 4 rectangles on the paper, using the squares to help them. Ask them to find different ways of colouring in half of the shape in blue and one quarter in red. When they have completed four of these rectangles, invite pairs to demonstrate what they have done using the interactive activity 'Fractions of shapes'. They should drag and drop coloured squares onto the screen to replicate their drawings. Finally, ask the children to draw irregular shapes on squared paper and repeat the activity, this time using the on-screen activity 'Make your own fractions of shapes'. Decide whether to use the self-assessment sheet for the children to record their achievements and what they need to do next.

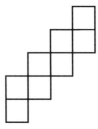

Teacher support

Less confident learners: Decide whether to ask the children to carry out the same task with a 4 × 3 array. Discuss how many squares would be ½ and how many for ¼.

More confident learners: Challenge the children to find other fractions that can be coloured using a 5 × 4 array, such as ²/₅ and ½.

Common misconceptions

Children do not understand the meaning of the denominator.
Explain that the denominator represents the number of parts into which the whole amount has been divided. Give simple examples using small numbers squares, such as a 4 × 2 array.

Probing questions

- What is ½ of 20?
- What is ¼ of 20?
- So what would ¾ of 20 be?
- What other fractions of 20 squares could we find?

Next steps

Support: Repeat the activity for other fractions, such as colouring in ¹/₃ and ½ of 12 squares. Refer back to Year 3 Block D Unit 1.

Extension: Ask the children to find simple fractions of other shapes, such as ⁵/₆ of 30 squares. Refer to Year 3 Block D Unit 2.

Unit 3 Securing number facts, understanding shape

Introduction
During this unit, encourage the children to discuss their work with a partner and with the whole class so that they have opportunities to use specific mathematics vocabulary in context. They extend their skills in using and applying mathematics by solving word problems, using what they know to investigate right-angled triangles. In this unit it is expected that children will have reasonable recall of the 2-, 3-, 4-, 5-, 6- and 10-times tables, and similarly they will be able to derive the related division facts. They are expected to have reasonable recall of addition and subtraction facts to 20 and to use these facts to derive others, including sums and differences of multiples of 10 and number pairs to make 100. They reinforce their understanding of fractions and of 2D and 3D shapes.

Framework objectives	Assessment focuses		Success criteria for Year 3	Learning outcomes
	Level 3	Level 2		
① Solve and check				
Solve one-step and two-step problems involving numbers, money or measures, including time, choosing and carrying out appropriate calculations	• select the mathematics they use in a wider range of classroom activities, e.g. • choose their own equipment appropriate to the task, including calculators • use mental recall of addition and subtraction facts to 20 in solving problems involving larger numbers	• select the mathematics they use in some classroom activities • choose the appropriate operation when solving addition and subtraction problems, e.g. • use repeated addition to solve multiplication problems • begin to use repeated subtraction or sharing equally to solve division problems • solve number problems involving money and measures	• Recognises which mathematics to use • Uses mental methods where appropriate • Uses paper and pencil and/or resources for larger number calculations • Identifies the steps to take to solve the problem • Checks answer using a different calculation	*I can solve a problem by writing down what calculation I should do.*
① Solve and check				
Use knowledge of number operations and corresponding inverses, including doubling and halving, to estimate and check calculations	• derive associated division facts from known multiplication facts, e.g. • use inverses to find missing whole numbers in problems such as 'I think of a number, double it and add 5. The answer is 35. What was my number?'	• use the knowledge that subtraction is the inverse of addition • understand halving as a way of 'undoing' doubling and vice versa	• Estimates answers using rounding, doubling and halving • Checks calculations using inverses, knowledge of number operations and doubling and halving	*I can estimate and check my calculations.*

Unit 3 ▢ Securing number facts, understanding shape

BLOCK B

Framework objectives	Assessment focuses		Success criteria for Year 3	Learning outcomes
	Level 3	Level 2		

② Make a sketch

Framework objectives	Level 3	Level 2	Success criteria for Year 3	Learning outcomes
Represent the information in a puzzle or problem using numbers, images or diagrams; use these to find a solution and present it in context, where appropriate using £.p notation or units of measure	• begin to organise their work and check results, e.g. • begin to develop own ways of recording • develop an organised approach as they get into recording their work on a problem • discuss their mathematical work and begin to explain their thinking • use and interpret mathematical symbols and diagrams	• discuss their work using mathematical language, e.g. with support • describe the strategies and methods they use in their work • listen to others' explanations, try to make sense of them, compare… evaluate… • begin to represent their work using symbols and simple diagrams	• Begins to develop ways of recording • Demonstrates an organised approach to the task and recording outcomes • Uses mathematical vocabulary appropriately when discussing their work • Uses mathematical symbols and diagrams to demonstrate their findings	*I can draw a picture to help make sense of a problem.*

③ 100-square hunt ⑩ Shape puzzle

Framework objectives	Level 3	Level 2	Success criteria for Year 3	Learning outcomes
Identify patterns and relationships involving numbers or shapes, and use these to solve problems	• understand a general statement by finding particular examples that match it, e.g. • make a generalisation with the assistance of probing questions and prompts	• predict what comes next in a simple number, shape or spatial pattern or sequence and give reasons for their opinions	• Predicts what comes next in a number sequence, shape or spatial pattern • Begins to make a generalisation with help	*I can find numbers or shapes that match a property.*

④ Fractions of shapes

Framework objectives	Level 3	Level 2	Success criteria for Year 3	Learning outcomes
Read and write proper fractions (e.g. $3/7$, $9/10$), interpreting the denominator as the parts of a whole and the numerator as the number of parts; identify and estimate fractions of shapes; use diagrams to compare fractions and establish equivalents	• use simple fractions that are several parts of a whole and recognise when two simple fractions are equivalent • begin to use decimal notation in contexts such as money, e.g. • order decimals with one dp, or two dp in context of money	• begin to use halves and quarters • relate the concept of half of a small quantity to the concept of half of a shape, e.g. • shade one half or one quarter of a given shape including those divided into equal regions	• Understands what each of the numbers in a fraction means, i.e. denominator and numerator • Can demonstrate that two fractions are equivalent by, for example, shading squares on a diagram	*I can say what fraction of a shape is shaded.*

⑤ Quick-fire add and subtract ⑥ Make a hundred

Framework objectives	Level 3	Level 2	Success criteria for Year 3	Learning outcomes
Derive and recall all addition and subtraction facts for each number to 20, sums and differences of multiples of 10 and number pairs that total 100	• add and subtract two-digit numbers mentally, e.g. • calculate 36 + 19, 63 − 26, and complements to 100 such as 100 − 24	• use mental recall of addition and subtraction facts to 10, e.g. • use addition/subtraction facts to 10 and place value to add or subtract multiples of 10, e.g. know 3 + 7 = 10 and use place value to derive 30 + 70 = 100	• Has quick recall of addition and subtraction facts to 20 • Has quick recall of sums and differences of multiples of 10 • Has mental methods for finding pairs that total 100	*I know and use all addition and subtraction facts to 20.* *I can find what to add to a number to make 100.*

Unit 3 ◻ Securing number facts, understanding shape

Framework objectives	Assessment focuses		Success criteria for Year 3	Learning outcomes
	Level 3	**Level 2**		
⑦ Multiplication square				
Derive and recall multiplication facts for the 2-, 3-, 4-, 5-, 6- and 10-times tables and the corresponding division facts; recognise multiples of 2, 5 or 10 up to 1000	• recognise a wider range of sequences, e.g. ● recognise sequences of multiples of 2, 5 and 10 • derive associated division facts from known multiplication facts • use mental recall of the 2, 3, 4, 5 and 10 multiplication tables	• recognise sequences of numbers, including odd and even numbers, e.g. ● recognise numbers from counting in tens or twos • use mental calculation strategies to solve number problems including those involving money and measures, e.g. ● recall doubles to 10 + 10 and other significant doubles, e.g. double 50p is 100p or £1 ● use knowledge of doubles to 10 + 10 to derive corresponding halves	• Has quick recall of the 2-, 3-, 4-, 5-, 6- and 10-times tables • Recognises, for example, that if 6 × 4 = 24 then 24 ÷ 4 = 6 and uses this to derive division facts • Recognises the patterns in the 2-, 5- and 10-times tables and can extend these to find multiples of 2, 5 or 10 to 1000	I know the 2-, 3-, 4-, 5-, 6- and 10-times tables and use them for division. I recognise multiples of 2, 5 and 10.
⑧ Shape sort				
Relate 2D shapes and 3D solids to drawings of them; describe, visualise, classify, draw and make the shapes	• classify 3D and 2D shapes in various ways using mathematical properties such as reflective symmetry for 2D shapes • begin to recognise nets of familar 3D shapes, e.g. cube, cuboid, triangular prism, square-based pyramid	• use mathematical names for common 3D and 2D shapes, e.g. ● identify 2D and 3D shapes from pictures of them in different orientations, e.g. square, triangle, hexagon, pentagon, octagon, cube, cylinder, sphere, cuboid, pyramid • describe their properties, including numbers of sides and corners	• Names drawings of 2D and 3D shapes • Sorts shapes by various criteria, including symmetry in 2D shapes • Draws shapes with some accuracy • Makes shapes from modelling materials and makes recognisable models	I can describe the properties of shapes. I can sort shapes using different properties.
⑨ Is it a right angle?				
Use a set-square to draw right angles and to identify right angles in 2D shapes; compare angles with a right angle; recognise that a straight line is equivalent to two right angles	• classify 3D and 2D shapes in various ways using mathematical properties such as reflective symmetry for 2D shapes, e.g. ● recognise right angles in shapes in different orientations ● recognise angles which are bigger/smaller than 90° and begin to know the terms 'obtuse' and 'acute' ● recognise right-angled and equilateral triangles • use a wider range of measures, e.g. ● recognise angles as a measure of turn and know that one whole turn is 360 degrees	• describe the properties of common 3D and 2D shapes, including numbers of sides and corners, e.g. ● sort 2D and 3D shapes according to a single criterion, e.g. shapes that are pentagons or shapes with a right angle	• Recognises a right angle in a 2D shape • Compares any angle in a 2D shape and can say whether it is larger or smaller than a right angle • Uses a set-square to draw and identify right angles • Understands that a straight line is equivalent to two right angles	I can say whether the angles of a 2D shape are right angles or whether they are smaller or bigger.

BLOCK B

BLOCK B

Activity ①

Prior learning
Children can solve a problem by writing down what calculation they should do and can estimate and check their calculations.

Framework objectives
● Solve one-step and two-step problems involving numbers, money or measures, including time, choosing and carrying out appropriate calculations
● Use knowledge of number operations and corresponding inverses, including doubling and halving, to estimate and check calculations

Vocabulary
problem, solution, calculate, calculation, operation, inverse, answer, method, explain, reasoning, pattern, predict, estimate, approximate

Resources
Worksheet: Solve and check

① Solve and check

Provide the worksheet 'Solve and check'. Ask the children to solve the word problems. They must write their calculation, show their working and then write a check calculation. They should work individually until they have completed the problems. Now ask them to work with a partner to compare how they have solved the problems and checked their solutions. If they have chosen different methods, ask them to discuss which they think is the better way, and why they think this.

Teacher support
Less confident learners: Decide whether to have these children work as a group with adult support to identify how they can solve the problems. Discuss how they can check their calculations.
More confident learners: Encourage these children to work quickly and accurately. Discuss how they solved the problems, and ask if they think they used the most efficient method to do so.

Common misconceptions
Children do not understand which words in the problem give the clue about the type of mathematics needed to solve it.
Read a word problem together. *Which word/s tell you what sort of problem this is?* Repeat this for different word problems so that the children recognise the language used within word problems.

Probing questions
● A box holds 35 nuts. John eats 17 nuts. How many nuts are left? How many people can have 5 nuts each? How many nuts are there in 3 boxes? What calculation did you do each time?
● Anna has a 50p coin and three 20p coins. How much is this altogether? Show how you worked out the answer. How did you decide what calculations to do?
● Half of 38 is 19. Use the word 'double' to make a sentence with the same numbers.
● Which two of these calculations are wrong?
A. Half of 34 is 18
B. 35 −19 = 16
C. 35 ÷ 5 = 12

Next steps
Support: Provide further experience of solving word problems and of checking calculations. Refer back to Year 3 Block B Units 1 and 2.
Extension: Challenge the children to write similar problems for each other to solve. Refer to Year 3 Block E Unit 3 and Year 4 Block B Unit 2.

Activity ②

Prior learning
Children can draw a picture to help make sense of a problem.

Framework objective
Represent the information in a puzzle or problem using numbers, images or diagrams; use these to find a solution and present it in context, where appropriate using £.p notation or units of measure

Vocabulary
problem, solution, calculate, calculation, operation, inverse, answer, method, explain, reasoning, pattern, predict, estimate, approximate, add, subtract, sum, total, difference, plus, minus, multiple

Resources
Worksheet: Make a sketch

② Make a sketch

Provide the worksheet 'Make a sketch'. Explain that there are problems to be solved and that you would like the children to use a sketch or a number line in order to show how they tackled them. Remind them that they should also show a number sentence to show how they solved each problem.

Teacher support
Less confident learners: Decide whether to have these children work as a group with an adult. Ask the adult to check that the children understand the problem and have a method for solving it.
More confident learners: Invite the children to discuss with each other how they solved the problem and what sketch helped them to do this.

Common misconceptions
Children do not recognise what type of problem they are dealing with.
Read the problem together, looking for key words to identify the mathematics needed to solve it. Encourage the children to draw a sketch or use an empty number line in order to move towards a solution.

Probing questions
● A spider has eight legs. How many legs do six spiders have in total? How did you find the answer? What did you write down or draw?
● Anna is 118cm tall. Her brother is 97cm tall. How much taller is Anna than her brother? Draw a picture or use a number line to help you to find the answer.
● Ali had 50 apples. He sold some and then had 20 left. Which of these number sentences shows this?
A. ▢ − 20 = 5
B. 20 − ▢ = 50
C. ▢ − 50 = 20
D. 50 − ▢ = 20

Next steps
Support: Provide further problems for the children to solve. Encourage them to use a number line or make a sketch to help them with their calculations. Refer back to Year 3 Block B Unit 2.
Extension: Challenge the children to work in pairs and to write word problems for each other. Ask them to sketch, write something down, or use an empty number line to show their thinking. Refer to Year 4 Block B Unit 2.

BLOCK B

BLOCK B

Activity

Prior learning
Children can find numbers that match a property.

Framework objective
Identify patterns and relationships involving numbers or shapes, and use these to solve problems

Vocabulary
problem, solution, calculate, calculation, operation, inverse, answer, method, explain, reasoning, pattern, predict, estimate, approximate

Resources
Worksheet: 100-square hunt

③ 100-square hunt

A number ending in 0 can be in the 2-, 3-, 4-, 5-, 6- and 10-times table. Ask the children to think about how they can check this statement to see if they believe it is true. Provide each child with the worksheet '100-square hunt'. Give them about 15 minutes to decide whether the statement is true and to provide some evidence.

Teacher support
Less confident learners: Decide whether to limit the search to just the 2-, 5- and 10-times tables.
More confident learners: Challenge the children to consider whether other tables that they have not learned yet, such as the 7-, 8- and 9-times tables, also fit the statement and why that is so.

Common misconceptions
Children do not have strategies for finding the solution.
Talk the problem through together. Simplify it, if necessary, and suggest that the children begin by looking at one aspect of the problem.

Probing questions
● Explain your findings. Which numbers could be shaded in the 100-square to show that the statement is true?
● What is special about the numbers that you have chosen?

Next steps
Support: Work together to find evidence for another statement, such as 'All numbers in the 4-times table have an even units number'. Refer back to Year 3 Block B Unit 2.
Extension: Encourage the children to write their own statement and then to find evidence to show whether or not it is true. Refer to Year 4 Block B Unit 1.

Activity ④

Prior learning
Children can say what fraction of a shape is shaded.

Framework objective
Read and write proper fractions (e.g. $3/7$, $9/10$), interpreting the denominator as the parts of a whole and the numerator as the number of parts; identify and estimate fractions of shapes; use diagrams to compare fractions and establish equivalents

Vocabulary
part, equal part, fraction, one whole, one half, two halves, one quarter, two/three/four quarters, one third, two thirds, one sixth, one tenth

Resources
Worksheet: Fractions of shapes

④ Fractions of shapes

Provide the worksheet 'Fractions of shapes'. This sets a challenge: shade in $1/6$ of six 12-square grids in different ways. Set a time limit and encourage the children to work quickly.

Teacher support
Less confident learners: Discuss with the children how to find $1/6$ of 12. Ask: *So how many squares should you shade each time?*
More confident learners: Challenge the children to repeat the activity, this time for shading $3/4$. Ask them to write down other fractions that are equivalent to $3/4$ such as $6/8$ and $9/12$.

Common misconceptions
Children think that a larger numerator means a larger fraction (for example, $1/6$ is larger than $1/3$).
Use practical apparatus to demonstrate, for example, cutting pre-divided circles into thirds and sixths, then comparing the shapes.

Probing questions
● How do you know that you have shaded $1/6$ each time?
● Can you say another fraction that is equivalent to $1/6$? (For example, $2/12$.)
● Imagine a square made from 16 squares. How many would you shade for $1/4$? $1/8$? $7/8$?

Next steps
Support: Repeat the activity for different numbers of squares and fractions until the children are confident. Refer back to Year 3 Block B Unit 2.
Extension: Ask the children to use squared paper, make their own shapes and shade in fractions such as $3/10$ in different ways. Refer to Year 4 Block E Unit 1.

BLOCK B

Activities

Prior learning
Children know and use all addition and subtraction facts to 20. They can find what to add to a number to make 100.

Framework objective
Derive and recall all addition and subtraction facts for each number to 20, sums and differences of multiples of 10 and number pairs that total 100

Vocabulary
add, subtract, sum, total, difference, plus

Resources
Resource sheets: Self-assessment sheet, 100-square
Classroom resources: coloured pencils, individual whiteboards and pens

⑤ Quick-fire add and subtract

Provide the children with whiteboards and pens. Explain that you will give them 20 questions for which you expect them to be able to quickly write down the answers. When you say *Show me,* they hold up their whiteboards. Ask questions such as: *What is 15 + 4; 19 − 12; 14 + 18; 18 − 11?* When this is finished, ask the children to complete the self-assessment sheet. The children should comment on how well they did and identify what they need to learn now.

Teacher support
Less confident learners: Decide whether to limit this activity to just addition questions, then a set of subtraction questions.
More confident learners: Give the children more complex calculations to do or quicken the pace as they get more and more confident.

Common misconceptions
Children do not use facts that they already know to derive new facts.
Write down 1 + 1 = 2 and 11 + 1 = 12 and so on. Discuss how these facts link. Repeat this for some subtraction facts, such as 2 − 1 and 12 − 1 (and so on).

Probing questions
● Tell me some addition and subtraction facts with the answer 12.
● Now tell me some facts that fit this: □ + 11 = □; □ − 11 = □.

Next steps
Support: Provide further experience of recalling these facts. Concentrate on addition, subtraction and then a mix of both. Refer back to Year 3 Block A Unit 3.
Extension: Ask the children to write some word problems that use these facts. These can be used by the other children in the class as part of an oral and mental starter. Refer to Year 4 Block A Unit 1.

⑥ Make 100

The children work in groups of three or four, with resource sheet '100-square' and a coloured pencil. They take turns to shade in one of the squares and to say the number to add to it to make 100. For example, if the number 77 is shaded, the corresponding shaded number would be 23. This is repeated around the group until all the numbers have been shaded, except for 50 and 100. Decide whether to use the self-assessment sheet for the children to record their achievements and what they need to do next.

Teacher support
Less confident learners: The children could use a 100-square to count up in order to find those totals that they do not yet recall.

More confident learners: Ask the children to repeat the activity, working as quickly as they can, in order to demonstrate their rapid recall of the facts.

Common misconceptions
Children do not have strategies for finding the additions that they do not know.
Use a 100-square with the children to count up to find the correct answer. When they are confident with this, ask them to repeat this, counting up mentally.

Probing questions
● Which two numbers have not been shaded on your 100-square? Why is that?
● Rick says 38 + 72 = 100. Is he right? What mistake has he made?

Next steps
Support: Ensure that the children have frequent opportunities to recall these additions, such as in oral and mental starters. Refer back to Year 3 Block A Unit 2.
Extension: Provide opportunities for the children to recall these facts in solving problems. Encourage them to recall quickly so that they demonstrate their competence in this. Refer to Year 4 Block A Unit 1.

Activity ⑦

Prior learning
Children know the 2-, 3-, 4-, 5-, 6- and 10-times tables and can use them for division. They can recognise multiples of 2, 5 and 10.

Framework objective
Derive and recall multiplication facts for the 2-, 3-, 4-, 5-, 6- and 10-times tables and the corresponding division facts; recognise multiples of 2, 5 or 10 up to 1000

Vocabulary
multiple of, times, product, multiply, multiplied by, share, divide, divided by, divided into

Resources
Interactive activity: Multiplication square
Worksheet: Multiplication square

⑦ Multiplication square

Reveal the interactive activity 'Multiplication square' (prepare the screen beforehand by selecting one square, such as 24 in the 3-times table, and leaving the rest hidden). Ask the children to say the multiplication and division facts for the number they see (for example, 8 × 3 = 24 and 24 ÷ 3 = 8). Invite them to fill in all the other numbers in the square up to 6 × 10. Provide the worksheet 'Multiplication square' for the children to record their answers.

Teacher support
Less confident learners: Decide whether to restrict this activity to finding multiples up to 4 × 10.
More confident learners: Once the children have found the multiples to 6 ×10, ask them to complete as much of the rest of the multiplication square as they can.

Common misconceptions
Children do not recognise the patterns in the multiplication table and so cannot find the multiples.
Spend time looking for patterns. For example, ask the children to write in all the numbers in the 2-times table, in the column under '2', then to do the same in the row across for '2'. Repeat this for the other tables that the children know. Ask them to look at what they have written and describe any patterns they find.

BLOCK B

Probing questions

● Twenty-four is the multiple of 8 and 3. In what other ways can we make the multiple 24?
● What is 45 divided by 5? How do you know this?
● Find a number between 20 and 30 that gives a remainder of, for example, 1 or 2, when divided by 3.
● If the answer of a division is 9, what could the starting division sentence have been? How many different answers can you find?

Next steps

Support: Provide oral and mental starter experience of recalling table facts and deriving the relevant division facts. Let children concentrate on one table at a time, committing the facts to memory. Refer back to Year 3 Block E Unit 2.
Extension: Encourage the children to use the multiplication and division facts that they know in solving problems. They can set problems for the others in the class to answer and these could be used as an oral and mental starter. Refer to Year 3 Block E Unit 3.

Activity ⑧

Prior learning
Children can describe the properties of shapes and sort shapes using different properties.

Framework objective
Relate 2D shapes and 3D solids to drawings of them; describe, visualise, classify, draw and make the shapes

Vocabulary
triangle, square, rectangle, quadrilateral, pentagon, hexagon, octagon, circle, semicircle, cube, cuboid, pyramid, cone, cylinder, prism, hemisphere, face, edge, vertex, surface, solid, side, straight, curved, diagram, right-angled

Resources
Worksheet: Shape sort (3) (two copies for each pair of children)
Classroom resources: sets of 2D shape tiles (triangle, square, rectangle, quadrilateral, pentagon, hexagon, octagon, circle, semicircle), sets of 3D models of solids (cube, cuboid, pyramid, cone, cylinder, prism, hemisphere)

⑧ Shape sort

Provide each child with the worksheet 'Shape sort (3)'. They should work in pairs and decide on sorting criteria for the set of shapes that they have been given. This could be either a set of 2D shape tiles or 3D models. They should record their sorting on the worksheet. There is room to do this in two different ways. Then they swap their shape set with another pair, so that they have the other set, and repeat the activity using their second copy of their worksheet.

Teacher support
Less confident learners: Decide whether to limit the range of shapes that the children sort. Elicit from them the properties that they could use.
More confident learners: Challenge the children to include a wide range of properties, including line symmetry.

Common misconceptions
Children confuse 2D and 3D shapes.
Discuss how shapes such as prisms have rectangular or square faces and that a cone has a circular base. Children may find it useful to print with the 3D solids in order to see the 2D shapes in the faces.

Probing questions
- I dip a triangular prism in paint and make a print of each face. What shapes will I print?
- Use cubes to make these shapes:

Next steps
Support: Gradually extend the range of shapes and properties so that the children become familiar with these. Refer back to Year 3 Block B Unit 2.
Extension: Extend the range of shapes that the children use by asking them to combine shapes to make new ones. They then explore the properties of the shapes that they have made. Refer to Year 4 Block B Unit 1.

Activity ⑨

Prior learning
Children can say whether the angles of a 2D shape are right angles or whether they are smaller or bigger.

Framework objective
Use a set-square to draw right angles and to identify right angles in 2D shapes; compare angles with a right angle; recognise that a straight line is equivalent to two right angles

Vocabulary
right angle, right-angled, vertex, vertices

Resources
Interactive activity: Sorting machine – shapes
Worksheet: Is it a right angle?
Classroom resources: set-squares

⑨ Is it a right angle?

Begin with the interactive activity 'Sorting machine – shapes'. Ask the children to help you sort the angles marked on the shape into those that are right angles and those that are not. Discuss each shape and how the children made their decision. Then provide the worksheet 'Is it a right angle?' and ask the children to use their set-square to help them to identify right angles, angles that are smaller and those that are larger than a right angle.

Teacher support
Less confident learners: Decide whether to work as a group to complete the worksheet. Check that children use their set-square correctly.
More confident learners: Invite the children to draw some more shapes, showing angles that are right angles as well as some that are larger or smaller than right angles.

Common misconceptions
Children do not recognise right angles.
Check that the children can use their set-square correctly. Discuss where they might find right angles in the environment and ask them to do a search for right angles, angles that are larger and those that are smaller than a right angle.

Probing questions
- Find a quadrilateral that has two angles that are smaller than a right angle and two that are bigger than a right angle.
- Which shapes always have four right angles?

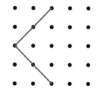

● Draw two lines to complete the square (see diagram, right).

Next steps
Support: Ask the children to draw shapes that contain a variety of angle sizes. They should say which are right angles, and which are smaller/larger than a right angle. Refer back to Year 2 Block B Unit 3.
Extension: Invite the children to make their own 2D shapes by combining shape tiles. Ask them to explore the angles of the shapes they make and to classify these. Refer to Year 4 Block B Unit 1.

Activity ⑩

Prior learning Children can find shapes that match a property.	**Framework objective** Identify patterns and relationships involving numbers or shapes, and use these to solve problems
	Vocabulary problem, solution, method, explain, reasoning, pattern
	Resources **Worksheet:** Shape puzzle **Classroom resource:** safety scissors

⑩ Shape puzzle

Provide each child with the worksheet 'Shape puzzle'. They should cut the two triangles from the bottom of the sheet and combine these to make new shapes. Ask them to sketch the shapes that they make and to find the shapes which have a right angle.

Teacher support
Less confident learners: Ask the children to describe the angles of the two triangles so that they are clear that one of these triangles has a right angle.
More confident learners: Ask the children to feed back their results to the rest of the class. Tell them to prepare their results so that they can do this in a systematic and logical way.

Common misconceptions
Children do not work systematically.
Ask the children how they can keep track of what they have discovered. Discuss how, by changing just one thing each time (such as the position of one of the shapes) they can be sure of what they have explored.

Probing questions
● Look at this set of 2D shapes. Identify the shapes in the set that have one right angle, two right angles, more than two right angles.

Next steps
Support: Provide further experience of solving shape puzzles. For example, ask the children to find ways of combining the two triangles so that the combined shape has no right angles. Refer back to Year 3 Block B Unit 2.
Extension: Ask the children to repeat the activity, this time combining a right-angled triangle with another shape of their choice. Ask them to find which shapes will allow them to have at least one right angle in their combined shape. Refer to Year 4 Block B Unit 1.

BLOCK B

Periodic assessment

These activities can be used at any time during the teaching of this block to assess those children that you think have achieved the objective. A grid highlighting the related assessment focuses and expected learning outcomes for each activity can be found on the CD-ROM.

Solving problems

Framework objective
Solve one-step and two-step problems involving numbers, money or measures, including time, choosing and carrying out appropriate calculations

Learning outcome
- I can explain how I solve problems.

Provide the children with the worksheet 'Solving problems'. Ask them to work individually to find the solutions. Encourage them to show their working. Review the problems together and discuss how the children found the solutions.

Addition and subtraction

Framework objective
Derive and recall all addition and subtraction facts for each number to 20, sums and differences of multiples of 10 and number pairs that total 100

Learning outcomes
- I know and use addition and subtraction facts for all numbers to 20.
- I can add and subtract multiples of 10 in my head.
- I can find what to add to a number to make 100.

Addition and subtraction to 20: Use the questions on the worksheet 'Addition and subtraction (1)'. Read these twice and ask the children to write down the answers. Give no more than about 5–7 seconds for each question. This can be marked together so that the children can see which facts they know.
Multiples of 10: Provide children with the interactive activity 'Totals and differences' and ask them to complete this individually. Mark together so that the children can see which facts they know.
Number pairs that total 100: Provide children with the interactive activity 'Number pairs'. Ask them to complete the task. Discuss with them the strategies that they used to find the solutions.

Reflective symmetry

Framework objective
Draw and complete shapes with reflective symmetry; draw the reflection of a shape in a mirror line along one side

Learning outcomes
- I can draw a symmetrical shape.
- I can reflect a shape when the mirror line is one of its sides.

Provide children with the worksheet 'Line symmetry' and ask them to complete this. Discuss how they tackled each shape and found its reflection. If any children find this difficult, provide a safety mirror so that they can see the reflection of the original shape and compare this with their sketch.

BLOCK B

Name   Date

BLOCK B

Solving problems

Find the answers to these problems.

◼ Show how you worked them out.

1. There are 70 books in one parcel and 50 in another.
How many books are there altogether?.....................................

2. Petra has 15 stickers.
She gives six stickers to Fay.
Suzy gives Petra 12 stickers.
How many stickers does Petra have now?..............................

3. There are eight packs of chocolate in a box.
Ten boxes fit into a crate.
How many packs of chocolate are there in a crate? ....

4. Peter has 24 postage stamps in his collection.
His father gives him another 23 stamps.
How many more does Peter need to make 100 stamps?....................

◼ Use the box below to show your working out.

How easy?

Red
Amber
Green

How do you think you have done?

_____

_____

Name   Date

Addition and subtraction (1)

Read each question twice.

■ Give the children no more than 5−7 seconds to write each answer.

1. 12 + 6 .... ☐

2. 3 + 19 .... ☐

3. 18 − 15 .... ☐

4. 16 − 4 .... ☐

5. 17 + 19 .... ☐

6. 17 − 3 .... ☐

7. 7 + 9 .... ☐

8. 16 + 3 .... ☐

9. 13 − 7 .... ☐

10. 20 − 14 .... ☐

How easy?

Red
Amber
Green

How do you think you have done?

_____

_____

BLOCK B

Name   Date

Line symmetry

Draw in the lines of symmetry.

◢ Reflect each shape in the mirror line.

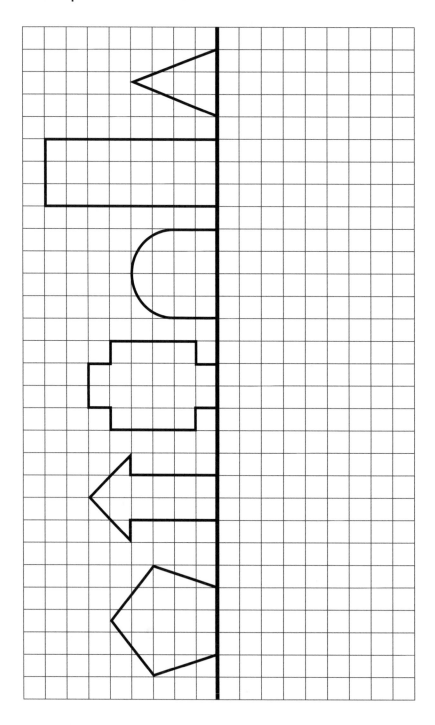

How easy?

Red

Amber

Green

How do you think you have done?

_____

_____

BLOCK C
Handling data and measures

Expected prior learning
Check that children can already:
- collect and record the data needed to answer questions
- begin to organise results and solutions, and present data as block graphs and pictograms
- sort objects using lists, tables and diagrams
- explain decisions, methods and results in words, pictures or written form
- choose and use standard units (m, cm, kg, litre) to estimate and measure
- choose and use suitable instruments and equipment to measure and collect data
- recognise multiples of 10 and derive and recall the 10-times table
- read scales with numbered divisions and interpret the divisions shown
- identify and use units of time and work out time intervals
- begin to use ICT to organise and present data.

Objectives overview
The text in this diagram identifies the focus of mathematics learning within the block.

Key aspects of learning
- Enquiry
- Problem solving
- Reasoning
- Information processing
- Social skills
- Communication

Collecting, organising, presenting and interpreting data to follow a line of enquiry

Identifying further questions

Sorting information using lists, tables and diagrams

Presenting data in frequency tables and bar charts

Choosing and using appropriate units of measurement

BLOCK C: Handling data and measures

Reading times and calculating time intervals

Knowing relationships between units of measure

Using ICT

Unit 1 Handling data and measures

Introduction
In this unit, children decide on information to collect, record and organise, when sorting data onto Carroll and Venn diagrams. They work in pairs and groups for some activities, and should be encouraged to discuss who will take which roles and carry out what specific actions. Children collect data about their own measurements. This should be kept safe for use again during the summer term.

BLOCK C

Framework objectives	Assessment focuses		Success criteria for Year 3	Learning outcomes
	Level 3	Level 2		
① Using a ruler ② Jug investigation				
Follow a line of enquiry by deciding what information is important; make and use lists, tables and graphs to organise and interpret the information	• begin to organise their work and check results, e.g. • begin to develop own ways of recording • develop an organised approach as they get into recording their work on a problem • discuss their mathematical work and begin to explain their thinking • use and interpret mathematical symbols and diagrams	• discuss their work using mathematical language, e.g. with support • describe the strategies and methods they use in their work • listen to others' explanations, try to make sense of them, compare.... evaluate... • begin to represent their work using symbols and simple diagrams	• Explains what information is important and should be collected • Decides how to collect the information, organise and record it	*I can decide what information to collect to answer a question.*
① Using a ruler ② Jug investigation				
Read, to the nearest division and half-division, scales that are numbered or partially numbered; use the information to measure and draw to a suitable degree of accuracy	• use non-standard units and standard metric units of length, capacity and mass in a range of contexts, e.g. • read simple scales, e.g. increments of 2, 5 or 10	• begin to use everyday non-standard and standard units to measure length and mass, e.g. • read scales to the nearest labelled division	• Uses a ruler, tape or metre stick to measure a given length to the nearest ½cm • Explains how to place the ruler, tape or metre stick against the item to be measured in order to give a reasonably accurate reading	*I can use a ruler or a tape measure to measure a length to the nearest ½cm.*
③ How do we measure it?				
Know the relationships between kilometres and metres, metres and centimetres, kilograms and grams, litres and millilitres; choose and use appropriate units to estimate, measure and record measurements	• use non-standard units and standard metric units of length, capacity and mass in a range of contexts, e.g. • measure a length to the nearest ½cm	• begin to use everyday non-standard and standard units to measure length and mass, e.g. • begin to understand that numbers can be used not only to count discrete objects but also to describe continuous measures, e.g. length • know which measuring tools to use to find, e.g., how much an object weighs, how tall a child is, how long it takes to run around the edge of the playground... • begin to use a wider range of measures	• Makes sensible suggestions for units to measure given lengths • Knows the metric system for length and understands the relationships between the units	*I can suggest sensible units to measure lengths.*

Unit 1 ⬜ Handling data and measures

Framework objectives	Assessment focuses		Success criteria for Year 3	Learning outcomes
	Level 3	Level 2		
④ Frequency chart				
Answer a question by collecting, organising and interpreting data; use tally charts, frequency tables, pictograms and bar charts to represent results and illustrate observations; use ICT to create a simple bar chart	• gather information, e.g. • decide what data to collect to answer a question, e.g. what is the most common way to travel to school • make appropriate choices for recording data, e.g. a tally chart or frequency table • extract and interpret information presented in simple tables, lists, bar charts and pictograms	• sort objects and classify them using more than one criterion, e.g. • sort a given set of shapes using two criteria such as triangle/not triangle and blue/not blue • understand vocabulary relating to handling data, e.g. • understand vocabulary such as sort, group, set, list, table, most common, most popular • collect and sort data to test a simple hypothesis, e.g. • count a show of hands to test the hypothesis 'Most children in our class are in bed by 7:30pm' • record results in simple lists, tables, pictograms and block graphs • communicate their findings, using the simple lists, tables, pictograms and block graphs they have recorded, e.g. • respond to questions about the data they have presented, e.g. 'How many of our names have five letters?' • pose similar questions about their data for others to answer	• Makes a frequency chart from data they have collected • Interprets the frequency chart, explaining what the data means	*I can explain what a frequency chart tells me.*
⑤ Venn diagram				
Use Venn diagrams or Carroll diagrams to sort data and objects using more than one criterion	• use Venn and Carroll diagrams to record their sorting and classifying of information, e.g. • represent sorting using one or two criteria typical of Level 2 and 3 mathematics, e.g. shapes sorted using properties such as right angles and equal sides	• sort objects and classify them using more than one criterion, e.g. • sort a given set of shapes using two criteria such as triangle/not triangle and blue/not blue • understand vocabulary relating to handling data, e.g. • understand vocabulary such as sort, group, set, list, table, most common, most popular	• Makes a Venn diagram • Knows what criteria are needed in order to be able to place an item into the intersection of the Venn diagram	*I can place objects on a Venn diagram.*

BLOCK C

Activities

Prior learning
Children can decide what information to collect to answer a question. They can use a ruler or a tape measure to measure a length to the nearest ½cm.

Framework objectives
● Follow a line of enquiry by deciding what information is important; make and use lists, tables and graphs to organise and interpret the information
● **Read, to the nearest division and half-division, scales that are numbered or partially numbered; use the information to measure and draw to a suitable degree of accuracy**

Vocabulary
problem, enquiry, solution, calculate, calculation, method, explain, reasoning, reason, metric unit, standard unit, millimetre (mm), centimetre (cm), metre (m), ruler, tape measure, length, width

Resources
Interactive activity (ITP): Fixing points
Worksheet: Using a ruler
Resource sheet: Self-assessment
Classroom resources: measuring tapes, rulers marked in 0.5cm, jugs, strips of paper

① Using a ruler

Reveal the ITP 'Fixing points'. Click on any two points of the grid to create a line between them. Drag the ruler to the correct position for measuring the line. Ask: *How long is this line?* Encourage the children to explain where a ruler should be placed against a line in order to make a measurement. Repeat this for another line length, then provide the children with a ruler each and ask them to complete the worksheet 'Using a ruler'.

Teacher support
Less confident learners: Check that the children understand where to place the ruler against what they are measuring. Check that they are confident with using a ruler marked in 0.5cm.
More confident learners: Decide whether to provide rulers marked in millimetres and ask the children to measure the lines to the nearest millimetre.

Common misconceptions
Children start to measure a line using the 'dead' part of the ruler, rather than at the 0cm point.
Discuss how measuring from the beginning of the ruler, rather than from the 0cm mark, leads to inaccurate measuring. Provide further experience of placing a ruler onto a line in order to measure accurately.

Probing questions
● Where should the ruler be placed to begin the measurement?
● How do you write a measurement that is half way between 5cm and 6cm?

Next steps
Support: Provide further experience of measuring the lengths, widths, heights, depths of objects in the classroom. Include measuring around the circumference using a measuring tape, so that children see that objects 'in the round' can also be measured. Refer back to Year 2 Block C Unit 3.
Extension: Include further experience of measuring with increasing accuracy, including measuring in millimetres. Refer to Year 3 Block C Unit 2.

② Jug investigation

Ask the children to work in pairs. Provide each pair with three differently shaped jugs, or similar containers, with a capacity of between 500ml and 1 litre. Ask the children to find out everything they can about the length, height, width and circumference of the container. Remind them that there are various tools available for measuring length. Provide paper for the children to record what they have found out. Give each child the self-assessment sheet to record their learning and what they need to do next.

Teacher support
Less confident learners: Check that the children understand how to use a ruler and a measuring tape with accuracy. Discuss with the children how they will record what they find out.
More confident learners: Challenge the children to collect the results from other groups and make a record of the results. Ask them to decide how to record the collected results.

Common misconceptions
Children may be unsure of how to use a ruler.
Look together at a ruler. Ask the children to say how they would use this to measure the length of a strip of paper. Discuss where they place the ruler and how to deal with the 'dead' end of it, where there are no measuring marks.

Probing questions
- Where should the ruler be placed to begin the measurement?
- How do you write a measurement that is half way between 5cm and 6cm?

Next steps
Support: Provide further experience of practical measuring. Check that the children understand how to use rulers and tape measures. Refer back to Year 2 Block C Unit 3.
Extension: Introduce measuring in millimetres. Refer to Year 3 Block C Unit 2.

BLOCK C

Activity ③

Prior learning
Children can suggest sensible units to measure lengths.

Framework objective
Know the relationships between kilometres and metres, metres and centimetres, kilograms and grams, litres and millilitres; choose and use appropriate units to estimate, measure and record measurements

Vocabulary
metric unit, standard unit, millimetre (mm), centimetre (cm), metre (m), kilometre (km)

Resources
Worksheet: How do we measure it?

③ How do we measure it?

Explain that you would like the children to answer the questions on the worksheet 'How do we measure it?'. Ask them to think carefully about each question and choose the most sensible answer. *What would you use to measure the height of a table: centimetres, metres or kilometres? Why do you think this is the most appropriate?*

Teacher support
Less confident learners: Check that the children are familiar with millimetres. Decide whether to complete the activity as a group. Discuss each part of the activity and why the children think their answers are sensible.
More confident learners: Challenge the children to think of three different answers to the final question on the activity sheet. Ask them to explain why they think that their answers are sensible.

Common misconceptions
Children do not understand the size of each measure of length.
Provide further experience in estimating and measuring lengths. Discuss which units are appropriate for each item that the child measures and why this is so.

Probing questions
● A metre stick is how many centimetres long?
● Which is the most sensible estimate for the length of your hand span?
  A. 80cm   B. 16m   C. 14cm   D. 12km
● Suggest something you would measure in kilograms, in millilitres, in kilometres.

Next steps
Support: Give further experience in choosing the units when measuring length. Ask the children to explain their choices each time. Refer back to Year 2 Block C Unit 2.
Extension: Encourage the children to measure length with a wider variety of equipment (callipers, depth gauges, and so on). Refer to Year 3 Block C Unit 2.

Activity ④

Prior learning
Children can explain what a frequency chart tells them.

Framework objective
Answer a question by collecting, organising and interpreting data; use tally charts, frequency tables, pictograms and bar charts to represent results and illustrate observations; use ICT to create a simple bar chart

Vocabulary
problem, enquiry, solution, calculate, calculation, method, explain, reasoning, reason, predict, collect, organise, compare, sort, classify, represent, interpret, effect, information, data, survey, table, frequency table, block graph, bar chart, label, title

Resources
Interactive activity: Frequency chart: favourite snacks
Worksheet: Frequency chart

④ Frequency chart

Reveal the interactive activity 'Frequency chart: favourite snacks'. Ask the children to study the chart on the screen, then ask the following questions:
● Which is the most popular snack?
● Which snack do the children like least?
● Which snack is more popular than Funny faces potato shapes but not as popular as Smoked apple and lamb crisps?
● How many children are there altogether in Class 3?
Check who gives positive responses and who is unsure. Once the children have answered the questions, give out the worksheet 'Frequency chart'. Ask the children to complete the frequency chart and answer the questions.

Teacher support

Less confident learners: Decide whether to work together to answer the questions. Read the statements on the chart, then ask the children to explain what information they have gleaned and where it goes in the chart.

More confident learners: When the children have completed the worksheet successfully, ask them to work in pairs to compile a new frequency chart that they can use with the rest of the class in order to collect data.

Common misconceptions

Children do not understand how to interpret the frequency chart.
Provide a simpler chart, in which the children collect their own data. Then ask questions about the data. If children are unsure, show them how the answers are derived from the data. Repeat this to check their understanding.

Probing questions

● You have to find out what sport your class prefers. Explain what you would do. How would you record the information?
● Say three things that you can tell from this frequency table.
● Why might so few children have chosen to have school dinner on Thursday?

School dinners for Class 4

Day	Number of school dinners
Monday	11
Tuesday	13
Wednesday	17
Thursday	8
Friday	13

Next steps

Support: Suggest to the children that they write their own frequency chart, collecting the data from the rest of the class (for example, on favourite ice-cream flavours). Check that the children understand the data they have collected and how this should be recorded. Ask them questions about their data to check that they can interpret the data. Refer back to Year 2 Block C Unit 2.

Extension: Ask the children to decide upon the information that they can collect and to carry this out, gaining information from the rest of the class. They should record using a frequency chart, then look carefully at their chart to see what information they can glean. Ask them to write three sentences to explain the information that they have from their chart. Refer to Year 3 Block C Unit 2.

BLOCK C

Activity ⑤

Prior learning
Children can place objects on a Venn diagram.

Framework objective
Use Venn diagrams or Carroll diagrams to sort data and objects using more than one criterion

Vocabulary
problem, enquiry, solution, calculate, calculation, method, explain, reasoning, reason, predict, collect, organise, compare, sort, classify, represent, interpret, effect, information, data, survey, Venn diagram, label, title

Resources
Interactive activity: Sorting numbers
Worksheet: Venn diagram (2)

⑤ Venn diagram

Reveal the interactive activity 'Sorting numbers'. Ask the children to place the numbers 0 to 30 in the correct areas of the Venn diagram. They should decide where each number should go, and why. Stop them at regular intervals and ask questions such as: *Where would the number 17 fit? Why does it go there? Where does the number 26 fit? Why does it go into the rectangle? What sort of numbers fit into the intersection?* (Numbers that are both odd and a multiple of 3, such as 3, 9, 15…) Now provide the worksheet 'Venn diagram (2)'. Ask the children to work individually to complete the Venn diagram and then answer the questions on the sheet.

Teacher support
Less confident learners: Decide whether to have the children work as a group to complete the Venn diagram. Children may find it helpful to say all the multiples of 4, from 0 to 50, in order to see the pattern that these multiples make.

More confident learners: Challenge the children to think of some more questions to ask about the completed Venn diagram.

Common misconceptions
Children do not understand what goes into the intersection of a Venn diagram. Make a simple Venn diagram using the numbers 2 to 20 and the criteria 'Multiples of 2' and 'Multiples of 5'. Ask the children to say where the numbers should go. If they have not understood that 10 and 20 are both multiples of 2 and of 5, then explain that these two numbers go into the intersection because they belong to both sets of numbers. Repeat this for another simple Venn diagram.

Probing questions
● Where would you place these numbers on the diagram: 13, 20, 10, 7?

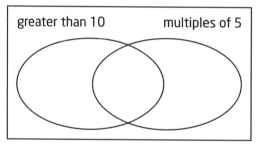

greater than 10   multiples of 5

● What number could go into the intersection?

Next steps
Support: Provide further opportunities for making and interpreting Venn diagrams. This could include sorting objects such as shapes, as well as sets of numbers.

Extension: Ask the children to decide upon their own sets of numbers to sort on a Venn diagram. Then ask them to think of some questions that could be asked about their diagram. They should pass their diagram to another child, then ask their questions about it. Refer to Year 3 Block C Unit 2.

Unit 2 Handling data and measures

Introduction

In this unit, children report on their work, making their communication succinct and clear. They develop their skills in handling data. They build on their skills in measuring, whilst concentrating on mass for this unit. They continue to develop their skills in telling the time and calculate intervals of time. They make Carroll diagrams, and use these to sort numbers, including multiples. They make pictograms of data that they collect for themselves

Framework objectives	Assessment focuses		Success criteria for Year 3	Learning outcomes
	Level 3	Level 2		
① Reading a thermometer ② Temperature ④ Car colour				
Follow a line of enquiry by deciding what information is important; make and use lists, tables and graphs to organise and interpret the information	● begin to organise their work and check results, e.g. ● begin to develop own ways of recording ● develop an organised approach as they get into recording their work on a problem ● discuss their mathematical work and begin to explain their thinking, e.g. ● use appropriate mathematical vocabulary ● talk about their findings by referring to their written work ● use and interpret mathematical symbols and diagrams	● discuss their work using mathematical language, e.g. with support ● describe the strategies and methods they use in their work ● listen to others' explanations, try to make sense of them, compare... evaluate... ● begin to represent their work using symbols and simple diagrams, e.g. with support ● use pictures, diagrams and symbols to communicate their thinking, or demonstrate a solution or process ● begin to appreciate the need to record and develop their own methods of recording	● Explains what information is important and should be collected ● Decides how to collect the information, organise and record it	*I can decide what information to collect to answer a question.*
① Reading a thermometer ② Temperature				
Know the relationships between kilometres and metres, metres and centimetres, kilograms and grams, litres and millilitres; choose and use appropriate units to estimate, measure and record measurements	● use non-standard units and standard metric units of length, capacity and mass in a range of contexts, e.g. ● measure a length to the nearest ½cm	● begin to use everyday non-standard and standard units to measure length and mass, e.g. ● begin to understand that numbers can be used not only to count discrete objects but also to describe continuous measures, e.g. length ● know which measuring tools to use to find, e.g., how much an object weighs, how tall a child is, how long it takes to run around the edge of the playground, how much water it takes to fill the water tray ● begin to use a wider range of measures	● Uses a thermometer to measure temperature in degrees Celsius	*I know that temperature can be measured in degrees Celsius.*

BLOCK C

Unit 2 📖 Handling data and measures

Framework objectives	Assessment focuses		Success criteria for Year 3	Learning outcomes
	Level 3	Level 2		
① Reading a thermometer ② Temperature				
Read, to the nearest division and half-division, scales that are numbered or partially numbered; use the information to measure and draw to a suitable degree of accuracy	● use non-standard units and standard metric units of length, capacity and mass in a range of contexts, e.g. ● read simple scales, e.g. increments of 2, 5 or 10	● begin to use everyday non-standard and standard units to measure length and mass, e.g. ● read scales to the nearest labelled division	● Measures temperature on a thermometer to the nearest degree Celsius	*I can read the temperature on a thermometer to the nearest degree.*
③ How long does it take?				
Read the time on a 12-hour digital clock and to the nearest 5 minutes on an analogue clock; calculate time intervals and find start or end times for a given time interval	● use standard units of time, e.g. ● read a 12-hour clock and generally calculate time durations that do not go over the hour	There is no assessment focus for this level.	● Reads time on a clock face to the nearest 5 minutes ● Calculates time taken to the nearest 5 minutes	*I can find how long a journey took if I know the start and end times.*
④ Car colour				
Answer a question by collecting, organising and interpreting data; use tally charts, frequency tables, pictograms and bar charts to represent results and illustrate observations; use ICT to create a simple bar chart	● gather information, e.g. ● decide what data to collect to answer a question, e.g. what is the most common way to travel to school ● make appropriate choices for recording data, e.g. a tally chart or frequency table ● extract and interpret information presented in simple tables, lists, bar charts and pictograms	● sort objects and classify them using more than one criterion ● understand vocabulary relating to handling data, e.g. ● understand vocabulary such as sort, group, set, list, table, most common, most popular ● collect and sort data to test a simple hypothesis ● record results in simple lists, tables, pictograms and block graphs ● communicate their findings, using the simple lists, tables, pictograms and block graphs they have recorded	● Makes a pictogram with a scale of one picture to two objects ● Can interpret the data in a pictogram with a scale of 1:2	*I can show information in a pictogram where each picture represents two people.*
⑤ Carroll diagram				
Use Venn diagrams or Carroll diagrams to sort data and objects using more than one criterion	● use Venn and Carroll diagrams to record their sorting and classifying of information, e.g. ● represent sorting using one or two criteria typical of Level 2 and 3 mathematics, e.g. shapes sorted using properties such as right angles and equal sides	● sort objects and classify them using more than one criterion, e.g. ● sort a given set of shapes using two criteria such as triangle/not triangle and blue/not blue ● understand vocabulary relating to handling data, e.g. ● understand vocabulary such as sort, group, set, list, table, most common, most popular	● Makes a Carroll diagram ● Knows how to label the regions in a four-region Carroll diagram ● Understands where objects will go in a four-region Carroll diagram	*I can place objects on a Carroll diagram.*

BLOCK C

Activities

Prior learning
Children can decide what information to collect to answer a question. They know that temperature can be measured in degrees Celsius and can read the temperature on a thermometer to the nearest degree.

Framework objectives
● Follow a line of enquiry by deciding what information is important; make and use lists, tables and graphs to organise and interpret the information
● Know the relationships between kilometres and metres, metres and centimetres, kilograms and grams, litres and millilitres; choose and use appropriate units to estimate, measure and record measurements
● **Read, to the nearest division and half-division, scales that are numbered or partially numbered; use the information to measure and draw to a suitable degree of accuracy**

Vocabulary
problem, enquiry, solution, calculate, calculation, method, explain, reasoning, reason, degree, Celsius (° C), thermometer, temperature

Resources
Display page: Reading a thermometer
Worksheets: Reading a thermometer, Temperature
Classroom resources: five beakers of water (from ice-cold to about 40°C) for each group, thermometers marked in degrees from 0°C to at least 50°C

① Reading a thermometer

Reveal the display page 'Reading a thermometer'. Ask the children to look at the example on the first screen and to agree the temperature reading. Invite a child to explain how to write degrees Celsius in the shortened form (°C). Repeat this for the further examples on the subsequent screens. Make a note of who responds confidently and who is not yet certain about how to make an accurate reading of a temperature. Now provide the worksheet 'Reading a thermometer' and ask the children to complete it individually.

Teacher support
Less confident learners: Check that the children understand what the intermediate marks on the thermometer, between the decade markings, stand for.
More confident learners: Discuss how the temperature can be less than 0°C. Ask the children to show where temperatures such as −5°C would be marked on the thermometer. Ask questions such as: *If the temperature rises to 3°C, how much warmer is that?*

Common misconceptions
Children do not understand how to read the scale on the thermometer.
Provide further experience of reading thermometer scales. Point out the divisions between the multiples of 10 on the scale. Ask the children to count up to the next 10 so that they understand how the scale is read.

Probing questions
● What measuring instrument would you choose to measure temperature in the classroom?
● The temperature outside is 15°C and the temperature inside is 19°C. What is the difference between the outside and inside temperatures?
● Show me on this thermometer where 25°C is marked.

Next steps
Support: Provide further experience of reading thermometers. This can be done as a practical activity with, for example, the children taking the indoor and outdoor temperatures each day. Refer back to Year 3 Block C Unit 1.

BLOCK C

Extension: Give further examples of comparing two temperatures where one of them is a negative temperature. Discuss how to make the comparison and find the difference between the temperatures, such as 16°C and −1°C. Refer to Year 3 Block C Unit 3.

② Temperature

Ask the children to work in groups of three or four. Each group will need a set of five beakers, each half-filled with water of varying temperatures, and thermometers. Ask: *How warm is the water in each beaker? Find the answer to the question and record the information you gather. You will be expected to explain what you have found out, and why you chose your method of recording.* Provide each child with the worksheet 'Temperature' which sets out the task for them. Check as they work that the children are taking accurate readings of temperature and recording these appropriately.

Teacher support

Less confident learners: Decide whether to have these children work as a group to solve the problem. Check that the children can use the thermometers effectively and take accurate readings of temperature.

More confident learners: Ask the children to repeat their readings of the water temperature after about 15 minutes. Ask them to explain any changes that they find in the temperature and to record their work in such a way that their results will be clear to others.

Common misconceptions

Children do not understand how to read the scale on the thermometer. Provide further experience of reading thermometer scales. Point out the divisions between the multiples of 10 on the scale. Ask the children to count up to the next 10 so that they understand how the scale is read.

Probing questions

● What are you trying to find out? What information will you collect? How? How did you record your results? Why did you choose this sort of table/graph? What did it show?

● Holly estimates that the temperature outside today is 1°C. Do you think that this is a good estimate?

● What temperature does this thermometer show?

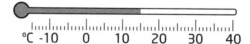

Next steps

Support: Provide further experience of reading thermometer scales. If necessary, use a thermometer scale marked in ones, then progress to those marked in tens, with intermediate marks shown. Refer back to Year 2 Block C Unit 3.

Extension: Provide thermometers marked in tens, with intermediate marks in twos or fives. Ask the children to read these as accurately as they can. Refer to Year 3 Block C Unit 3.

BLOCK C

Activity ③

Prior learning
Children can find how long a journey took if they know the start and end times.

Framework objective
Read the time on a 12-hour digital clock and to the nearest 5 minutes on an analogue clock; calculate time intervals and find start or end times for a given time interval

Vocabulary
time, clock, minute, hour, before, after, start time, end time, how long…?

Resources
Display page: How long does it take?
Worksheet: How long does it take?
Classroom resources: individual clock faces

③ How long does it take?

Reveal the display page 'How long does it take?' Explain that the first clock shows when Peter leaves home and the second one shows when he arrives at school. Ask: *How long does it take for Peter to get to school?* Repeat this questioning for the next set of clocks displayed on the second screen. Check which children are confident with reading clocks and which need more support. Provide the worksheet 'How long does it take?'. This contains a selection of time word problems, where children are asked to record the correct time on illustrations of digital clocks. The final question on the worksheet requires the children to work mentally.

Teacher support
Less confident learners: If children are unsure about reading clocks, provide individual clock faces so that the children can set the times for themselves and count in fives around the clock face to find the answers.
More confident learners: Challenge the children to answer questions where the time is across the hour, such as: *My train journey started at half past 5. I arrived at my destination at a quarter past 6. How long did my journey take?*

Common misconceptions
Children cannot count on or back to find the difference between two times. Count together in fives around the clock face. Discuss how the numbers 1 to 12 mark the hours and five-minute intervals. Choose simple times for the children to calculate, such as the difference between five past and quarter past the hour.

Probing questions
● How would this time appear on a 12-hour digital clock?

● My watch is 25 minutes slow. It shows half past 5. What is the real time?

Next steps
Support: Provide further experience of reading the clock – for example, in an oral and mental starter. Children may benefit from using individual clock faces to set the time to what you say, then the second time, so that they can count on in fives to find the difference between the two times. Say, for example: *Jon left*

home at 10 minutes past 9. He arrived at the bus stop at 25 minutes past 9. How long did it take him to get from home to the bus stop? Refer back to Year 2 Block C Unit 3.
Extension: Continue to set time problems which cross the hour, such as:
I caught the bus into town at 5 minutes to 10. The bus arrived in town at 20 minutes past 10. How long did my journey take? Refer to Year 4 Block D Unit 1.

Activity ④

Prior learning
Children can collect and record the data needed to answer questions.

Framework objectives
● Follow a line of enquiry by deciding what information is important; make and use lists, tables and graphs to organise and interpret the information
● Answer a question by collecting, organising and interpreting data; use tally charts, frequency tables, pictograms and bar charts to represent results and illustrate observations; use ICT to create a simple bar chart

Vocabulary
problem, enquiry, solution, calculate, calculation, method, explain, reasoning, reason, predict, pattern, relationship, collect, organise, compare, sort, classify, represent, interpret, effect, information, data, survey, table, label, title, scale, interval, how often?, how frequently?, more/less, most/least, most/least popular, most/least frequent, greatest/least value

Resources
Interactive activity: Frequency chart: car colour
Worksheet: Car colour

④ Car colour

Ask the children to test the suggestion: 'Most children in this class have a silver-coloured car at home'. Ask the children to work in groups of four to six to plan how they would carry out the task. Give them five minutes to do the planning. Now ask a spokesperson from each group to feed back on their plan. Discuss how they will collect the data and present it as a pictogram. Collect the data by a show of hands, giving children extra 'votes' if they have more than one car. Use the interactive activity 'Frequency chart: car colour' to record votes for the car colours. Ask the children to suggest labels and a title for the frequency chart. Leave the completed table visible and provide the worksheet 'Car colour'. Ask the children to use the data from the frequency table to complete a pictogram, using one icon to represent two cars.

Teacher support
Less confident learners: Decide whether to have these children work as a group to complete the pictogram. Discuss how one icon can represent two cars and how to count up in twos to find totals.
More confident learners: Challenge the children to draw another pictogram, this time with a scale of one icon to five cars.

Common misconceptions
Children cannot transfer data from a frequency chart to a pictogram.
Discuss what data the frequency chart shows and how this can be transferred to a pictogram. Give children more experience of this, beginning with a scale of 1:1, then transferring the same data to a scale of 1:2.

BLOCK C

Probing questions
● You have to test the suggestion 'We think most children in our class walk to school'. What information will you collect? How?
● This pictogram shows how the children in a class came to school this morning:

car	◯ ◖			
bus	◯	◯	◯	◯	◯
walk	◯	◯	◯	◯	◯
bike	◯	◯	◖		
	Number of children			

◯ = 2 children

● How many children came to school by car? On foot? By bike? By bus?
● Explain how to work out how many children there are in the class.
● Did most of the class walk? How can you tell?

Next steps
Support: Provide further suggestions to test, such as 'Most children in the class like plain crisps best'. Ask the children how they would carry out the investigation. Begin with a pictogram scale of 1:1, working together to transfer the data to a pictogram with a scale of 1:2. Refer back to Year 2 Block C Unit 3.
Extension: Challenge the children to test further statements, such as 'Most children in the class have a pet at home'. They should discuss in their group how to carry out the investigation. Ask them to think about scale and to choose one that is appropriate for their pictogram. Refer to Year 3 Block C Unit 3.

Activity ⑤

Prior learning	**Framework objective**
Children can place objects on a Carroll diagram.	Use Venn diagrams or Carroll diagrams to sort data and objects using more than one criterion

Framework objective
Use Venn diagrams or Carroll diagrams to sort data and objects using more than one criterion

Vocabulary
problem, enquiry, solution, calculate, calculation, method, explain, reasoning, reason, predict, pattern, relationship, collect, organise, compare, sort, classify, represent, interpret, effect, information, data, Carroll diagram

Resources
Interactive activity: Carroll number sort
Worksheet: Carroll diagram

⑤ Carroll diagram

Explain that you would like the children to complete the Carroll diagram that you will show them. Reveal the interactive activity 'Carroll number sort' and provide the worksheet 'Carroll diagram' for each child . Ask the children to complete the task on their worksheet. Give two or three minutes for the task to be completed. Now invite them to fill in the answers on the Carroll diagram on the screen, by dragging and dropping the numbers into the correct areas of the diagram. Ask: *What is special about the numbers in the 'Not odd' column?* Next, ask the children to complete the second Carroll diagram on their worksheet (give them about ten minutes to do this). Next, reveal the second screen of the interactive activity. Invite suggestions for where each number should go. Invite children to come to the board to drag and drop them into the Carroll diagram. Discuss where the numbers that are both a multiple of 3 and of 4 go, and where the numbers that are neither a multiple of 3 nor 4 fit.

Teacher support

Less confident learners: Decide whether to work only with two-region Carroll diagrams with these children until they are confident with these.

More confident learners: Ask the children to complete another Carroll diagram with four regions. The children can decide on their own criteria.

Common misconceptions

Children do not understand that Carroll diagrams have 'is' and 'is not' statements for pairs of regions.

Work with simple two-region Carroll diagrams. Discuss how everything that is being sorted must fit into the diagram. Use a criterion such as 'is even', so that the children can see that if a number is not even it must fit into the 'not even' region. Choose other criteria, such as 'is less than 10'.

Probing questions

● Is a cylinder a prism? Does it have any vertices? Where should it be placed on this Carroll diagram?

	prism	not a prism
has vertices		
does not have vertices		

● Draw a Carroll diagram for these statements: is less than 20; is even. Where would the number 19 fit? What about 24?

Next steps

Support: Continue with the simpler Carroll diagrams with just two regions until the children deal with these confidently. Then introduce four-region diagrams and the idea of two criteria that can both be expressed as 'is' and 'is not'. Refer back to Year 3 Block B Unit 1.

Extension: Provide further experiences of using Carroll diagrams. Encourage the children to use them for sorting numbers or shapes and to find their own pairs of criteria. Refer to Year 4 Block C Unit 1.

Unit 3 Handling data and measures

Introduction

In this unit, children are encouraged to work cooperatively in groups and to present their information. They ask questions about their data of the rest of the class so that they become more fluent with the relevant vocabulary. They develop their data-handling skills, including using a scale for bar charts and using tallies and frequencies. They also further develop their understanding of measures, including the relationship between the units.

Framework objectives	Assessment focuses		Success criteria for Year 3	Learning outcomes
	Level 3	Level 2		
① Choosing measures				
Know the relationships between kilometres and metres, metres and centimetres, kilograms and grams, litres and millilitres; choose and use appropriate units to estimate, measure and record measurements	● use non-standard units and standard metric units of length, capacity and mass in a range of contexts, e.g. ● measure a length to the nearest ½cm	● begin to use everyday non-standard and standard units to measure length and mass ● begin to understand that numbers can be used not only to count discrete objects but also to describe continuous measures, e.g. length ● know which measuring tools to use to find, e.g. how much an object weighs, how tall a child is, how much water it takes to fill the water tray ● begin to use a wider range of measures	● Makes suitable choices of units to estimate, then measure, lengths ● Records the estimates and measurements appropriately	*I can choose suitable units to estimate and measure length.*
② How large is it?				
Read, to the nearest division and half-division, scales that are numbered or partially numbered; use the information to measure and draw to a suitable degree of accuracy	● use non-standard units and standard metric units of length, capacity and mass in a range of contexts, e.g. ● read simple scales, e.g. increments of 2, 5 or 10	● begin to use everyday non-standard and standard units to measure length and mass ● read scales to the nearest labelled division	● Reads scales to the nearest division or half division ● Records the measurement appropriately ● Draws a line accurately to the nearest division or half division	*I can read a scale to the nearest division or half division.*
③ Favourite fruits				
Follow a line of enquiry by deciding what information is important; make and use lists, tables and graphs to organise and interpret the information	● begin to organise their work and check results, e.g. ● begin to develop own ways of recording ● discuss their mathematical work and begin to explain their thinking ● use and interpret mathematical symbols and diagrams	● discuss their work using mathematical language, e.g. with support ● describe the strategies and methods they use in their work ● listen to others' explanations, try to make sense of them, compare... evaluate... ● begin to represent their work using symbols and simple diagrams	● Explains what information is important and should be collected ● Decides how to collect the information, organise and record it	*I can decide what information to collect to answer a question.* *I can choose how to show others what I have found out.*

Unit 3 ▭ Handling data and measures

Framework objectives	Assessment focuses		Success criteria for Year 3	Learning outcomes
	Level 3	**Level 2**		
③ Favourite fruits				
Describe and explain methods, choices and solutions to puzzles and problems, orally and in writing, using pictures and diagrams	● begin to organise their work and check results, e.g. ● begin to develop own ways of recording ● develop an organised approach as they get into recording their work on a problem ● discuss their mathematical work and begin to explain their thinking, e.g. ● use appropriate mathematical vocabulary ● talk about their findings by referring to their written work	● discuss their work using mathematical language, e.g. with support ● describe the strategies and methods they use in their work ● listen to others' explanations, try to make sense of them, compare... evaluate... ● begin to represent their work using symbols and simple diagrams, e.g. with support ● use pictures, diagrams and symbols to communicate their thinking, or demonstrate a solution or process ● begin to appreciate the need to record and develop their own methods of recording	● Explains orally methods chosen and why these choice were made ● Can use writing, pictures and diagrams to record evidence	*I can explain how the class used information to solve a problem.*
③ Favourite fruits				
Answer a question by collecting, organising and interpreting data; use tally charts, frequency tables, pictograms and bar charts to represent results and illustrate observations; use ICT to create a simple bar chart	● gather information, e.g. ● decide what data to collect to answer a question, e.g. What is the most common way to travel to school? ● make appropriate choices for recording data, e.g. a tally chart or frequency table ● extract and interpret information presented in simple tables, lists, bar charts and pictograms	● sort objects and classify them using more than one criterion, e.g. ● sort a given set of shapes using two criteria such as triangle/not triangle and blue/not blue ● understand vocabulary relating to handling data, e.g. ● understand vocabulary such as sort, group, set, list, table, most common, most popular ● collect and sort data to test a simple hypothesis, e.g. ● count a show of hands to test the hypothesis 'Most children in our class are in bed by 7:30pm' ● record results in simple lists, tables, pictograms and block graphs ● communicate their findings, using the simple lists, tables, pictograms and block graphs they have recorded, e.g. ● respond to questions about the data they have presented, e.g. 'How many of our names have five letters?' ● pose similar questions about their data for others to answer	● Makes a tally chart that accurately records information ● Accurately makes a bar chart with a simple scale of 1:1 or 1:2	*I can show information in a tally chart or bar chart.*

BLOCK C

Activity ①

Prior learning
Children can choose suitable units to estimate and measure length.

Framework objective
Know the relationships between kilometres and metres, metres and centimetres, kilograms and grams, litres and millilitres; choose and use appropriate units to estimate, measure and record measurements

Vocabulary
problem, enquiry, solution, calculate, calculation, method, explain, reasoning, reason, predict, pattern, relationship, kilometre (km), metre (m), centimetre (cm), litre (l), millilitre (ml), kilogram (kg), gram (g)

Resources
Resource sheet: Self-assessment
Classroom resources: individual whiteboards and pens

① Choosing measures

Provide the children with whiteboards and pens. Explain that you will ask the children some measures questions and that you would like them to write their answers on their whiteboards. When you say *Show me,* they must hold up their boards for you to see. Check who has answered correctly and who still needs more experience. Ask questions about all of the measures in order to give the children the opportunity to show what they know about the relationships between units. Ask, for example:
- How many 20-centimetre strips could you cut from 1 metre of ribbon?
- How many millilitres in half a litre?
- How tall is the cupboard over there: 20 centimetres or 2 metres?
- How tall would you expect a table to be? 1 metre or 500cm?
- How much do you think a bag of sugar would weigh? 500g, 2kg or 1kg?

Decide whether to use the self-assessment sheet for the children to record their achievements and what they need to do next.

Teacher support
Less confident learners: Decide whether to ask an adult to work with this group and to ask the same questions, discussing each one and why each answer is correct.
More confident learners: Challenge these children to think of some similar, sensible questions to ask the rest of the class.

Common misconceptions
Children do not know the relationships between the units.
Begin with length and look together at a metre rule. Discuss centimetres and how many there are in a metre. Then look at mass and capacity in the same way.

Probing questions
- Complete this table:

kg	0	½	2	5	7	4	6	9
g								

- How many 10cm strips could you cut from 1 metre of tape? How do you know?
- Would you expect:
  a door to be 1, 2 or 5 metres tall?
  a handspan to be 5, 15 or 50cm wide?
  a teapot to hold 1 litre, 10 litres or 100 litres?

▷ **Next steps**

Support: Provide further experience for the children to compare units, including practical experience of measuring length, weighing and finding capacities. Refer back to Year 3 Block B Unit 1.

Extension: Encourage the children to use their knowledge of units in solving problems, such as finding the height, mass and capacity (perhaps using displacement) of a brick, and choosing appropriate units in which to make the measurements. Refer to Year 4 Block C Unit 1.

Activity ②

Prior learning

Children can read a scale to the nearest division or half division.

Framework objective

Read, to the nearest division and half-division, scales that are numbered or partially numbered; use the information to measure and draw to a suitable degree of accuracy

Vocabulary

problem, enquiry, solution, calculate, calculation, method, explain, reasoning, reason, predict, pattern, relationship, kilometre (km), metre (m), centimetre (cm), litre (l), millilitre (ml), kilogram (kg), gram (g)

Resources

Resource sheet: Self-assessment
Classroom resources: access to water or sand for finding capacity; jugs marked in 100ml; paper for recording; rulers marked in half centimetres, tapes and metre sticks; three different sized plastic boxes for each group; weighing scales marked in grams and kilograms

② How large is it?

Provide each group of about four children with three different-sized plastic boxes. Ask them to find each box's height, width, depth, mass and capacity. Show them the resources available. Ask each child to record their findings. Observe how children measure and the level of accuracy that they can achieve. Decide whether to use the self-assessment sheet for the children to record their achievements and what they need to do next.

Teacher support

Less confident learners: Decide whether to have these children work as a group with adult input. Ask the children what they intend to do and why, and watch carefully as they make their measurements.

More confident learners: Challenge the children to measure to the nearest millimetre.

Common misconceptions

Children do not read the scale accurately.

Work together with measuring equipment. Check how the children make their measurements and correct any inaccuracies or misunderstandings about how to read the scale. For example, children may, with a weighing scale, just read to the nearest kilogram. Point out the intermediate marks and discuss what these mean and how to interpret them.

Probing questions

● [Show the children a line that is 5cm long.] Draw a line that is 2cm longer than this one.
● [Show a measuring jug with 500ml of water in it.] Pour 200ml of water into

BLOCK C

this jug. Now how much water is there?
- What measurement is shown on this weighing scale? (See illustration, right.)

Next steps
Support: Provide further experience of measuring, using length, mass and capacity. For example, the children can find the length, width and depth of reading books, and find their mass. They can find how much various cups hold, measuring to the nearest 100ml. Refer back to Year 3 Block C Unit 1.

Extension: Ask the children to measure the length of longer items, such as the length of the netball pitch, the corridor or the school hall. Ask them to plan how they will do this, the equipment they need to use, the units they will need to use to make the measurement, then make an estimate. Ask them to measure as accurately as they can. Refer to Year 4 Block C Unit 1.

Activity ③

Prior learning
Children can decide what information to collect to answer a question and choose how to show others what they have found out. They can explain how the class used information to solve a problem. They can show information in a tally chart or bar chart.

Framework objectives
- Follow a line of enquiry by deciding what information is important; make and use lists, tables and graphs to organise and interpret the information
- Describe and explain methods, choices and solutions to puzzles and problems, orally and in writing, using pictures and diagrams
- Answer a question by collecting, organising and interpreting data; use tally charts, frequency tables, pictograms and bar charts to represent results and illustrate observations; use ICT to create a simple bar chart

Vocabulary
problem, enquiry, solution, calculate, calculation, method, explain, reasoning, reason, predict, pattern, relationship, collect, organise, compare, sort, classify, represent, interpret, effect, information, data, survey, questionnaire, table, frequency table, block graph, bar chart, axis, axes, horizontal axis, vertical axis, label, title, scale, interval, division, how often?, how frequently?, more/less, most/least, most/least popular, most/least frequent, greatest/least value, approximately, close, about the same as, ten times, hundred times

Resources
Interactive activity: Frequency chart: favourite fruits
Worksheet: Favourite fruits (part 1 and part 2)
Classroom resources: computer with data-handling software

③ Favourite fruits

Explain the task: work as a class to collect data about favourite fruits, then make a tally chart and a bar graph. Give the children five minutes to work in small groups, planning how they would carry out the task. Ask for feedback from each group. If there are a number of different suggestions, challenge individuals to explain their choice of method. Agree that a class vote on favourite fruits, with the responses entered as tallies will be the way forward. Reveal the interactive activity 'Frequency chart: favourite fruits'. This contains a list of common fruits, but there is room to add other fruits if necessary. Children then work individually on the worksheet 'Favourite fruits (parts 1 and 2)' to complete the tally and frequency chart. They use the data to compile a bar chart. Remind them to decide on the scale for this. When this is complete, ask questions such as: *Which is the favourite/least favourite fruit? Which fruit received three more/ fewer votes than ___?*

BLOCK C

▷ ### Teacher support
Less confident learners: Decide whether to work as a group to prepare a group chart and bar chart. Discuss the scale, such as 1:2.
More confident learners: Provide a data-handling program on the class computer. Ask the children to make their bar chart using this software, enter labels for axes and chart title, and to identify the scale that they used. This can be used during the plenary session.

Common misconceptions
Children do not understand how to transfer the information that they have collected into a bar chart.
Discuss how to make a bar chart. Begin with a scale of 1:1. Ask the children where to write the names of the fruit, the scale numbers, and so on. Discuss how to make the bars. Using a different-coloured pencil for each bar and its label can help the children to identify each part of the chart.

Probing questions
● What are you trying to find out? What information will you collect? How?
● How did you record your results? Why did you choose this sort of table/graph? What did it show?
● Did anything you found out surprise you?
● What did you write down?
● How did making a tally and frequency chart help you to make your bar chart?
● Complete this tally chart:

Transport	Tally	Frequency
Bus	|||	3
Bike	||	2
Car		12
Walk	⧄ |||	

● Look at this bar chart:

Packed lunches brought to school

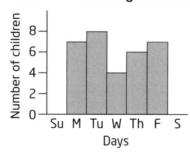

● On which day were most packed lunches brought to school?
● How many packed lunches were brought in the whole week?
● Why do you think that there are different numbers of packed lunches on different days?

Next steps
Support: Provide more experience of collecting data in this way, such as finding out the class's favourite television programmes. Refer back to Year 3 Block C Units 1 and 2.
Extension: Challenge the children to use other scales such as 1:5 or 1:10. They could collect data on the numbers of brothers and sisters the children in the class have, for example. Refer to Year 4 Block C Unit 1.

BLOCK C

Units 1, 2 & 3 ◻ Periodic assessment

These activities can be used at any time during the teaching of this block to assess those children that you think have achieved the objective. A grid highlighting the related assessment focuses and expected learning outcomes for each activity can be found on the CD-ROM.

Various measures

Framework objective
Read, to the nearest division and half-division, scales that are numbered or partially numbered; use the information to measure and draw to a suitable degree of accuracy

Learning outcomes
- I can use a ruler or a tape measure to measure a length to the nearest ½cm.
- I can read the temperature on a thermometer to the nearest degree.
- I can read a scale to the nearest division or half division.

Provide rulers and tape measures which measure to the nearest ½cm. Ask the children to find two items in the classroom that measure about 20cm in length, two that are longer, and two that are shorter. Ask them to measure these accurately to the nearest ½cm and to record their findings on paper.
   Provide thermometers marked in °C, with the decades numbered. Over a week, children must take the classroom and the outside temperature. Ask them to record this on paper in their own way.
   Provide rulers marked in ½cm, weighing scales in 100g and jugs marked in 100ml. Ask the children to find the dimensions (width, height and depth), mass and capacity of a plastic box. They must record their findings on paper. Ask the children to complete the self-assessment sheet.

Venn and Carroll diagrams

Framework objective
Use Venn diagrams or Carroll diagrams to sort data and objects using more than one criterion

Learning outcomes
- I can place objects on a Venn diagram.
- I can place objects on a Carroll diagram.

Provide the worksheets 'Venn and Carroll diagrams (parts 1 and 2)'. The activity is in two parts – each part can be undertaken separately, or completed together. The first is a Venn diagram for multiples of 4 and multiples of 5. Check that the children are clear about which numbers go into the intersection and in the area outside the diagram. The second is a Carroll diagram for multiples of 3 and multiples of 5. Check that the children understand what must go into each of the four regions.

Finding out

Framework objective
Follow a line of enquiry by deciding what information is important; make and use lists, tables and graphs to organise and interpret the information

Learning outcomes
- I can decide what information to collect to answer a question.
- I can choose how to show others what I have found out.

Provide the worksheet 'Finding out'. This asks children to find out the favourite type of pen that the others in the class prefer to use, such as gel pens, ballpoints or fountain pens. The children will need to decide how to collect, display and interpret the data. Children would benefit from using a data-handling program to display their data.

Name _____ Date _____

Venn and Carroll diagrams (part 1)

Complete the Venn diagram.

■ Place the numbers 1 to 40 onto this Venn diagram.

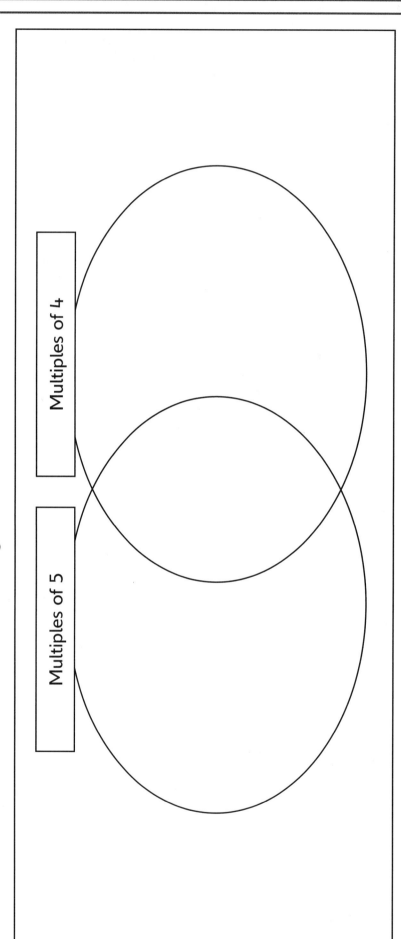

Multiples of 4

Multiples of 5

How easy?

Red

Amber

Green

How do you think you have done?

_____

_____

PHOTOCOPIABLE ◼ SCHOLASTIC

Name   Date

Venn and Carroll diagrams (part 2)

Complete the Carroll diagram.

◼ Place the numbers 1 to 40 into this Carroll diagram.

	Multiples of 3	Not multiples of 3
Multiples of 5		
Not multiples of 5		

How easy?

Red
Amber
Green

How do you think you have done?

_____

_____

Name   Date

Finding out

- Which type of pen do children in your class prefer?
Do they like gel pens, ballpoint pens or fountain pens?

- Collect data and record it in a table.
- Then make a chart of your findings.

- You can use graph paper or plain paper, or use a data-handling program on the computer.

- Write three sentences to say what you have found out.

_____

_____

_____

_____

_____

_____

_____

_____

_____

How easy?

Red

Amber

Green

How do you think you have done?

_____

_____

BLOCK D
Calculating, measuring and understanding shape

Expected prior learning
Check that children can already:
- identify the operations needed in simple one-step word problems
- recognise and use the value of coins and measures of length, weight and capacity
- read numbered and unnumbered divisions on simple scales
- add and subtract mentally a one-digit number to or from a two-digit number
- record informally the addition and subtraction of two-digit numbers
- recognise simple fractions and find halves and quarters of numbers and quantities
- understand multiplication as repeated addition and division as repeated subtraction
- use symbols to record simple number sentences
- follow instructions using vocabulary related to position, direction and movement
- recognise and use right angles to describe turns and corners of shapes.

Objectives overview
The text in this diagram identifies the focus of mathematics learning within the block.

Key aspects of learning
- Problem solving
- Reasoning
- Creative thinking
- Information processing
- Communication

Developing written methods of calculation for all four operations

Finding unit fractions of numbers and quantities

Solving problems and representing information; setting solutions in the context of the problem

Using measures and scales

Comparing angles with right angles

BLOCK D: Calculating, measuring and understanding shape

Understanding multiplication and division as inverse operations

Using inverses to estimate and check calculations

Using the vocabulary of position, direction and movement

Unit 1 ▨ Calculating, measuring and understanding shape

Introduction

In this unit, children solve one- and two-step problems involving addition and subtraction of one- and two-digit numbers, fractions and for measures. They listen carefully to instructions for position, direction and movement, where they will need to interpret the vocabulary. Children may need reminding that forward movements on a graph or chart should be interpreted as 'up' and backward movements as 'down'.

BLOCK D

Framework objectives	Assessment focuses		Success criteria for Year 3	Learning outcomes
	Level 3	**Level 2**		
(1) Joshua's homework (8) Telling the time (9) Time problems				
Solve one-step and two-step problems involving numbers, money or measures, including time, choosing and carrying out appropriate calculations	• select the mathematics they use in a wider range of classroom activities • use mental recall of addition and subtraction facts to 20 in solving problems involving larger numbers	• select the mathematics they use in some classroom activities • choose the appropriate operation when solving addition and subtraction problems • solve number problems involving money and measures	• Solves one-step problems and explains how the answer was found in the context of measuring • Solves two-step problems and explains the steps to find the answer in the context of measuring	*I can explain how I found the answer to a word problem that involves measurements.*
(2) Function machine – addition and subtraction				
Add or subtract mentally combinations of one-digit and two-digit numbers	• add and subtract two-digit numbers mentally, e.g. • calculate 36 + 19, 63 – 26, and complements to 100 such as 100 – 24	• use mental recall of addition and subtraction facts to 10, e.g. • use addition/subtraction facts to 10 and place value to add or subtract multiples of 10, e.g. know 3 + 7 = 10 and use place value to derive 30 + 70 = 100	• Adds and subtracts mentally combinations of one-digit and two-digit numbers • Adds and subtracts multiples of 10 to and from a two-digit number	*I can add or subtract a one-digit number to or from a two-digit number. I can add or subtract a multiple of 10 to or from a two-digit number.*
(3) Halves and quarters				
Find unit fractions of numbers and quantities (e.g. $1/2$, $1/3$, $1/4$ and $1/6$ of 12 litres)	• use simple fractions that are several parts of a whole and recognise when two simple fractions are equivalent • begin to use decimal notation in contexts such as money	• begin to use halves and quarters • relate the concept of half of a small quantity to the concept of half of a shape	• Uses fractions in the context of measuring • Finds simple given fractions of measures • Explains what calculations were carried out and why	*I can find ½ or ¼ of a measurement.*

Unit 1 Calculating, measuring and understanding shape

Framework objectives	Assessment focuses		Success criteria for Year 3	Learning outcomes
	Level 3	Level 2		
④ Compass points ⑤ Find the cat – coordinates				
Read and record the vocabulary of position, direction and movement, using the four compass directions to describe movement about a grid	• describe position and movement, e.g. ○ use terms such as left/right, clockwise/anticlockwise, quarter turn/90° to give directions along a route	• distinguish between straight and turning movements, e.g. ○ distinguish between left and right and between clockwise and anticlockwise and use these when giving directions ○ instruct a programmable robot, combining straight-line movements and turns, to move along a defined path or reach a target destination ○ recognise right angles in turns	• Finds the position of a square on a grid and names it correctly • Recognises the compass points and uses these to describe a position	I can describe the position of a square on a grid. I can use the compass points (north, south, east and west) to describe a direction.
⑥ 100g compare				
Know the relationships between kilometres and metres, metres and centimetres, kilograms and grams, litres and millilitres; choose and use appropriate units to estimate, measure and record measurements	• use non-standard units and standard metric units of length, capacity and mass in a range of contexts	• begin to use everyday non-standard and standard units to measure length and mass, e.g. ○ begin to understand that numbers can be used not only to count discrete objects but also to describe continuous measures, e.g. length ○ begin to use a wider range of measures	• Makes suitable choices of units to estimate, then measure masses • Records the estimates and measurements appropriately	I know how many grams are the same as 1kg. I can estimate whether an object is lighter than a 100g weight.
⑦ Reading scales				
Read, to the nearest division and half-division, scales that are numbered or partially numbered; use the information to measure and draw to a suitable degree of accuracy	• use non-standard units and standard metric units of length, capacity and mass in a range of contexts, e.g. ○ read simple scales, e.g. increments of 2, 5 or 10	• begin to use everyday non-standard and standard units to measure length and mass, e.g. ○ read scales to the nearest labelled division	• Reads scales to the nearest division or half division • Records the measurement appropriately • Draws a line accurately to the nearest division or half division	I can say what one division on a scale is worth. I can read a scale to the nearest division or half division.
⑧ Telling the time ⑨ Time problems				
Read the time on a 12-hour digital clock and to the nearest 5 minutes on an analogue clock; calculate time intervals and find start or end times for a given time interval	• use standard units of time, e.g. ○ read a 12-hour clock and generally calculate time durations that do not go over the hour	• begin to use a wider range of measures, e.g. ○ use a time line to order daily events and ordinal numbers (first, second, third...) to describe the order of some regular events	• Reads time on a clock face to the nearest 5 minutes • Calculates time taken to the nearest 5 minutes	I can tell the time to the nearest 5 minutes. I can work out the start or end time for an activity.

Activity ①

Prior learning
Children can explain how they found the answer to a word problem that involves measurements.

Framework objective
Solve one-step and two-step problems involving numbers, money or measures, including time, choosing and carrying out appropriate calculations

Vocabulary
problems, solution, methods, sign, operation, symbol, number sentence, equation, mental calculation, written calculation, informal method, jottings, diagrams, add, plus, total, subtract, take away, minus, difference, fraction

Resources
Worksheet: Joshua's homework

① Joshua's homework

Provide each child with a copy of the worksheet 'Joshua's homework'. Explain that Joshua has finished his homework. Ask the children to check his answers. Explain that they will need to work out each answer for themselves and then if they think the homework is correct they tick it. If it is incorrect, they need to write in the correct answer.

Teacher support
Less confident learners: Decide whether to have these children work as a group to check the homework answers. Ask the children to explain how they work out each of the answers.
More confident learners: Ask the children to find another way to check the answers and to explain both of their methods.

Common misconceptions
Children do not recognise the key words in the word problem that tell them what sort of number operation they need to use.
Work together to answer some word problems. Read the problem through, then ask the children to identify the key words and the number operation that is needed.

Probing questions
● Ella buys one toy costing 35p and another costing 48p. She pays with a £5 note. How much change does she get?
● What two calculations do you need to do to answer this problem? What does the answer to the first calculation tell you?
● Make up a word problem that would lead to the calculation 8 × 4. How do you recognise that this problem involves multiplication?

Next steps
Support: Encourage the children to recognise what number operation is needed. Discuss whether there are one or two steps to the problem and how the children know that. Provide more experience of solving word problems such as: *Pat has used half of her pencil. It was 20cm long. How long is it now?* Refer back to Year 2 Block D Unit 3.
Extension: Challenge the children to write some one-step, then two-step, word problems that involve measures. They can swap these with others in the class to find the answers. Refer to Year 3 Block B Unit 3.

■SCHOLASTIC

BLOCK D

Activity ②

Prior learning
Children can add or subtract a one-digit number to or from a two-digit number. They can add or subtract a multiple of 10 to or from a two-digit number.

Framework objective
Add or subtract mentally combinations of one-digit and two-digit numbers

Vocabulary
problems, solution, methods, sign, operation, symbol, number sentence, equation, mental calculation, written calculation, informal method, jottings, diagrams, add, plus, total, subtract, take away, minus, difference

Resources
Interactive activity: Function machine – addition and subtraction
Resource sheet: Self-assessment
Classroom resources: a pile of counters for each child

② Function machine – addition and subtraction

Provide each child with a pile of counters. Open the interactive activity 'Function machine – addition and subtraction'. Use the tabs on the left-hand side of the screen to select which function (addition or subtraction, or a combination of both) to focus upon. Decide which two windows on the machine to reveal to the children each time. Ask them to calculate the answer mentally before you click 'go' to reveal the answer. Tell them to take a counter from their pile for each correct answer. This activity can be used as a starter or during a plenary session. Note which children can respond quickly and accurately and which need more experience of recalling or deriving these number facts. At the end of the activity provide each child with the self-assessment sheet.

Teacher support
Less confident learners: Invite the children to explain how they derived the answer. If they have difficulty, discuss strategies that they can use.
More confident learners: Decide whether to set up the activity for this group of children without the others. Set a time limit and ask the children to see how many questions they can answer correctly within this time limit.

Common misconceptions
Children do not have strategies for adding one-digit numbers to two-digit numbers.
Ask the children to consider, say, 26 + 8. How can we calculate this? One way is to break the number sentence into chunks, such as 26 + 4 + 4. Alternatively, children may know that 6 + 8 = 14, so then this becomes 20 + 14 = 34. Repeat for a subtraction example, such as 36 − 5; then 36 − 8.

Probing questions
● Look at this problem. Explain how to work it out. Wilf has 68p in his money bank. He adds another 5p. How much is in his money bank now?
● What is the missing number on the number line shown below? What calculation is represented on the number line?

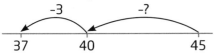

● Sam adds a 50g weight to scales containing 45g. What is the weight on the scales now?

BLOCK D

▷ Next steps

Support: Provide further experience of adding or subtracting a one-digit number to or from a two-digit number and a multiple of 10 to any two-digit number. Each time, ask the children to explain how they calculated. Write number sentences to show the calculation, such as 36 + 40 = 30 + 40 + 6 = 70 + 6 = 76. Refer back to Year 3 Block A Unit 1.

Extension: Run the 'Function machine – addition and subtraction' activity in random mode, so that some of the questions will include the addition or subtraction of any two two-digit numbers. Give a time limit and ask the children to keep a record of how many correct answers they had and any difficulties that they encountered. Refer to Year 3 Block A Unit 2.

Activity ③

Prior learning Children can find ¹/₂ or ¹/₄ of a measurement.	**Framework objective** Find unit fractions of numbers and quantities (for example, ¹/₂, ¹/₃, ¹/₄ and ¹/₆ of 12 litres) **Vocabulary** fraction, part, equal parts, one whole, one half, one quarter **Resources** **Worksheet:** Halves and quarters **Classroom resources:** rulers with ½cm marked as a line

③ Halves and quarters

Provide the worksheet 'Halves and quarters'. Explain that the sheet contains measurements of various items. Ask the children to find the fractions of the measurements.

Teacher support
Less confident learners: Decide whether to have these children work as a group. Ask the children to explain how they worked out the answers. Discuss any questions that they found difficult.
More confident learners: When the children have finished the activity sheet, ask them to use a ruler to find half, then a quarter, of a line measuring 18cm.

Common misconceptions
Children do not read the markings on a scale. They do not understand that the line between two numbers represents a reading of 'halfway between'.
Use a weighing scale, a jug marked in 100ml with each 50ml marked as lines, and a ruler with every ½cm represented by a line. Ask the children to read the scale for measurements that you point to. Discuss what the halfway lines represent each time.

Probing questions
- What calculation would you do to find one quarter of 12 litres?
- One half of 32p is 16p. What is one quarter of 32p?
- This line is 10cm long. Use a ruler to divide it into quarters. Find ¼ of 10cm.

Next steps
Support: Provide further experience of taking measurements in practical activities. Ask the children to record each measurement and discuss what the half marks represent each time. Refer back to Year 2 Block D Unit 3.
Extension: Challenge the children to find quarter measurements of lines

BLOCK D

that they draw themselves. They can work in pairs and give each other whole number measurements between 3cm and 20cm. They must draw these lines, then find a quarter of each line. Refer to Year 3 Block D Unit 2.

Activities ④ ⑤

Prior learning
Children can describe the position of a square on a grid. They can use the compass points (north, south, east and west) to describe a direction.

Framework objective
Read and record the vocabulary of position, direction and movement, using the four compass directions to describe movement about a grid

Vocabulary
grid, row, column, up, down, right, left, journey, route, map, plan, forward, backward, sideways, across, next to, clockwise, anticlockwise, right angle, ascend, descend, compass point, north (N), south (S), east (E), west (W)

Resources
Interactive activity: Coordinates – find the cat
Resource sheet: Self-assessment
Classroom resources: the word 'North' written on a sheet of paper and placed on the appropriate wall in the classroom

④ Compass points

Ask the children to stand up and to face north. Now give commands and ask questions such as: *Turn south. How many right angles did you turn through? Now face east. Which way did you turn: clockwise or anticlockwise? If you turned clockwise through two right angles which way would you face now?* As the children respond to the commands and questions, observe which children are confident with the compass points and which need more experience. Provide the self-assessment sheet for the children to record their strengths and growth points for this objective.

Teacher support
Less confident learners: Children may need reminding of the position of the points of the compass.
More confident learners: Ask the children to give some commands to the rest of the class to follow.

Common misconceptions
Children do not know the positions of the points of the compass.
Put up labels with all four points marked. Ask the children to turn to each point, as above. Repeat this with the labels removed. Draw a 'N, S, W, E' diagram of the compass points and put this on the wall to act as a reminder until the children are confident.

Probing questions
● Face north; turn anticlockwise through a right angle. Which way are you facing now?
● Now turn clockwise to the south. How many right angles did you turn through? What if you had turned anticlockwise? How many right angles then?

Next steps
Support: Use opportunities in PE, for example, to give children directions using the compass points. Refer back to Year 2 Block D Unit 2.
Extension: Challenge the children to use compass points in giving directions for turning. Refer to Year 3 Block D Unit 2.

BLOCK D

⑤ **Find the cat – coordinates**

Reveal the interactive activity 'Coordinates – find the cat'. Invite the children to suggest coordinates, and input the horizontal (*x*-axis) then the vertical (*y*-axis) coordinates. When the cat has been found, and the other items in the picture revealed, ask children to give the coordinates of things that you ask for. Check which children are confident with using coordinates and which need further experience. Provide the self-assessment sheet for the children to record their strengths and growth points for this objective.

Teacher support
Less confident learners: Use squared paper and draw *x* and *y* axes, both numbered from 1 to 4. Now invite the children to say a grid reference and point to that square. Invite them to write their initials in the square if they are correct. When they are confident, repeat the 'Find the cat' game.
More confident learners: Invite the children to play the game as a group. Each child takes a turn to point to the square that they want uncovered, then to enter the coordinates. The other children check that the correct coordinates were entered.

Common misconceptions
Children confuse the x and y coordinates and are unsure which is first.
Repeat the 'Find the cat' game. This time ask the children to point to the square that they want uncovered, then say the coordinates, pointing to the *x*-axis number, then the *y*-axis number. Repeat this until they have understood that the order of the numbers for coordinates is very important.

Probing questions
● Which square lies halfway between squares A3 and E3?

4					
3					
2					
1					
	A	B	C	D	E

● Move a counter from square B4 to square E2. Describe each move you make, using the words north, south, east and west.

Next steps
Support: Provide more opportunities to name squares using coordinates, such as taking turns to name a square and point to it. If their partner agrees that the square has been named correctly using coordinates, they can place a counter in that square. Refer back to Year 2 Block D Unit 1.
Extension: Provide larger grids for the children to work with, such as *x* and *y* axes labelled 1 to 10, and ask them to play battleships. Refer to Year 3 Block D Unit 2.

Activity ⑥

Framework objective
Know the relationships between kilometres and metres, metres and centimetres, kilograms and grams, litres and millilitres; choose and use appropriate units to estimate, measure and record measurements

Vocabulary
kilograms (kg), grams(g), estimate, weigh, balance, scales, weight

Resources
Worksheet: 100g compare
Classroom resources: 100g weights, scales marked in 100g intervals, tray of items for each group (some about 100g, some heavier and some lighter than 100g)

⑥ 100g compare

Begin by asking questions such as: *How many grams are in 1kg? So how many 100g are there in 1kg? How did you work that out?* Check that all the children know the relationship between grams and kilograms. Now provide each group with a set of scales, some 100g weights and a tray of items. Ask the children to estimate which items are lighter, which about the same as and which heavier than the 100g weight. They should record their estimates on the worksheet '100g compare', then check their estimates by weighing.

Teacher support
Less confident learners: Ask the children to explain how they decided on their estimates. Check that they can use the scales appropriately to take accurate readings.
More confident learners: Provide scales that measure in 50g increments. Ask the children to weigh their items as accurately as they can, then to place them in order of mass.

Common misconceptions
Children do not know the relationship between kilograms and grams.
Discuss how many grams there are in 1 kilogram, then in ½kg. Ask the children to say how many grams there are in 100g, 500g, and so on.

Children do not make good estimates of mass comparison.
Ask these children to demonstrate how they make an estimate of mass. Provide a 100g weight and something to compare it with. Check how they carry this out. Discuss how comparing with two hands (that is, the mass in one and the item in the other) can work as long as they keep still and concentrate on how the two items 'feel' in their hands.

Probing questions
● A sack of rice weighs 5kg. How many grams is this?
● Compare the mass of this book with this bag of sugar and with this 100g weight. Suggest an estimate for the mass of the book.
● Which is a newborn baby more likely to weigh?
  A. 30g
  B. 3kg
  C. 30kg

Next steps
Support: Provide further opportunities for making estimates, such as comparing items with a 200g weight. Refer back to Year 2 Block D Unit 3.

BLOCK D

Extension: Provide opportunities for the children to read scales to the nearest 50g, such as when weighing out foodstuffs for cooking. Refer to Year 4 Block C Unit 1.

Activity ⑦

Prior learning
Children can say what one division on a scale is worth. They can read a scale to the nearest division or half division.

Framework objective
Read, to the nearest division and half-division, scales that are numbered or partially numbered; use the information to measure and draw to a suitable degree of accuracy

Vocabulary
scale, enough, not enough, too much, too little, too many, too few, nearly, roughly, about, close to, about the same as, approximately, just over, close to, measure, division

Resources
Worksheet: Reading scales
Classroom resources: weighing scales, measuring jugs, rulers, thermometers

⑦ Reading scales

Provide the children with the worksheet 'Reading scales'. Ask them to write the measurements, measuring to the nearest division. Check that they recognise the scale and what the 'lines' between numbers represent.

Teacher support
Less confident learners: Provide further experience of reading scales using weighing scales, measuring jugs, rulers and thermometers. For each item, check that the children recognise the scale and what the lines in between the numbers represent.
More confident learners: Ask the children to use measuring instruments with more complex scales, such as a ruler with millimetres marked. Ask the children to explain the scale and to show how accurately they can measure with it.

Common misconceptions
Children cannot interpret the scale.
Use real measuring instruments. Discuss the numbered scale. Ask the children to say what the marks in between the numbers mean. For example, use a ruler marked in centimetres, with half-centimetres represented by a line.

Probing questions
● [Show children some weighing scales.] Point to where the dial would go if it showed a mass of 45g. How do you know?
● [Show children a measuring jug.] What is each division on this jug worth?
● [Pour 400ml of water into a measuring jug.] How much water is in this jug? How do you know?

Next steps
Support: Provide further experience of using real measuring instruments and interpreting scales, such as weighing scales marked in 100g increments between the kilograms. Refer back to Year 3 Block C Unit 1.
Extension: Encourage the children to make more accurate readings, using more complex scales. Refer to Year 3 Block C Unit 3.

Activities

Prior learning
Children can tell the time to the nearest five minutes. They can work out the start or end time for an activity. They can explain how they found the answer to a word problem that involves measurements.

Framework objectives
- Read the time on a 12-hour digital clock and to the nearest 5 minutes on an analogue clock; calculate time intervals and find start or end times for a given time interval
- Solve one-step and two-step problems involving numbers, money or measures, including time, choosing and carrying out appropriate calculations

Vocabulary
time, how long ago?, how long will it be to...?, how long will it take to...?, hour, minute, second, o'clock, half past, quarter to, quarter past, digital/analogue clock/watch

Resources
Worksheet: Time problems
Resource sheets: Time cards (photocopied onto card for each pair and cut out, keeping pairs of cards together), Self-assessment
Classroom resources: individual whiteboards and pens, teaching clock face with geared hands

Telling the time

Provide each child with a whiteboard and pen. Explain that you will set the teaching clock to a time. Ask the children to write the time on their whiteboards in digital format, then, when you say *Show me*, they should hold up their boards for you to see. Check who is confident with telling the time to the nearest five-minute interval and who needs further support. Set the clock to times such as 8.20, 9.35, 10.55 and 1.05. Then set to nearly a five-minute interval, such as 3.04 and ask the children to read this to the nearest five minutes. Decide whether to provide the self-assessment sheet for the children to record what they know and can do and what they need to improve.

Teacher support
Less confident learners: Repeat the activity with this group, concentrating on times with the minutes in tens: 10, 20, half past and so on. Then repeat this with five-minute intervals.
More confident learners: Challenge the children to read the time to the nearest minute.

Common misconceptions
Children do not understand time beyond the half hour: 25 to 11, quarter to 12, and so on.
Use the teaching clock. Explain how the way we say time changes after 'half past'. Move the minute hand to show each five-minute interval and demonstrate how it is said. Discuss how the hour hand gradually moves to the next hour. Repeat the activity 'Telling the time', this time putting the minute hand on the five-minute intervals and concentrating on times 'to the hour'.

Probing questions
- How would a digital clock show the time twenty minutes to six?
- [Set the clock hands to 8.40.] What time is this? How can you tell?
- How would you write this time in digital time?

Next steps
Support: Provide further experience of telling the time, concentrating on the aspects that the children are still unsure about. Refer back to Year 2 Block D Unit 3.

BLOCK D

Extension: Ask the children to work as a group, setting the teaching clock and reading the time to the nearest five-minute interval. The others must say or write the time in digital format, then check that each other's responses are correct. Refer to Year 3 Block D Unit 3.

⑨ Time problems

Provide pairs of children with the worksheet 'Time problems' and the cards cut out of the resource sheet 'Time cards'. The children must make up a problem to fit the times on pairs of clocks, one analogue and one digital. They write a problem and the answer, then tell their partner the problem, who says the answer. They must check that they both have the correct answer. If there is a difference of opinion, ask the children to check their answers. Observe who is confident in finding the time answers.

Teacher support

Less confident learners: Decide whether to have these children work as a group and to find the difference in time between the two clocks. Children may benefit from using real clocks, turning the hands, and counting in five-minute intervals between the two times to find the answer.

More confident learners: Challenge the children to cut up the pairs of clocks and shuffle them. They can repeat the activity, using pairs of clocks drawn at random.

Common misconceptions

Children have difficulty with pairs of times that cross the hour.
Use a teaching clock and set the clock to, say, 9.45. Now explain that you will move the hands to another time, such as 10.00. Ask the children to count in five-minute intervals to find the time difference. Extend this to find the time difference between 9.45 and 10.10.

Probing questions

● I leave the house at 5 past 8 and arrive at school at 10 to 9. How long does my journey take?
● If I leave school at 4 o'clock, what time will I get home?
● The car journey to work takes Rob 20 minutes. He needs to be at work at 9 o'clock. Move the hands on this clock face to show the time that he should leave.
● How did you work out the answers to the questions?

Next steps

Support: Provide further opportunities for children to respond to time word problems. Keep the problems simple to begin with, such as: *I leave home at 10 past 9 and arrive at the shops at 25 past 9. How long did it take me to walk to the shops? Show me the two times on this clock.* This could form part of an oral and mental starter. Refer back to Year 2 Block D Unit 3.

Extension: Encourage the children to invent more time problems for their partners to solve. Refer to Year 3 Block D Unit 3.

BLOCK D

Unit 2 Calculating, measuring and understanding shape

Introduction

In this unit, children follow instructions, such as giving and following instructions for position and movement. They solve word problems, using diagrams and number equations to help them. They reinforce their knowledge and use of addition and subtraction, multiplication and division calculation strategies and develop methods of recording their work. They link finding fractions of quantities to division. They find reflections of shapes. They use a set-square to find and draw right angles.

Framework objectives	Assessment focuses		Success criteria for Year 3	Learning outcomes
	Level 3	Level 2		
① Pairs of numbers				
Add or subtract mentally combinations of one-digit and two-digit numbers	• add and subtract two-digit numbers mentally, e.g. • calculate 36 + 19, 63 – 26, and complements to 100 such as 100 – 24	• use mental recall of addition and subtraction facts to 10, e.g. • use addition/subtraction facts to 10 and place value to add or subtract multiples of 10, e.g. know 3 + 7 = 10 and use place value to derive 30 + 70 = 100	• Adds two two-digit numbers using an efficient and effective method • Subtracts a two-digit number from a two-digit number using an efficient and effective method • Finds the difference between two two-digit numbers using an efficient and effective method	*I can add or subtract two two-digit numbers.* *I know how to find the difference between two two-digit numbers.*
② Written methods for addition and subtraction				
Represent the information in a puzzle or problem using numbers, images or diagrams; use these to find a solution and present it in context, where appropriate using £.p notation or units of measure	• begin to organise their work and check results, e.g. • begin to develop own ways of recording • develop an organised approach as they get into recording their work on a problem • discuss their mathematical work and begin to explain their thinking • use and interpret mathematical symbols and diagrams	• discuss their work using mathematical language, e.g. with support • describe the strategies and methods they use in their work • listen to others' explanations, try to make sense of them, compare... evaluate... • begin to represent their work using symbols and simple diagrams	• Has strategies to help to solve a problem, such as drawing a picture, making jottings, and/or writing a calculation	*I can draw a picture, make jottings or write calculations to help me answer a problem.*
② Written methods for addition and subtraction				
Develop and use written methods to record, support or explain addition and subtraction of two-digit and three-digit numbers	• add and subtract three-digit numbers using written methods, e.g. • use written methods that involve bridging 10 or 100 • add and subtract decimals in the context of money, where bridging is not required	• record their work in writing, e.g. • record their mental calculations as number sentences	• Records an addition or subtraction calculation • Shows calculation strategies • Shows working out for each stage	*I can record how I work out an addition or subtraction calculation showing each step.*

Unit 2 Calculating, measuring and understanding shape

Framework objectives	Assessment focuses		Success criteria for Year 3	Learning outcomes
	Level 3	Level 2		
③ Recording multiplication and division				
Use practical and informal written methods to multiply and divide two-digit numbers (e.g. 13 × 3, 50 ÷ 4); round remainders up or down, depending on the context	• solve whole number problems including those involving multiplication or division that may give rise to remainders, e.g. • identify appropriate operations to use • round up or down after simple division, depending on context	• choose the appropriate operation when solving addition and subtraction problems, e.g. • use repeated addition to solve multiplication problems • begin to use repeated subtraction or sharing equally to solve division problems	• Uses practical and informal recording methods to multiply a teen number by a one-digit number • Uses practical and informal recording methods to divide a two-digit number by a one-digit number • Recalls appropriate known table facts for both multiplication and division	*I can multiply a 'teen' number by a one-digit number.* *I can divide a two-digit number by a one-digit number.*
④ Fraction challenge				
Find unit fractions of numbers and quantities (e.g. $\frac{1}{2}$, $\frac{1}{3}$, $\frac{1}{4}$ and $\frac{1}{6}$ of 12 litres)	• use simple fractions that are several parts of a whole and recognise when two simple fractions are equivalent, e.g. • understand and use unit fractions such as $\frac{1}{2}$, $\frac{1}{4}$, $\frac{1}{3}$, $\frac{1}{5}$, $\frac{1}{10}$ and find those fractions of shapes and sets of objects	• begin to use halves and quarters, e.g. • use the concept of a fraction of a number in practical contexts such as sharing sweets between two to get $\frac{1}{2}$ each, among four to get $\frac{1}{4}$ each	• Recognises that table facts can be used to find unitary fractions of $\frac{1}{2}$, $\frac{1}{3}$, $\frac{1}{4}$, $\frac{1}{5}$ and $\frac{1}{6}$ • Uses table facts for the 2-, 3-, 4-, 5- and 6-times tables and derives the appropriate division fact to find fractions of a measurement	*I can use division to find $\frac{1}{2}$, $\frac{1}{3}$, $\frac{1}{4}$, $\frac{1}{5}$ and $\frac{1}{6}$ of a measurement.*
⑤ Make it symmetrical				
Draw and complete shapes with reflective symmetry; draw the reflection of a shape in a mirror line along one side	• recognise shapes in different orientations • reflect shapes, presented on a grid, in a vertical or horizontal mirror line	• describe the position of objects, e.g. • recognise and explain that a shape stays the same even when it is held up in different orientations	• Reflects a shape that has straight edges and one edge along the mirror line, whether the reflection is horizontal or vertical	*I can reflect a shape in one of its sides.*
⑥ Moving using the compass				
Read and record the vocabulary of position, direction and movement, using the four compass directions to describe movement about a grid	• describe position and movement, e.g. • use terms such as left/right, clockwise/anticlockwise, quarter turn/90° to give directions along a route	• distinguish between straight and turning movements, e.g. • distinguish between left and right and between clockwise and anticlockwise and use these when giving directions • instruct a programmable robot, combining straight-line movements and turns, to move along a defined path or reach a target destination • recognise right angles in turns	• Can follow instructions to make right-angled turns (or combinations of right angles) • Can give clear and concise instructions for making turns	*I can follow and give instructions to make turns.*

Unit 2 📖 Calculating, measuring and understanding shape

Framework objectives	Assessment focuses		Success criteria for Year 3	Learning outcomes
	Level 3	Level 2		
⑦ Using a set-square				
Use a set-square to draw right angles and to identify right angles in 2D shapes; compare angles with a right angle; recognise that a straight line is equivalent to two right angles	• classify 3D and 2D shapes in various ways using mathematical properties such as reflective symmetry for 2D shapes, e.g. ● recognise right angles in shapes in different orientations ● recognise angles which are bigger/smaller than 90° and begin to know the terms 'obtuse' and 'acute' ● recognise right-angled and equilateral triangles • use a wider range of measures, e.g. ● recognise angles as a measure of turn and know that one whole turn is 360 degrees	• describe the properties of common 3D and 2D shapes, including numbers of sides and corners, e.g. ● sort 2D and 3D shapes according to a single criterion, e.g. shapes that are pentagons or shapes with a right angle	• Uses a set-square effectively and accurately to draw right angles • Recognises right angles in shapes • Uses a set-square to check whether or not a shape is a right angle	*I can identify right angles in shapes and use a set-square to check.*
⑧ Which units of length?				
Know the relationships between kilometres and metres, metres and centimetres, kilograms and grams, litres and millilitres; choose and use appropriate units to estimate, measure and record measurements	• use non-standard units and standard metric units of length, capacity and mass in a range of contexts, e.g. ● measure a length to the nearest ¹/₂cm	• begin to use everyday non-standard and standard units to measure length and mass, e.g. ● begin to understand that numbers can be used not only to count discrete objects but also to describe continuous measures ● know which measuring tools to use to find, e.g., how much an object weighs, how tall a child is, how long it takes to run around the edge of the playground, how much water it takes to fill the water tray • begin to use a wider range of measures	• Knows the metric equivalents for length for centimetres, metres and kilometres • Makes a sensible decision about the units of length to choose for items which may not have their length estimated or measured	*I know how many centimetres make 1 metre and how many metres make 1 kilometre.* *I can decide whether a length should be measured in centimetres, metres or kilometres.*

Activity ①

Prior learning
Children can add or subtract two two-digit numbers and know how to find the difference between two two-digit numbers.

Framework objective
Add or subtract mentally combinations of one-digit and two-digit numbers

Vocabulary
problem, solution, puzzle, pattern, methods, sign, operation, symbol, number sentence, equation, mental calculation, written calculation, informal method, jottings, diagrams, pictures, images, add, plus, sum, total, subtract, take away, minus, difference

Resources
Worksheet: Pairs of numbers

① Pairs of numbers

Ask the children to work in pairs with the worksheet 'Pairs of numbers'. They must take turns to choose two numbers then, working mentally, add the pair and find the difference between them.

Teacher support
Less confident learners: Encourage the children to concentrate on addition of pairs of numbers first, using resources such as an empty number line to help them. When they are confident, they can find the differences between pairs of numbers.
More confident learners: Challenge the children to complete as many additions and differences as they can in, say, 15 minutes.

Common misconceptions
Children do not use the mental strategies that they know when adding or subtracting (finding the difference between) pairs of numbers.
Choose a pair of numbers and ask the children where they could start with adding the pair of numbers. Write out the calculation. For example, for 45 and 73: 45 + 73 = (40 + 70) + (5 + 3) = 110 + 8 = 118. Repeat this for other pairs of numbers – first for addition, then for subtraction (finding the difference).

Probing questions
● A 95g orange is placed in some balance scales. There is 35g in the other pan. How much needs to be added to the 35g so that the scales balance? How did you work this out?
● The difference between the heights of two children is 37cm. What could their heights be? Are your suggestions reasonable? Roughly how old do you think the children would be?
● Find the different totals you can make by adding pairs of these numbers:
  47 50 8 29
● Choose two calculations where you used different strategies to find the totals. Explain why you chose different strategies.

Next steps
Support: Provide further opportunities for adding or subtracting pairs of numbers, such as during an oral and mental starter. Refer back to Year 3 Block A Unit 2.
Extension: Encourage the children to use recall where possible and to derive answers for those that they do not know as quickly as possible. Ask them to explain their calculation strategies. Refer to Year 4 Block A Unit 3.

BLOCK D

■SCHOLASTIC

Activity ②

Prior learning
Children can record how they work out an addition or subtraction calculation showing each step. They can draw a picture, make jottings or write calculations to help them answer a problem.

Framework objectives
● Develop and use written methods to record, support or explain addition and subtraction of two-digit and three-digit numbers
● Represent the information in a puzzle or problem using numbers, images or diagrams; use these to find a solution and present it in context, where appropriate using £.p notation or units of measure

Vocabulary
problem, solution, puzzle, pattern, methods, sign, operation, symbol, number sentence, equation, mental calculation, written calculation, informal method, jottings, diagrams, pictures, images, add, plus, sum, total, subtract, take away, minus, difference

Resources
Worksheet: Written methods for addition and subtraction

② Written methods for addition and subtraction

Explain that you would like the children to find the solutions to the word problems on the worksheet 'Written methods for addition and subtraction'. Tell them that they will need to show their methods for solving each problem.

Teacher support
Less confident learners: Decide whether to work as a group. Ask the children to explain what sort of calculation the problem needs and how they know that.
More confident learners: Challenge the children to invent some similar problems, solve them, then ask their partner to solve the problems.

Common misconceptions
Children do not recognise the type of calculation needed to solve a problem.
Ask the children to pick out key words that identify what type of calculation is needed. If they are unsure, read the problem together and ask the children to explain it. This will help them to recognise the required calculation.

Probing questions
● Find the total cost of a book costing £2.50 and a comic costing 99p. Jot down your method, showing each step.
● Bill records these steps to work out a calculation: 263 − 40 = 223; 223 − 5 = 218. What calculation did he work out? What did you write down to help you answer this?
● Look at this problem: Two snakes are 56cm and 83cm long. What is the difference between their lengths? Draw a picture that will help you to solve the problem. What part of your picture shows the difference?
● Becky has three £1 coins and four 1p coins in her purse. Write down the amount of money she has altogether. What did you write down to help you answer this problem?

Next steps
Support: Provide further word problems. Ask the children to point out the word/s which tell them what sort of calculation they need to perform. Remind the children to write down their method as they work and check that they choose appropriate methods. Refer back to Year 3 Block B Unit 2.
Extension: Decide whether to teach a more formal method of recording addition and subtraction problems. Refer to Year 3 Block E Unit 3.

Activity ③

Prior learning
Children can multiply a 'teen' number by a one-digit number. They can divide a two-digit number by a one-digit number.

Framework objective
Use practical and informal written methods to multiply and divide two-digit numbers (for example, 13 × 3, 50 ÷ 4); round remainders up or down, depending on the context

Vocabulary
double, halve, inverse, multiply, times, multiplied by, product, share, share equally, divide, divided by, divided into, left, left over, remainder, round up, round down

Resources
Resource sheet: Self-assessment
Classroom resources: individual whiteboards and pens

③ Recording multiplication and division

Explain that you are going to say a multiplication or division problem. The children must record their calculations on their individual whiteboards, which they must hold up when you say *Show me*. Say: *A square pond has sides of 11 metres each. If you walked all around the edge of the pond, how far would you walk? Show me.* Ask individuals to explain how they worked out the answer. Repeat with: *There are 45 cakes on a tray. A box holds four cakes. How many cakes can be put into boxes?* Discuss how to deal with the remainder (1). *What if all the cakes had to be put into boxes. How many boxes would be needed?* Now say: *There are 15 boxes of notepads. Each box contains three notepads. How many notepads is that in total?* When the children have finished, ask them to hold up their whiteboards. *How did you work this out? How did you record what you did?* Provide the self-assessment sheet for the children to record their achievements and what they need to do next.

Teacher support
Less confident learners: Suggest that the children try using empty number lines to help them to calculate the answers.
More confident learners: Ask the children to invent a new problem and to find the answer. They can say their problem for the other children to solve. Ask them to explain how to solve it and to show their working out.

Common misconceptions
Children do not recognise the type of calculation needed to solve a problem. Discuss the problem. Ask the children to find the key vocabulary that tells them what sort of problem it is. If they are still unsure, ask them to put the problem into their own words and to say what sort of calculation it is.

Probing questions
● A square pool has sides 12m long. If you walked around the edge of it, how far would you walk? What calculation did you do? How did you work it out?
● Altogether the four sides of a square picture frame are 60cm long. How long is each side? What calculation did you do? How did you work it out?
● What two multiplication facts could you use to work out 13 × 3?

Next steps
Support: Provide further examples of problems. Keep these simple, with multiplication and division of a one-digit number by a one-digit number. Check each time that the children have understood the key vocabulary and what sort

of problem it is. When the children are confident, move to the problem types above. Refer back to Year 2 Block E Unit 1.

Extension: Decide whether to teach a more formal method of recording. Refer to Year 3 Block E Unit 3.

Activity ④

Prior learning
Children can use division to find $\frac{1}{2}$, $\frac{1}{3}$, $\frac{1}{4}$, $\frac{1}{5}$ and $\frac{1}{6}$ of a measurement.

Framework objective
Find unit fractions of numbers and quantities (for example, $\frac{1}{2}$, $\frac{1}{3}$, $\frac{1}{4}$ and $\frac{1}{6}$ of 12 litres)

Vocabulary
fraction, part, equal parts, one whole, one half, one third, one quarter, one fifth, one sixth

Resources
Resource sheet: Self-assessment
Classroom resources: counters or interlocking cubes

④ Fraction challenge

Write these fractions and numbers on the board:

$\frac{1}{2}$ $\frac{1}{3}$ $\frac{1}{4}$ $\frac{1}{5}$ $\frac{1}{6}$ 24   30   90

Ask the children to use division to find which of the fractions can be found exactly for the numbers 24, 30 and 90. They write each response as either a number sentence or a sentence to say whether it is possible to find the fraction exactly. Keep the pace of this sharp so that the children derive quickly the division facts that they need. Decide whether to use the self-assessment sheet for the children to record their success and learning points, and what they need to do next.

Teacher support
Less confident learners: Decide whether to give counters or cubes to the children to model the divisions.
More confident learners: Ask the children to find any other fractions that they can of 24 ($\frac{1}{12}$, $\frac{1}{8}$, $\frac{1}{24}$), of 30 ($\frac{1}{10}$, $\frac{1}{15}$, $\frac{1}{30}$) and of 90 ($\frac{1}{9}$, $\frac{1}{10}$, $\frac{1}{45}$, $\frac{1}{90}$).

Common misconceptions
Children do not understand that they can use division to find unitary fractions of quantities.
Provide counters to model finding half of 6. Ask the children to separate a set of six counters into half, or into two piles. Discuss how finding half is the same as dividing by 2. Repeat for other fractions, keeping the quantities smaller.

Probing questions
● How would you find one third of 27? One quarter of 56? What about one tenth of 250?
● Milly has a 100ml bottle of medicine. She takes one fifth of the medicine each day. How many days does she take the medicine for? How much medicine does she take each day? What calculations did you do to work this out?
● John has a 120g bar of chocolate. He cuts it into six equal pieces. How much does each piece weigh? What fraction of the bar is this?

Next steps
Support: Provide further experience of finding fractions of numbers that lie within the table facts that the children know, such as a quarter of 36. Over time,

BLOCK D

> extend this to quantities such as finding one sixth of 60, 120 and so on. Refer back to Year 3 Block D Unit 1.
> **Extension:** Challenge the children to repeat the activity using numbers such as 120, 160, 400... Refer to Year 4 Block E Unit 1.

Activity ⑤

Prior learning
Children can reflect a shape in one of its sides.

Framework objective
Draw and complete shapes with reflective symmetry; draw the reflection of a shape in a mirror line along one side

Vocabulary
line of symmetry, fold, match, mirror line, reflection

Resources
Resource sheets: Centimetre-squared paper, Self-assessment
Classroom resources: safety mirrors

Figure 1

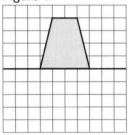

Figure 2

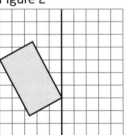

Figure 3

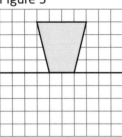

⑤ Make it symmetrical

Ask the children to work in pairs. Provide centimetre-squared paper for each child. They should take turns to draw a mirror line, vertically or horizontally, along one of the lines on the squared paper. Then they should draw a shape with straight lines and one line along the mirror line (see Figure 1, left). Ask the children to swap papers and draw in the reflection of the shape, then repeat this four more times. Each time they should check each other's work. If there is a disagreement, suggest that they check their work using a mirror. Decide whether to use the self-assessment sheet for the children to record their achievements and growth points, and what they need to do next.

Teacher support
Less confident learners: Use simple shapes such as squares, rectangles and right-angled triangles for the activity.
More confident learners: Challenge the children to try more complex reflections (as in Figure 2).

Common misconceptions
Children repeat the shape without reflecting it in the mirror line.
Draw a mirror line and a simple shape (such as a right-angled triangle) on squared paper, with one side touching the mirror line. Use a mirror to show the reflection. Repeat with other shapes, discussing the position of each line in the reflection. Use a mirror to check each time that the reflection is correct.

Probing questions
● Draw the reflection of this shape in the mirror line. (See Figure 3.)
● A letter 'd' is reflected in its straight side. Its reflection is a different letter. Which one?

Next steps
Support: Repeat the activity with the children working in pairs. Check that they understand that the reflection is along the mirror line. Discuss where the line of symmetry is of the whole shape (the mirror line). Ask: *Are there any other lines of symmetry of your whole shape?* Refer back to Year 3 Block B Unit 2.
Extension: Challenge the children to draw more complex shapes which they can give to a partner to reflect. They should check using a mirror. Refer to Year 4 Block B Unit 1.

BLOCK D

Activity ⑥

Prior learning
Children can follow and give instructions to make turns.

Framework objective
Read and record the vocabulary of position, direction and movement, using the four compass directions to describe movement about a grid

Vocabulary
map, plan, compass point, north (N), south (S), east (E), west (W), turn, whole turn, half turn, quarter turn, right, left, up, down, ascend, descend, forward, backward, sideways, across, angle, right angle

Resources
Resource sheet: Self-assessment
Resource sheet: Centimetre-squared paper

⑥ Moving using the compass

On the board, draw the compass with the four points marked with lines and N for north. Ask: *Which line shows south? East? West?* Provide centimetre-squared paper for each child. Ask them to draw the compass as it is on the board. Now ask them to take turns to draw a route, with right-angled turns, without their partner seeing. They must then give directions for drawing their route. If it is a straight-line move, they say how many centimetres long the line is, using the squared paper and counting squares. They then compare papers, checking carefully. They then swap roles, repeating the activity three times in total, so that each child has taken the lead twice in giving instructions. Decide whether to use the self-assessment sheet for the children to record their achievements and what they need to do next.

Teacher support
Less confident learners: Decide whether to have these children work as a group. Encourage them to describe each move carefully, using the vocabulary of position, direction and movement, and referring to the compass points.
More confident learners: Challenge the children to make more complicated routes for others to draw from their descriptions.

Common misconceptions
Children do not know the compass points.
Draw a compass on a large sheet of paper. (If the children find it difficult to refer to a diagram placed in the vertical rather than the horizontal plane, you could try drawing the compass on the playground floor instead, using chalk – this way the children can place their feet in the direction of the compass points.) Give instructions, for example: *Face south. Now face east. Through how many right angles did you turn?* Then say: *Face north. Take three steps forwards. Turn west. Take three steps backwards* (and so on).

Probing questions
● If you stand facing north, then make a half turn, what direction would you be facing?
● Give instructions to draw this route. Use the direction words: north, south, east and west. Give the exact length of each line.

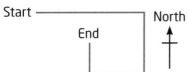

Next steps
Support: Provide opportunities for the children to move, using compass points, a series of right-angled turns and counted steps in PE. Refer back to Year 3 Block D Unit 1.
Extension: Introduce the eight-point compass and ask children to repeat the

BLOCK D

activity using NW, NE, SW and SE. They then measure the diagonal lines to provide more information about the length of the line. Refer to Year 4 Block D Unit 1.

Activity ⑦

Prior learning
Children can identify right angles in shapes and use a set-square to check.

Framework objective
Use a set-square to draw right angles and to identify right angles in 2D shapes; compare angles with a right angle; recognise that a straight line is equivalent to two right angles

Vocabulary
angle, right angle, set-square

Resources
Resource sheet: Self-assessment
Classroom resources: plain paper, rulers, set-squares

⑦ Using a set-square

Provide each child with paper, a ruler and a set-square. Explain to the children that you will ask them to use the ruler and set-square to draw a shape. Say: *Draw a square with sides of 9cm. Draw a rectangle with one pair of sides of 6cm and the other of 8cm. Draw a right-angled triangle. The two sides that form the right angle should each be 7cm.* The children should then swap with their partners, who check the lengths of lines and accuracy of right angles. Ask the children to complete the self-assessment sheet, writing how accurately they drew their right angles and their lines with a ruler.

Teacher support
Less confident learners: Have the children draw simple shapes such as squares initially. Check that they can use the set-square accurately.
More confident learners: Challenge the children to draw more complex shapes, such as a house-shaped pentagon with a base of 8cm and sides (walls) of 6cm. Ask them to measure the lengths of the other two lines and to check with their set-square whether the angle at the top of the 'roof' is a right angle.

Common misconceptions
Children do not understand how to use a set-square.
Ask the children to examine a set-square. What shape is it? Where is its right angle? Provide them with opportunities to draw right angles using the set-square. Then show them how to use it to check whether or not an angle is a right angle.

Probing questions
● Use a set-square and a ruler to draw a square with sides of 12cm.
● How many right angles are there in this pentagon? How could you check?

Next steps
Support: Provide opportunities for the children to use a set-square, such as asking them to draw rectangles of given sizes, or to complete a shape using the set-square to draw right-angled vertices. Refer back to Year 2 Block D Unit 3.
Extension: Challenge the children to give each other instructions for drawing shapes that involve using a set-square and ruler. Refer to Year 3 Block B Unit 3.

Activity ⑧

Prior learning
Children know how many centimetres make 1 metre and how many metres make 1 kilometre. They can decide whether a length should be measured in centimetres, metres or kilometres.

Framework objective
Know the relationships between kilometres and metres, metres and centimetres, kilograms and grams, litres and millilitres; choose and use appropriate units to estimate, measure and record measurements

Vocabulary
centimetres (cm), metres (m), kilometres (km), millimetres (mm)

Resources
Display page: Which units of length?
Resource sheet: Self-assessment
Classroom resources: individual whiteboards and pens

⑧ Which units of length?

Reveal the first screen of the display page 'Which units of length?'. Ask the children to find the answer and write it on their whiteboards. When you say *Show me,* they hold up their boards. Discuss the units that the children chose. Now reveal the next question and ask the children to display their answer on their whiteboards. Repeat for the further questions on the following pages. Observe the answers and check to see who is confident and who needs further help. Decide whether to use the self-assessment sheet for the children to record their ability to use units of length appropriately.

Teacher support
Less confident learners: Read the words on the screen and check that the children have understood the question or statement.
More confident learners: Ask the children to suggest more items that can be measured in millimetres, centimetres, metres and kilometres.

Common misconceptions
Children do not understand the relationship between the units of length.
Begin with centimetres. Use a metre rule and ask the children: *How many centimetres are there? How long is this rule? So how many centimetres make a metre?* Explain that there are 1000m in a kilometre. Leave millimetres for now.

Probing questions
● A bench is 2m and 40cm long. How many centimetres is this? Explain your working.
● How many 100-metre runs would you need to do to run a total of 1 kilometre? What calculation did you use to work this out?
● Suggest an object whose length would be measured in metres. What about centimetres? And millimetres?
● Match the measurement to the appropriate unit:
the amount of water in a cup	kilogram
the length of a road	millilitre
the mass of a dog	kilometre

Next steps
Support: Give further practical experience of measuring in centimetres and metres. Ask the children to explain their choice of unit each time. Give word problems that use kilometres, before moving on to some that use both kilometres and metres. Refer back to Year 3 Block C Unit 1.
Extension: Provide examples of problems that use mixed units, so that children have to decide how to represent their answer. Refer to Year 3 Block C Unit 3.

BLOCK D

Unit 3 ▫ Calculating, measuring and understanding shape

Introduction

In this unit, children are encouraged to present information in a logical sequence, using appropriate mathematical vocabulary and be prepared to answer questions from other children. They solve problems which involve addition, subtraction, multiplication or division and use appropriate methods to record their work. They develop their understanding that division is the inverse of multiplication and use this understanding to solve problems. They sketch shapes, and recognise right angles. They read scales for capacity, make estimates and checks in practical situations. They tell the time in five-minute intervals, and record times using digital time. They also write sentences about time intervals.

BLOCK D

Framework objectives	Assessment focuses		Success criteria for Year 3	Learning outcomes
	Level 3	**Level 2**		
① Checking solutions				
Solve one-step and two-step problems involving numbers, money or measures, including time, choosing and carrying out appropriate calculations	• select the mathematics they use in a wider range of classroom activities • use mental recall of addition and subtraction facts to 20 in solving problems involving larger numbers	• select the mathematics they use in some classroom activities • choose the appropriate operation when solving addition and subtraction problems • solve number problems involving money and measures	• Recognises that some problems need two steps, rather than one, to find the answer • Explains how a problem was solved	*I can explain how I found the answer to a word problem that involves measurements.*
① Checking solutions				
Use knowledge of number operations and corresponding inverses, including doubling and halving, to estimate and check calculations	• derive associated division facts from known multiplication facts, e.g. ● use inverses to find missing whole numbers in problems such as 'I think of a number, double it and add 5. The answer is 35. What was my number?'	• use the knowledge that subtraction is the inverse of addition, e.g. ● given 14, 6 and 8, make related number sentences 6 + 8 = 14, 14 − 8 = 6, 8 + 6 = 14, 14 − 6 = 8 ● understand halving as a way of 'undoing' doubling and vice versa	• Has checking strategies for assessing whether the answer is correct • Uses these strategies regularly in order to check that the answer is correct	*I can check whether the answer to a calculation is correct.*
② Add and subtract				
Develop and use written methods to record, support or explain addition and subtraction of two-digit and three-digit numbers	• add and subtract three-digit numbers using written methods, e.g. ● use written methods that involve bridging 10 or 100 ● add and subtract decimals in the context of money, where bridging is not required	• record their work in writing, e.g. ● record their mental calculations as number sentences	• Has an effective written method for addition of two-digit and three-digit numbers • Has an effective written method for subtraction of two-digit and three-digit numbers	*I can write down my method to add or subtract two-digit or three-digit numbers.*

■■SCHOLASTIC

Unit 3 Calculating, measuring and understanding shape

Framework objectives	Assessment focuses		Success criteria for Year 3	Learning outcomes
	Level 3	**Level 2**		
③ Multiply and divide				
Use practical and informal written methods to multiply and divide two-digit numbers; round remainders up or down, depending on the context Understand that division is the inverse of multiplication and vice versa; use this to derive and record related multiplication and division sentences	● solve whole-number problems including those involving multiplication or division that may give rise to remainders, e.g. ● identify appropriate operations to use ● round up or down after simple division, depending on context ● derive associated division facts from known multiplication facts, e.g. ● use inverses to find missing whole numbers in problems	● choose the appropriate operation when solving addition and subtraction problems, e.g. ● use repeated addition to solve multiplication problems ● begin to use repeated subtraction or sharing equally to solve division problems	● Uses practical or informal written methods for multiplying and dividing a two-digit number by a one-digit number ● Understands that multiplication facts help to derive division facts, and vice versa	*I can multiply or divide a two-digit number by a one-digit number.* *I can say what multiplication fact I would use for a division calculation.*
④ Angle size				
Use a set-square to draw right angles and to identify right angles in 2D shapes; compare angles with a right angle; recognise that a straight line is equivalent to two right angles	● classify 3D and 2D shapes in various ways using mathematical properties ● use a wider range of measures, e.g. ● recognise angles as a measure of turn and know that one whole turn is 360 degrees	● describe the properties of common 3D and 2D shapes, including numbers of sides and corners, e.g. ● sort 2D and 3D shapes according to a single criterion, e.g. shapes that are pentagons or shapes with a right angle	● Uses a set-square effectively and accurately to draw right angles ● Recognises right angles in shapes ● Uses a set-square to check whether or not a shape is a right angle	*I can test whether an angle is equal to, bigger than or smaller than a right angle.*
⑤ Using measuring equipment				
Read, to the nearest division and half-division, scales that are numbered or partially numbered; use the information to measure and draw to a suitable degree of accuracy	● use non-standard units and standard metric units of length, capacity and mass in a range of contexts, e.g. ● read simple scales, e.g. increments of 2, 5 or 10	● begin to use everyday non-standard and standard units to measure length and mass, e.g. ● read scales to the nearest labelled division	● Reads scales to the nearest division or half division ● Records the measurement appropriately ● Draws a line accurately to the nearest division or half division	*I can say what one division on a scale is worth.* *I can read a scale to the nearest division or half division.*
⑥ Time problems				
Read the time on a 12-hour digital clock and to the nearest 5 minutes on an analogue clock; calculate time intervals and find start or end times for a given time interval	● use standard units of time, e.g. ● read a 12-hour clock and generally calculate time durations that do not go over the hour	● begin to use a wider range of measures, e.g. ● use a time line to order daily events and ordinal numbers (first, second, third...) to describe the order of some regular events	● Reads time on a clock face to the nearest 5 minutes ● Calculates time taken to the nearest 5 minutes	*I can tell the time to the nearest 5 minutes.* *I can work out the start or end time for an activity.*

BLOCK D

Activity ①

Prior learning
Children can explain how they found the answer to a word problem that involves measurements. They can check whether the answer to a calculation is correct.

Framework objectives
● Solve one-step and two-step problems involving numbers, money or measures, including time, choosing and carrying out appropriate calculations
● Use knowledge of number operations and corresponding inverses, including doubling and halving, to estimate and check calculations

Vocabulary
problem, solution, puzzle, pattern, methods, sign, operation, symbol, number sentence, equation, add, plus, sum, total, subtract, take away, minus, difference, double, halve, inverse, multiply, times, multiplied by, product, share, share equally, divide, divided by, divided into, left, left over, remainder

Resources
Worksheet: Checking solutions

① Checking solutions

Provide copies of the worksheet 'Checking solutions'. Ask the children to solve the problems and write a checking calculation to check their answers. When they have finished, ask individuals how they worked out specific answers.

Teacher support
Less confident learners: Remind the children of ways of calculating: working mentally; making jottings; drawing pictures such as an empty number line.
More confident learners: Ask the children to compare their answers, working out and check calculations with a partner. Ask them to discuss which method/s they think are the more efficient, and why they think that.

Common misconceptions
Children do not recognise what sort of mathematics is needed for the problem.
Read the problem together. Invite the children to say what sort of problem they think it is and which words help them. If they are not sure, ask them to say the problem in their own words.

Children do not recognise that they can use inverse calculations to check answers.
Discuss how an inverse calculation helps them to check answers, such as for doubling: halve; for addition: subtract; for multiplication: divide.

Probing questions
● Ella buys one toy costing 35p and another 48p. She pays with a £5 note. How much change does she get? What two calculations will help you to answer this problem? What does the answer to the first calculation tell you?
● Make up a word problem that would lead to the calculation 8 × 4. How do you recognise that this problem involves multiplication?
● Joe says that 92cm − 48cm = 56cm. How could you check his answer?
● I think of a number, double it and then subtract 2. I get the answer 6. What was my number? How did you find it?
● Will the answer to £6.78 + £2.84 be closer to £8, £9 or £10?

Next steps
Support: Provide further word problems, such as: *Mark has 40 marbles. He decides to share them between his five friends. How many marbles does each friend have?* Discuss the key words in the problem and also which method to use to check the calculation. Refer back to Year 3 Block D Unit 1 and Block B Unit 3.

> **Extension:** Offer more complex problems, such as: *John, Ali and Sue are going on a class outing. The outing will cost £160. The school has received £60 towards the costs. There are 25 children in their class. How much will each child have to pay?* Refer to Year 3 Block E Unit 3 and Year 4 Block A Unit 1.

Activity ②

Prior learning
Children can write down their method to add or subtract two-digit or three-digit numbers.

Framework objective
Develop and use written methods to record, support or explain addition and subtraction of two-digit and three-digit numbers

Vocabulary
problem, solution, puzzle, pattern, methods, sign, operation, symbol, number sentence, equation, mental calculation, written calculation, informal method, jottings, diagrams, pictures, images, add, plus, sum, total, subtract, take away, minus, difference

Resources
Resource sheet: Self-assessment

② Add and subtract

Explain that you will say a problem that involves adding or subtracting. Ask the children to write down their calculation, find the answer, and be able to explain their working to others. *I have £7.56 in my purse. I spend £4.88 on fruit. How much money do I have left?* Repeat the problem so that the children have time to write down their calculation. Ask individuals to explain their workings, writing their responses on the board. Invite discussion about the method and whether it is efficient. Repeat with: *In one school there are 654 children. In another school there are 567 children. Which school has more children? How many more?* And another problem: *Will has £3.47 in his money box. He receives £6.78 from his uncle. How much money has he now?* Decide whether to use the self-assessment sheet for the children to record their achievements and what they need to do next.

Teacher support
Less confident learners: Check that the children are clear about whether the problem requires an addition or subtraction method to be used. If necessary, give the children problems with smaller numbers.
More confident learners: Ask the children to discuss methods and answers with a partner and write a check calculation to confirm their answer.

Common misconceptions
Children do not set out the calculation correctly, so they add or subtract the wrong digits.
Work through some examples of addition using a written method. Check that the children understand how to set out the written method. Provide an example for the children to try for themselves. Repeat for subtraction.

Probing questions
● I spend £6.78 and £2.84 on my shopping. Work out how much I have spent altogether. Explain each step of your calculation.
● Work out 91 − 37. Decide how to record your working.

Next steps
Support: When children are confident with written methods for addition and

BLOCK D

▷ subtraction with two two-digit numbers, include a three-digit number in the calculations. Refer back to Year 3 Block D Unit 2.
Extension: When children are confident with written methods for addition and subtraction with two three-digit numbers, extend to writing a three-digit and four-digit addition or subtraction. Refer to Year 3 Block E Unit 3.

Activity ③

Prior learning
Children can multiply and divide a two-digit number by a one-digit number. They can say what multiplication fact they would use for a division calculation.

Framework objectives
- Use practical and informal written methods to multiply and divide two-digit numbers (for example, 13 × 3, 50 ÷ 4); round remainders up or down, depending on the context
- Understand that division is the inverse of multiplication and vice versa; use this to derive and record related multiplication and division number sentences

Vocabulary
problem, solution, puzzle, pattern, methods, sign, operation, symbol, number sentence, equation, mental calculation, written calculation, informal method, jottings, diagrams, pictures, images, double, halve, inverse, multiply, times, multiplied by, product, share, share equally, divide, divided by, divided into, left, left over, remainder

Resources
Worksheet: Multiply and divide (1)

---

③ Multiply and divide

Say: *I have 64 pencils to share between 3 children. How would you work out the answer?* Discuss the children's methods and their use of multiplication facts to derive division facts. Provide the worksheet 'Multiply and divide (1)' for each child and ask them to record their methods for working out the answer.

Teacher support
Less confident learners: If necessary, work together to solve the problems. Remind children that multiplication facts can be used to derive division facts.
More confident learners: Challenge these children to write their own word problems. They should swap problems with their partners, then compare answers and methods, deciding which method is more efficient and saying why they think that.

Common misconceptions
Children do not understand that multiplication facts can be used to help them to derive division facts.
Ask: *What is 4 × 3? And 3 × 4? So what is 12 ÷ 3? And 12 ÷ 4?* Discuss how the numbers 3, 4 and 12 make a 'family' for two multiplication and division facts and that if the multiplication is known then the division fact can be derived.

Children do not have an efficient method for multiplying or dividing a two-digit by a one-digit number.
Ask the children to show how they can multiply 24 by 3. If necessary, teach a method such as: 24 × 3 = (20 × 3) + (4 × 3) = 60 + 12 = 72. Similarly, teach a division method - for example, 40 ÷ 3:
$10 \times 3 = 30 \qquad 3 \times 3 = 9$
$13 \times 3 = (10 \times 3) + (3 \times 3) = 30 + 9 = 39$
So $40 \div 3 = 13$ remainder 1

Repeat for other examples until the children are confident with this method. Also check that they can use known multiplication facts to derive division facts.

Probing questions
- An egg weighs about 50g. Roughly, how much do six eggs weigh? Jot down how you worked this out.
- What is 20 × 4? What is 6 × 4? What is 26 × 4?
- What is the remainder when 35 is divided by 3?
- Thirty-five crayons are shared fairly into three pots. How many crayons are in each pot? How did you decide on your answer?
- How many five-minute cartoons can I watch in 20 minutes? What division calculation matches this problem? What multiplication fact can help to find the answer?
- Charlie starts with the number 20. He multiplies it by 6 then divides the answer by 6. What number does he get? How do you know?

Next steps
Support: Provide further experience of multiplying or dividing a two-digit number by a one-digit number. Check that the children understand that they can use the multiplication facts that they know to derive division facts and vice versa. Refer back to Year 3 Block D Unit 2.

Extension: Challenge the children to continue to write word problems for their partner involving multiplication and division of two-digit by one-digit numbers. Refer to Year 3 Block E Unit 3 and Year 4 Block B Unit 2.

Activity ④

Prior learning
Children can test whether an angle is equal to, bigger than or smaller than a right angle.

Framework objective
Use a set-square to draw right angles and to identify right angles in 2D shapes; compare angles with a right angle; recognise that a straight line is equivalent to two right angles

Vocabulary
right angle, set-square

Resources
Resource sheet: Self-assessment
Classroom resources: rulers, set-squares

④ Angle size

Ask the children to work in pairs with a set-square and ruler between them. They take turns to draw two lines to make an angle and estimate whether their angle is a right angle, smaller than a right angle or larger than a right angle. Their partner uses the set-square to check up to five examples. Ask the children to record successes and learning points on the self-assessment sheet.

Teacher support
Less confident learners: Check that the children are clear about how to use a set-square. Teach this skill if necessary.
More confident learners: Ask the children to draw several right angles, but with different arm lengths. *Are these all the same angle? How do you know?*

Common misconceptions
Children are unsure about how to use a set-square.
Teach how to use a set-square, both for comparing the size of angles and for

BLOCK D

drawing right angles. Check that the children understand that they can use the set-square to identify angles that are right angles and angles that are greater than or smaller than a right angle.

Probing questions
● Paula says that angle A is smaller than angle B. Is she correct? Explain your answer.

● Place a set of shapes in the correct place in this table.

all right angles	some right angles	no right angles

Next steps
Support: Provide opportunities for using a set-square. Check that the children are confident about positioning the set-square and reading from the set-square. Refer back to Year 3 Block D Unit 2.
Extension: Ask the children to draw shapes using a ruler and set-square. Swap with their partner and assess the size of the shape angles. Say whether they are right angles, or smaller or larger than a right angle. Refer to Year 4 Block B Unit 1.

Activity ⑤

BLOCK D

Prior learning
Children can say what one division on a scale is worth. They can read a scale to the nearest division or half division.

Framework objective
Read, to the nearest division and half-division, scales that are numbered or partially numbered; use the information to measure and draw to a suitable degree of accuracy

Vocabulary
measure, estimate, unit, metre (m), centimetre (cm), kilogram (kg), gram (g), litre (l), millilitre (ml)

Resources
Resource sheet: Self-assessment
Classroom resources: set up three work stations as follows:
Capacity: jugs with scales marked in 200ml increments; sand or water, in unmarked containers
Mass: weighing scales marked in 100g increments to 1kg and items to weigh ranging from 50g to 1kg
Temperature: warm water in a jug and a thermometer where the scale is in 10°C increments, with even numbers (2, 4, 6, etc) marked as small lines

⑤ Using measuring equipment

Show the equipment. Ask children to work in groups. They move between the workstations to measure the items accurately and record measurements using appropriate units. Allow time for the children to complete each task, but keep the pace sharp. When they have finished, ask about each scale and how to read it. Provide the self-assessment sheet for the children to record their successes and areas of improvement.

Teacher support

Less confident learners: Decide whether to work with these children and to check that they can interpret each scale.
More confident learners: Decide whether to provide more complex scales for the children to read (eg scale marked in 100 grams with only 500g numbered).

Common misconceptions

Children do not recognise how to read a scale.
Look together at a scale. Ask the children to read the numbers and to identify the scale. Invite them to look at the marks between the numbered parts of the scale and to say what these represent. Repeat for other scales until the children are confident.

Probing questions

● [Show children some weighing scales.] Point to where the dial would go if it showed a mass of 45g. How do you know?
● [Show children a measuring jug.] What is each division on this jug worth?
● [Pour 400 ml of water into a measuring jug.] How much water is in this jug? How do you know?

Next steps

Support: Provide further opportunities for the children to use a range of measuring equipment. They should measure as accurately as they can, reading the scale with care. Refer back to Year 3 Block D Unit 1.
Extension: Give specific amounts to be weighed or measured and check each other's measurements. Provide equipment with scales that involve the children working with unnumbered divisions. Refer to Year 4 Block C Unit 1.

Activity ⑥

Prior learning
Children can tell the time to the nearest five minutes. They can work out the start or end time for an activity.

Framework objective
Read the time on a 12-hour digital clock and to the nearest five minutes on an analogue clock; calculate time intervals and find start or end times for a given time interval

Vocabulary
time, clock, watch, hours (h), minutes (min), seconds (s)

Resources
Display page: Time problems
Resource sheet: Self-assessment
Classroom resources: individual whiteboards and pens, clock faces

⑥ Time problems

Reveal the first screen of the display page 'Time problems'. Read the problem together then ask the children to write the answer on their whiteboards and hold them up when you say *Show me*. Check for correct answers and methods used. Repeat for the further questions on the following pages. Decide whether to provide the self-assessment sheet for the children to record their successes and areas for improvement.

Teacher support

Less confident learners: Decide whether to provide clock faces with moveable hands to help the children to count on/back to find the time taken.
More confident learners: Invite children to explain their solutions.

Unit 3 ◻ Calculating, measuring and understanding shape

Common misconceptions
Children are unsure about calculating periods of time.
Work within the hour. Set the hands on a clock face to 5 o'clock and ask: *What time will it be in 5 minutes? 10 minutes?* (and so on). Now say: *I leave home at 5 o'clock. I walk for 20 minutes. What time is it now?* Set the clock hands to show the time. Repeat for other questions, gradually moving to other time differences.

Probing questions
● How would a digital clock show the time twenty minutes to six?
● The journey to work takes Rob 20 minutes. He needs to be at work at 9 o'clock. Move the hands on this clock face to show the time that he should leave.

Next steps
Support: Provide clock faces for the children to use as counting aids. Work together to move away from the clock face to counting mentally in five- or ten-minute intervals in order to find solutions. Refer back to Year 3 Block D Unit 1.
Extension: Ask the children to write their own time problems for a partner to solve. Encourage them to explain to each other how they solved the problems. Refer to Year 4 Block D Unit 1.

BLOCK D

◼ SCHOLASTIC

Periodic assessment

These activities can be used at any time during the teaching of this block to assess those children that you think have achieved the objective. A grid highlighting the related assessment focuses and expected learning outcomes for each activity can be found on the CD-ROM.

Adding and subtracting

Framework objective

Add or subtract mentally combinations of one-digit and two-digit numbers

Learning outcomes
- I can add or subtract a one-digit number to or from a two-digit number.
- I can add or subtract a multiple of 10 to or from a two-digit number.
- I can add or subtract two two-digit numbers.
- I know how to find the difference between two two-digit numbers.

The first two learning outcomes are tested through an oral and mental session. Provide Part 1 of the worksheet 'Adding and subtracting' for the children to write their answers on. Part 2 is a teacher's sheet containing the questions and answers. Ask the children to listen to the question, then to write the answer in the relevant part of the sheet. (Both these sheets are available on the CD-ROM.)

   Provide the worksheet 'Add and subtract two two-digit numbers'. Ask the children to find the answers to the word problems and to record their working out as well as their answers.

Reading scales

Framework objective

Read, to the nearest division and half-division, scales that are numbered or partially numbered; use the information to measure and draw to a suitable degree of accuracy

Learning outcomes
- I can say what one division on a scale is worth.
- I can read a scale to the nearest division or half division.

Provide the worksheet 'Reading scales'. Ask the children to complete this, looking carefully at the scales and where each pointer or level is.

Reflecting shapes

Framework objective

Draw and complete shapes with reflective symmetry; draw the reflection of a shape in a mirror line along one side

Learning outcome
- I can reflect a shape in one of its sides.

Provide the worksheet 'Reflecting shapes'. Ask the children to complete the shape by drawing its reflection in the marked mirror line. The reflections need to be accurately completed.

Name	Date

Add and subtract two two-digit numbers

Write the answers to these word problems.

◼ Write some jottings to show how you added or subtracted.

Word problem	Jottings	Answer
1. There are 34 dogs and 47 cats in the animal sanctuary. How many animals is that in total?		
2. Each day the animal sanctuary uses 55 large tins of dog food and 49 very large tins of cat food. How many tins of food does the animal sanctuary use each day?		
3. A tin of dog food costs 98p and a tin of cat food costs 88p. What is the cost of a tin of dog food and a tin of cat food?		
4. At the weekend more dogs and cats come into the animal sanctuary. Now there are 45 dogs and 53 cats. How many more cats are there than dogs?		
5. A local pet shop gives the animal sanctuary 86 tins of dog food. On that day the dogs eat 59 tins of food. How many tins of dog food are there left?		

How easy?

Red
Amber
Green

How do you think you have done?

_____

_____

Name   Date

Reading scales

Write the readings shown on these scales.

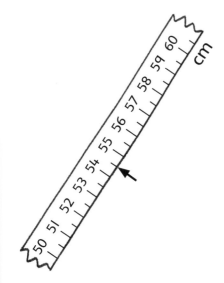 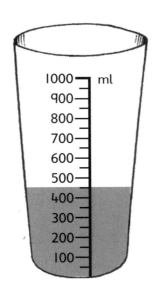 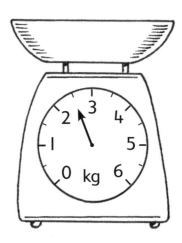

_____ _____ _____

◼ Mark each of these scales with the reading.

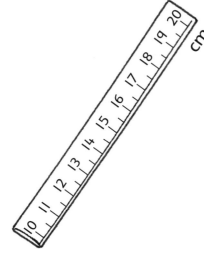 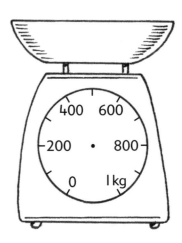

17cm   300ml   900g

_____ _____ _____

How easy?

Red
Amber
Green

How do you think you have done?

_____

_____

Name	Date

Reflecting shapes

Draw the reflection of each shape in the mirror line.

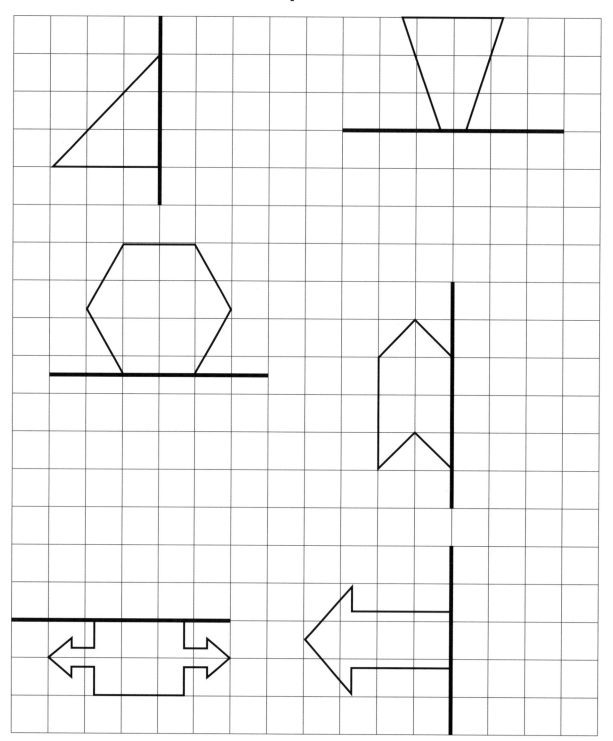

How easy?

Red

Amber

Green

How do you think you have done?

_____

_____

BLOCK D

BLOCK E
Securing number facts, relationships and calculating

Expected prior learning

Check that children can already:
- solve one-step word problems involving all four operations
- choose and use suitable equipment when following a given line of enquiry
- select, organise and present information in lists, tables and simple diagrams
- partition two-digit numbers and recognise the importance of place value
- recognise simple fractions and find halves and quarters of sets of objects and small numbers
- recall addition and subtraction facts for all numbers to 10 and multiples of 10
- understand inverse operations and use the inverse relationships of addition and subtraction to generate number facts
- understand multiplication and division, and derive and recall multiplication and division facts for 2, 5 and 10.

Objectives overview

The text in this diagram identifies the focus of mathematics learning within the block.

Key aspects of learning
- Enquiry
- Problem solving
- Reasoning
- Creative thinking
- Social skills
- Communication
- Motivation

Following lines of enquiry and solving problems

Solving problems by identifying patterns and relationships in numbers

Deriving and consolidating knowledge of number facts for all four operations

**BLOCK E:
Securing number facts, relationships and calculating**

Interpreting and using proper fractions

Finding unit fractions of quantities

Developing practical and written methods for adding, subtracting, multiplying and dividing two-digit numbers

Interpreting remainders in context

BLOCK E

Unit 1 Securing number facts, relationships and calculating

Introduction
In this unit children develop their ability to make decisions when solving problems, and to use tables and charts to make clear the data they have collected. They use and apply mathematics in problem-solving situations. The using and applying aspect of mathematics is included in all work in this unit. Children are encouraged throughout the unit to explain their thinking and to give their view and choices. When working with a partner or in small groups encourage them to discuss their work, and to sustain their conversation so that they develop their abilities to discuss in more detail.

Framework objectives	Assessment focuses		Success criteria for Year 3	Learning outcomes
	Level 3	Level 2		
① Multiplication by 2, 5 and 10 ② Multiply and divide				
Follow a line of enquiry by deciding what information is important; make and use lists, tables and graphs to organise and interpret the information	• begin to organise their work and check results, e.g. • begin to develop own ways of recording • develop an organised approach as they get into recording their work on a problem • discuss their mathematical work and begin to explain their thinking, e.g. • use appropriate mathematical vocabulary • talk about their findings by referring to their written work • use and interpret mathematical symbols and diagrams	• discuss their work using mathematical language, e.g. with support • describe the strategies and methods they use in their work • listen to others' explanations, try to make sense of them, compare… evaluate… • begin to represent their work using symbols and simple diagrams, e.g. with support • use pictures, diagrams and symbols to communicate their thinking, or demonstrate a solution or process • begin to appreciate the need to record and develop their own methods of recording	• Decides what information is important • Makes tables, lists, graphs, as appropriate • Organises the information and interprets it	*I can make a table to record my results.*
① Multiplication by 2, 5 and 10 ② Multiply and divide				
Derive and recall multiplication facts for the 2-, 3-, 4-, 5-, 6- and 10-times tables and the corresponding division facts; recognise multiples of 2, 5 or 10 up to 1000	• recognise a wider range of sequences, e.g. • recognise sequences of multiples of 2, 5 and 10 • derive associated division facts from known multiplication facts, e.g. • given a number sentence, use understanding of operations to create related sentences, e.g. given 14 × 5 = 70, create 5 × 14 = 70, 70 ÷ 5 = 14, 70 ÷ 14 = 5, 14 × 5 = 10 × 5 add 4 × 5 • use mental recall of the 2, 3, 4, 5 and 10 multiplication tables	• recognise sequences of numbers, including odd and even numbers, e.g. • recognise numbers from counting in tens or twos • use mental calculation strategies to solve number problems including those involving money and measures, e.g. • recall doubles to 10 + 10 and other significant doubles, e.g. double 50p is 100p or £1 • use knowledge of doubles to 10 + 10 to derive corresponding halves	• Has quick recall of multiplication facts for 2-, 5- and 10-times tables • Uses multiplication facts to find related division facts	*I know the 2-, 5- and 10-times tables.* *I can use multiplication facts to answer division questions.*

■SCHOLASTIC

Unit 1 📖 Securing number facts, relationships and calculating

Framework objectives	Assessment focuses		Success criteria for Year 3	Learning outcomes
	Level 3	Level 2		
③ Pattern of fives				
Identify patterns and relationships involving numbers or shapes, and use these to solve problems	• understand a general statement by finding particular examples that match it, e.g. • make a generalisation with the assistance of probing questions and prompts	• predict what comes next in a simple number, shape or spatial pattern or sequence and give reasons for their opinions	• Recognises the pattern in a series of numbers • Solves problems using number patterns	*I can describe the pattern when I count in fives.*
④ Addition and subtraction to 20 ⑤ Add and subtract multiples of 10				
Derive and recall all addition and subtraction facts for each number to 20, sums and differences of multiples of 10 and number pairs that total 100	• add and subtract two-digit numbers mentally, e.g. • calculate 36 + 19, 63 - 26, and complements to 100 such as 100 - 24	• use mental recall of addition and subtraction facts to 10, e.g. • use addition/subtraction facts to 10 and place value to add or subtract multiples of 10, e.g. know 3 + 7 = 10 and use place value to derive 30 + 70 = 100	• Knows all addition and subtraction facts to 20 • Recalls these facts quickly and accurately • Adds and subtracts multiples of 10	*I know addition and subtraction facts for numbers to 20. I can add and subtract multiples of 10.*
⑥ Multiply using teen numbers				
Use practical and informal written methods to multiply and divide two-digit numbers (e.g. 13 × 3, 50 ÷ 4); round remainders up or down, depending on the context	• solve whole number problems including those involving multiplication or division that may give rise to remainders, e.g. • identify appropriate operations to use • round up or down after simple division, depending on context	• choose the appropriate operation when solving addition and subtraction problems, e.g. • use repeated addition to solve multiplication problems • begin to use repeated subtraction or sharing equally to solve division problems	• Has practical or informal written methods for multiplying and dividing a two-digit number by a one-digit number	*I can multiply a 'teen' number by 2, 3, 4, 5 or 6.*
⑦ Fractions of numbers				
Find unit fractions of numbers and quantities (e.g. $1/2$, $1/3$, $1/4$ and $1/6$ of 12 litres)	• use simple fractions that are several parts of a whole and recognise when two simple fractions are equivalent, e.g. • understand and use unit fractions such as $1/2$, $1/4$, $1/3$, $1/5$, $1/10$ and find those fractions of shapes and sets of objects	• begin to use halves and quarters, e.g. • use the concept of a fraction of a number in practical contexts such as sharing sweets between two to get $1/2$ each, among four to get $1/4$ each • work out halves of numbers up to 20 and begin to recall them	• Recognises that table facts can be used to find unitary fractions of $1/2$, $1/3$, $1/4$, $1/5$ and $1/6$ • Uses table facts for the 2-, 3-, 4-, 5-, 6- or 10-times tables and derives the appropriate division fact to find fractions of a measurement	*I can find fractions of numbers by using division.*

BLOCK E

Activities

Prior learning

Children can make a table to record their results. They know the 2-, 5- and 10-times tables. They can use multiplication facts to answer division questions.

Framework objectives

● Follow a line of enquiry by deciding what information is important; make and use lists, tables and graphs to organise and interpret the information
● Derive and recall multiplication facts for the 2-, 3-, 4-, 5-, 6- and 10-times tables and the corresponding division facts; recognise multiples of 2, 5 or 10 up to 1000

Vocabulary

problem, solution, calculate, calculation, inverse, answer, method, explain, predict, estimate, reason, pattern, relationship, compare, order, information, test, list, table, diagram, double, halve, inverse, multiply, times, multiplied by, product, share, share equally, divide, divided by, divided into

Resources

Worksheets: Multiplication by 2, 5 and 10, Multiply and divide (2)
Resource sheet: Self-assessment
Classroom resources: centimetre-squared paper

① Multiplication by 2, 5 and 10

Introduce the activity by showing the worksheet 'Multiplication by 2, 5 and 10' on the whiteboard. Explain that you would like the children to find a way to record all the table facts for the 2-, 5- and 10-times tables and that the record should be easy for anyone else to use. Explain that there is squared paper on the worksheet to help them make a neat chart. Provide extra sheets of the centimetre-squared paper if necessary (there is a template available on the CD-ROM). When the children have made their charts, ask them to work in pairs to compare what they have done. *How can you use what you have done to find division facts?* Provide the self-assessment sheet for the children to record their achievements.

Teacher support

Less confident learners: Decide whether to have these children work as a group to make the chart. Invite the children to explain how they think the chart should be made and why they think that.
More confident learners: Extend the task to making a chart which also includes the 3-, 4- and 6-times tables.

Common misconceptions

Children are unclear about how to set out a multiplication grid.
Make the multiplication grid together. Discuss what numbers could go across the top of the grid and which ones could go down the side. Ask the children to help you to place the multiples into the grid. Once this is done, say: *Here is 14. Which numbers can divide into 14?* Read off the answer from the grid, by following the horizontal row and vertical column to build $7 \times 2 = 14$, so $14 \div 2 = 7$ and $14 \div 7 = 2$. Repeat for other multiples.

Probing questions

● What information will you find? How will you record it?
● What did you find out? Show me what in your results helped you to draw this conclusion.
● Why did you choose to record your results in a table?
● [Show grid on following page.] What number should go in the shaded square? What multiplication fact did you use?

■ SCHOLASTIC

×	2	3	4	5	6
2					
3					
4					
5					
6					

Next steps
Support: Encourage the children to make another chart, perhaps for the table facts for the 3, 4 and 6 multiplication tables. Continue to ask multiple and division questions for the 2-, 5- and 10-times tables, perhaps during oral and mental starters. Refer back to Year 3 Block C Unit 1 and Block B Unit 1.
Extension: Encourage the children to make a complete 2- to 10-times table chart. They can investigate counting in sevens, eights and nines to find the facts that they do not yet know. Refer to Year 3 Block E Unit 2 and Year 4 Block C Unit 1.

② Multiply and divide

Provide the worksheet 'Multiply and divide (2)'. Explain that this contains questions about multiplication and that the children should use the multiplication facts that they know in order to answer the division questions.

Teacher support
Less confident learners: Work with these children as a group to answer the questions. Note where children are unsure and teach the specific points.
More confident learners: Decide whether to include similar questions for the 3-, 4- and 6-times table facts.

Common misconceptions
Children do not understand that division is the inverse of multiplication.
Use multiplication arrays to show that, for example, $5 × 2 = 2 × 5$. Explain that the relevant division facts can be derived from this. Show, using the array, that $10 ÷ 2 = 5$ and $10 ÷ 5 = 2$. Repeat for other facts.

Probing questions
● How many fives make the same number as three tens?
● What multiplication and division facts does this array show?

● Complete this division fact in as many ways as you can: $12 ÷ □ = □$
● Is 113 a multiple of 5? How do you know?
● How many multiples of 2 are there between 175 and 183?

Next steps
Support: Provide further opportunities to recall multiplication facts and to derive the related division ones, such as during oral and mental starters. Refer back to Year 3 Block B Unit 1.
Extension: Extend the range of multiplication facts that the children should know to include the 3-, 4- and 6-times tables. Check that the children understand how they can derive the related division facts. Refer to Year 4 Block A Unit 1.

BLOCK E

Activity ③

Prior learning
Children can describe the pattern when they count in fives.

Framework objective
Identify patterns and relationships involving numbers or shapes, and use these to solve problems

Vocabulary
problem, solution, calculate, calculation, inverse, answer, method, explain, predict, estimate, reason, pattern, relationship

Resources
Resource sheet: Self-assessment

③ Pattern of fives

Pat says 'When you count from zero in fives, every other number has the units number of 5.' Is this true? Ask the children to investigate the pattern of fives. Ask them to record their thinking and to show as far as they can whether or not they think this is true. When they have completed the work ask them to work in pairs and to compare their findings. *How did you solve this problem? Was this an efficient way to do this?* Ask the children to review how well they did on the self-assessment sheet and to write down what they need to do next.

Teacher support
Less confident learners: Consider whether to ask the children to work in pairs on the task. Suggest that the children draw their own empty number line and use it as an aid to counting in fives.
More confident learners: If the children complete the task quickly, ask them to consider this statement: 'When I count in sixes, the units number is always even'.

Common misconceptions
Children do not understand how to record their attempts and findings.
Work with the children on the counting in fives statement. Ask them to suggest how to start the investigation, such as using an empty number line to count in fives. Suggest that they record on their empty number line each number that they say. Discuss that each has a unit number. Ask if they can say now whether or not the statement is true and why they think that. Repeat for another statement such as 'If I count in threes from zero, every other number is even'.

Probing questions
● What are the missing numbers in this pattern? How did you find them?
83, 78, ☐, 68, 63, 58, ☐
● Find $\frac{1}{2}$ of 16. Find $\frac{1}{4}$ of 16. Find $\frac{1}{8}$ of 16. What do you notice?
● Sam says, 'When you count from zero in fours, every number is even.' Is he right? How do you know?

Next steps
Support: Provide further statements for the children to prove, such as: 'If I count in tens from zero, every unit number is a zero'. Refer back to Year 3 Block C Unit 3.
Extension: Provide more challenging investigations, such as: 'If I count in sevens from zero, every other unit number is even'. Refer to Year 4 Block E Unit 1.

Activities

Prior learning
Children know addition and subtraction facts for numbers to 20. They can add and subtract multiples of 10.

Framework objective
Derive and recall all addition and subtraction facts for each number to 20, sums and differences of multiples of 10 and number pairs that total 100

Vocabulary
add, plus, sum, total, subtract, take away, minus, difference

Resources
Interactive activity: Number spinners
Resource sheet: Self-assessment
Classroom resources: individual whiteboards and pens

④ Addition and subtraction to 20

Use the interactive activity 'Number spinners' as an oral and mental starter or as a review activity. Use two six-sided spinners (they each include numbers up to 20). Click on the spinners to spin them, and ask the children to write on their whiteboards the answers to the addition of the two numbers produced by the spinners, then the difference between the two numbers. When you say *Show me,* they hold up their boards for you to see their answers. Repeat this several times. Note who is confident with recall of these number facts and who needs further help. Children can record their progress and what they still need to do on the self-assessment sheet.

Teacher support
Less confident learners: Decide whether to simplify the number range to 10. Check that the children are confident with these facts.
More confident learners: Use three spinners so that the children need to derive the answers to more complex additions.

Common misconceptions
Children do not use the number patterns that they know in order to derive what they cannot recall.
Write up 5 + 7 and ask for the answer. *How can this help us to find 15 + 7? 15 + 17?* Discuss the methods that the children suggest and agree on what is efficient. Repeat for subtraction. For example: *What is the difference between 9 and 7? How did you work that out? So what is the difference between 9 and 17? 19 and 7? 19 and 17?* Check that the children can see how to use what they know in order to find the differences.

Probing questions
● What is the missing number in this pattern? 4, 7, 10, 13, ☐, 19.
● What facts did you use to work this out? What other fact could you use?
● Put + or − symbols in the circles to make the answer to this calculation correct: 9 ○ 7 ○ 3 ○ 5 = 8

Next steps
Support: Repeat the activity several times, until children are confident with numbers to 10. Extend the range to, say, 15, then up to 20. Refer back to Year 3 Block B Unit 3.
Extension: Continue to extend the children's confidence, using three, four or five spinners, so that the children use their knowledge of number facts to 20 in order to derive addition of several numbers. Refer to Year 4 Block A Unit 1.

BLOCK E

⑤ Add/subtract multiples of 10

Ask the children to use their whiteboards and pens to write the answers to your questions and to hold their boards up for you to see when you say *Show me.* Say, for example: *What is 50 add 30? Two multiples of 10 total 120. What could they be? Three multiples of 10 total 100. Two of the numbers are 60 and 20. What is the third number?* Each time, ask: *How did you work that out?* Continue with similar questions and check each time who has answered correctly. Invite children to explain how they worked out the answer each time. Ask the children to record on the self-assessment sheet where they feel confident and where they need more experience of adding and subtracting multiples of 10.

Teacher support
Less confident learners: Provide simpler questions such as: *Two multiples of 10 total 50. What could they be? Two multiples of 10 total 80. What could they be?*
More confident learners: Challenge the children with more complex questions such as *Three multiples of 10 total 250. What could they be?*

Common misconceptions
Children do not have a successful strategy for adding and subtracting multiples of ten.
Teach a strategy. For example, write on the board: 4 + 3 = 7. So 40 + 30 = ? Repeat for other multiples of 10 for addition. Then write up: 9 − 6 = 3. So 90 − 60 = ? Check that the children can use this strategy quickly and successfully.

Probing questions
● Three numbers add up to 100. Two of the numbers are 50 and 20. What is the third number?
● The factory makes 30 cars on Monday, 70 cars on Tuesday and 50 cars on Wednesday. How many is that in total?
● The factory must make 300 cars each week. How many more must they make?

Next steps
Support: Continue to provide opportunities, such as oral and mental starter time, to ask the children questions involving addition and subtraction of multiples of 10. Check that the children have appropriate strategies to find the solutions and can explain how they found their answers. Refer back to Year 3 Block C Unit 3.
Extension: Ask the children to write some word problems that use addition and subtraction of multiples of 10. They can swap with their partner to check their answers, then use their word problems in a whole-class oral and mental session. Refer to Year 4 Block A Unit 1.

BLOCK E

■SCHOLASTIC

Activity ⑥

Prior learning
Children can multiply a 'teen' number by 2, 3, 4, 5 or 6.

Framework objective
Use practical and informal written methods to multiply and divide two-digit numbers (for example, 13 × 3, 50 ÷ 4); round remainders up or down, depending on the context

Vocabulary
double, halve, inverse, multiply, times, multiplied by, product, share, share equally, divide, divided by, divided into

Resources
Worksheet: Multiply using teen numbers

⑥ Multiply using teen numbers

Ask the children to work in pairs with a copy of the worksheet 'Multiply using teen numbers' each. They must take turns to choose a teen number from the grid and one of 2, 3, 4, 5, 6 or 10, then both multiply the teen number by the other number. The children should show their working out and compare methods and answers each time. Discuss their chosen methods and how efficient they think they are.

Teacher support
Less confident learners: Suggest to the children that they use an empty number line to help them.
More confident learners: Challenge the children to carry out as much of the calculation as they can mentally.

Common misconceptions
Children multiply either the tens or the digits number, but forget that both must be multiplied.
Teach the empty number line method of multiplying so that children have an efficient method. When they understand that, for example, 11 × 3 is 11 hops of 3 from zero along an empty number line, suggest to them that they already know that 10 × 3 is 30, so that they just need another 3 to add to 30 to make 33. Repeat this method for other calculations, such as 15 × 4, 18 × 6 and so on.

Probing questions
● Paul buys 12 lollies that cost 5p each. Work out how much this will cost altogether. How did you find the answer? Did you jot anything down?
● You know that 10 × 3 = 30 and 3 × 3 = 9. How many threes are there in 39?
● How many teams of three people can be made from ten people? Draw a picture that shows that your answer is correct.

Next steps
Support: Provide more experience of multiplying teen numbers, including word problems such as: *There are 15 cakes on a tray. How many cakes are there on five trays?* Refer back to Year 3 Block D Unit 2.
Extension: Extend multiplication to 20–29 using the same method. For example, for 25 × 6: (10 × 6) + (10 × 6) + (5 × 6) = 60 + 60 + 30 = 150. Refer to Year 4 Block D Unit 2.

BLOCK E

Activity ⑦

Prior learning
Children can find fractions of numbers by using division.

Framework objective
Find unit fractions of numbers and quantities (for example, $\frac{1}{2}$, $\frac{1}{3}$, $\frac{1}{4}$ and $\frac{1}{6}$ of 12 litres)

Vocabulary
fraction, part, equal parts, one whole, parts of a whole, number of parts, one half, one third, one quarter, one fifth, one sixth, one tenth, two thirds, three quarters, three fifths, unit fraction

Resources
Resource sheet: Self-assessment
Classroom resources: individual whiteboards and pens

⑦ Fractions of numbers

Write the number 24 and ask the children to use their knowledge of dividing to find $\frac{1}{4}$ of 24. Ask them to write their answer on their whiteboards, holding them up when you say *Show me.* Repeat this for finding $\frac{1}{2}$, $\frac{1}{3}$ and $\frac{1}{6}$ of 24. Now write 30 and ask the children to find $\frac{1}{3}$, $\frac{1}{5}$ and $\frac{1}{6}$ of 30. Challenge the more confident to find $\frac{1}{2}$ of 30 and to explain how they found that. Now write up 36 and challenge the children to work out $\frac{1}{2}$, $\frac{1}{3}$, $\frac{1}{4}$ and $\frac{1}{6}$ of it. Discuss how they found the answers. As the children work, note those who can confidently and accurately find unitary fractions of numbers and those who need more support. Decide whether to provide the self-assessment sheet for the children to write down where they are confident and what they need to do next.

Teacher support
Less confident learners: Decide whether to limit the range of numbers to 12 ($\frac{1}{2}$, $\frac{1}{3}$, $\frac{1}{4}$, $\frac{1}{6}$) and 10 ($\frac{1}{2}$, $\frac{1}{5}$).
More confident learners: Challenge the children with numbers such as 60, where $\frac{1}{2}$, $\frac{1}{3}$, $\frac{1}{4}$, $\frac{1}{5}$, $\frac{1}{6}$ and $\frac{1}{10}$ can be found.

Common misconceptions
Children do not see the link between division and finding fractions of numbers. Provide practical activities where children can find, say, $\frac{1}{2}$ of 12 using cubes or counters. Discuss how this can be seen as the same as dividing 12 by 2. Repeat for other examples until the children see that they can use table facts to find fractions of numbers.

Probing questions
● Which is heavier: $\frac{1}{2}$ of 18kg or $\frac{1}{4}$ of 32kg?
● What calculation would you do to work out $\frac{1}{8}$ of 32?
● Mary says that $\frac{1}{4}$ of the numbers on a 100-square are bigger than 60. Is she right? How do you know?

Next steps
Support: Gradually increase the size of the number used to find fractions and keep the number within the multiplication table facts range. Refer back to Year 3 Block D Unit 2.
Extension: Decide whether to include finding vulgar fractions such as $\frac{2}{3}$, $\frac{4}{5}$ and so on. Refer to Year 4 Block E Unit 1.

BLOCK E

Unit 2 Securing number facts, relationships and calculating

Introduction

In this unit, children develop and use mathematical vocabulary for solving problems, multiplication and division and for fractions. They solve word problems as well as writing their own for given equations. They develop their practical and written methods for division, including division involving remainders, and consolidate recall for table facts, including those for the 6-times table. They multiply one- and two-digit numbers by 10 or 100 and observe the effect. They begin to recognise that the same fraction can be expressed in different ways (equivalence) and that fractions can be ordered by their size.

Framework objectives	Assessment focuses		Success criteria for Year 3	Learning outcomes
	Level 3	**Level 2**		
① Solving multiplication and division problems				
Solve one-step and two-step problems involving numbers, money or measures, including time, choosing and carrying out appropriate calculations	• select the mathematics they use in a wider range of classroom activities • use mental recall of addition and subtraction facts to 20 in solving problems involving larger numbers	• select the mathematics they use in some classroom activities • choose the appropriate operation when solving addition and subtraction problems • solve number problems involving money and measures	• Recognises the key words in a problem that identify what type of mathematics is needed	*I can recognise when a word problem involves multiplication or division.*
② Shape fractions				
Read and write proper fractions (e.g. $^3/_7$, $^9/_{10}$), interpreting the denominator as the parts of a whole and the numerator as the number of parts; identify and estimate fractions of shapes; use diagrams to compare fractions and establish equivalents	• use simple fractions that are several parts of a whole and recognise when two simple fractions are equivalent, e.g. • understand and use unit fractions such as $^1/_2$, $^1/_4$, $^1/_3$, $^1/_5$, $^1/_{10}$ and find those fractions of shapes and sets of objects • recognise and record fractions that are several parts of the whole such as $^3/_4$, $^2/_5$ • recognise some fractions that are equivalent to $^1/_2$ • begin to use decimal notation in contexts such as money	• begin to use halves and quarters, e.g. • use the concept of a fraction of a number in practical contexts such as sharing sweets between two to get $^1/_2$ each, among four to get $^1/_4$ each • work out halves of numbers up to 20 and begin to recall them • relate the concept of half of a small quantity to the concept of half of a shape	• Understands what each of the numbers in a fraction, i.e. denominator and numerator, stands for • Knows that the bottom number represents how many pieces the whole is divided into	*I know that the number on the bottom of a fraction tells me how many pieces the whole is divided into.*
③ Times tables				
Derive and recall multiplication facts for the 2-, 3-, 4-, 5-, 6- and 10-times tables and corresponding division facts; recognise multiples of 2, 5 or 10 up to 1000	• recognise a wider range of sequences, e.g. • recognise sequences of multiples of 2, 5 and 10 • derive associated division facts from known multiplication facts • use mental recall of the 2, 3, 4, 5 and 10 multiplication tables	• recognise sequences of numbers, including odd and even numbers, e.g. • recognise numbers from counting in tens or twos • use mental calculation strategies to solve number problems including those involving money and measures	• Has quick recall of multiplication facts for 2-, 3-, 4-, 5-, 6- and 10-times tables	*I know the 2-, 3-, 4-, 5-, 6- and 10-times tables.*

BLOCK E

Unit 2 ▢ Securing number facts, relationships and calculating

Framework objectives	Assessment focuses		Success criteria for Year 3	Learning outcomes
	Level 3	Level 2		
④ Multiplying by 10 or 100				
Multiply one-digit and two-digit numbers by 10 or 100, and describe the effect	● understand place value in numbers to 1000, e.g. ● use understanding of place value to multiply/divide whole numbers by 10 (whole number answers)	● recognise sequences of numbers, including odd and even numbers, e.g. ● recognise numbers from counting in tens or twos	● Multiplies one-digit and two-digit numbers by 10 ● Multiplies one-digit and two-digit numbers by 100 ● Explains what happens and understands the place value effect	I can multiply a number by 10 or 100.
⑤ Multiplying by tens				
Use practical and informal written methods to multiply and divide two-digit numbers (e.g. 13 × 3, 50 ÷ 4); round remainders up or down, depending on the context	● solve whole number problems including those involving multiplication or division that may give rise to remainders, e.g. ● identify appropriate operations to use ● round up or down after simple division, depending on context	● choose the appropriate operation when solving addition and subtraction problems, e.g. ● use repeated addition to solve multiplication problems ● begin to use repeated subtraction or sharing equally to solve division problems	● Has practical or informal written methods for multiplying and dividing a two-digit number by a one-digit number ● Can explain how to multiply a multiple of 10 by a one-digit number	I can multiply a multiple of 10 by a one-digit number.
⑥ Multiplication and division facts				
Understand that division is the inverse of multiplication and vice versa; use this to derive and record related multiplication and division number sentences	● derive associated division facts from known multiplication facts, e.g. ● use inverses to find missing whole numbers in problems such as 'I think of a number, double it and add 5. The answer is 35. What was my number?'	There is no assessment focus for this level	● Understands that multiplication facts help to derive division facts ● Uses multiplication facts to find division facts	I can give the multiplication fact that is linked to a division fact.
⑦ Fraction problems				
Find unit fractions of numbers and quantities (e.g. ¹/₂, ¹/₃, ¹/₄ and ¹/₆ of 12 litres)	● use simple fractions that are several parts of a whole and recognise when two simple fractions are equivalent, e.g. ● understand and use unit fractions such as ¹/₂, ¹/₄, ¹/₃, ¹/₅, ¹/₁₀ and find those fractions of shapes and sets of objects	● begin to use halves and quarters, e.g. ● use the concept of a fraction of a number in practical contexts such as sharing sweets between two to get ¹/₂ each, among four to get ¹/₄ each ● work out halves of numbers up to 20 and begin to recall them	● Recognises that table facts can be used to find unitary fractions of ¹/₂, ¹/₃, ¹/₄, ¹/₅ and ¹/₆ ● Uses table facts for the 2-, 3-, 4-, 5-, 6- or 10-times tables and derives the appropriate division fact to find fractions of a measurement	I can find a fraction of a number by using division.

BLOCK E

Activity ①

Framework objective
Solve one-step and two-step problems involving numbers, money or measures, including time, choosing and carrying out appropriate calculations

Vocabulary
problem, solution, calculate, calculation, inverse, answer, method, explain

Resources
Worksheet: Solving multiplication and division problems

① Solving multiplication and division problems

Provide the worksheet 'Solving multiplication and division problems'. Explain to the children that the problems involve multiplication and division, but that they may find they need to do other calculations as well. Ask them to show their jottings as well as a number sentence and answer.

Teacher support
Less confident learners: Read the problems through together, one at a time. Discuss what sort of mathematics is needed for each and how the children can recognise this.
More confident learners: Ask the children to write some word problems involving multiplication and division that they can give to a partner to solve.

Common misconceptions
Children do not recognise the key vocabulary that tells them what type of calculations they need to do.
Read the problem together. Ask: *Which words tell you what sort of maths you need?* Repeat this for other problems until the children are confident.

Probing questions
● There are 20 legs. How many zebras is this? What calculation did you do? What was it about the problem that made you decide to use this operation?
● Make up your own word problem that would lead you to working out the calculation 32 ÷ 4. How do you recognise that this problem involves division?

Next steps
Support: Provide further experience of solving word problems. Read the problem together, then ask the children to identify the key words that tell them the type of mathematics they will need to use. Refer back to Year 3 Block D Unit 3.
Extension: Encourage the children to write some more complex word problems, where more than one type of calculation is needed. They can give these to a partner to solve. Refer to Year 3 Block E Unit 3.

Activity ②

Prior learning

Children know that the number on the bottom of a fraction tells them how many pieces the whole is divided into.

Framework objective

Read and write proper fractions (for example, $3/7$, $9/10$), interpreting the denominator as the parts of a whole and the numerator as the number of parts; identify and estimate fractions of shapes; use diagrams to compare fractions and establish equivalents

Vocabulary

one half, one third, one quarter, one fifth, one sixth, one tenth, two thirds, three quarters, three fifths, unit fraction, whole, denominator, numerator

Resources

Interactive activity: Shape fractions
Resource sheets: Self-assessment
Classroom resources: centimetre-squared paper, individual whiteboards and pens

② Shape fractions

Open the interactive activity 'Shape fractions'. Point to the first shape fraction on the screen and ask questions such as:
- What fraction of this shape is shaded?
- How did you work out your answer?
- Is there another way to write this fraction?
- What fraction is not coloured? Write this in as many ways as you can.
- What does the bottom number of a fraction tell you? And the top?

Ask the children to complete the activity on the screen by dragging the arrows to match each shape to the correct fraction. Decide whether to use the self-assessment sheet for the children to record their achievements and what they need to do next.

Teacher support

Less confident learners: If necessary, simplify the fractions of the shapes on the screen to $1/4$, $1/2$ and $1/3$ to begin with.
More confident learners: Challenge the children to draw, on squared paper, some shape fractions. They should swap their work with their partner and write the coloured fractions in as many ways as they can.

Common misconceptions

Children do not recognise that the denominator gives how many the shape or number is divided by and the numerator how many 'parts' of the fraction.
Start with simple fractions such as $1/2$, $1/3$, $1/4$, and discuss what half of 4 is, what half of 8 is, what is half of a shape made of 12 parts, and so on. Introduce the idea of how many 'parts' there are by using fractions with a numerator such as $2/3$, and discuss how this is two parts or two thirds. Repeat for other fractions.

Probing questions

- What fraction of this shape is shaded? How do you know? Is there another way that you can describe the fraction?

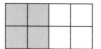

- Approximately what fraction of this shape is shaded? Explain how you decided on your answer.

BLOCK E

◼◼**SCHOLASTIC**

Next steps
Support: Extend children's experience of fractions by including fractions such as $^3/_4$ and $^5/_6$, using shapes and quantities. Refer back to Year 3 Block E Unit 1.
Extension: Encourage the children to work with quantities, finding, for example, $^3/_4$ of 24, $^5/_6$ of 30, and so on. Refer to Year 3 Block E Unit 3.

Activity ③

Prior learning
Children know the 2-, 3-, 4-, 5-, 6- and 10-times tables.

Framework objective
Derive and recall multiplication facts for the 2-, 3-, 4-, 5-, 6- and 10-times tables and the corresponding division facts; recognise multiples of 2, 5 or 10 up to 1000

Vocabulary
multiply, times, multiplied by, product, share, share equally, divide, divided by, divided into

Resources
Resource sheet: Self-assessment
Classroom resources: individual whiteboards and pens

③ Times tables

This activity can be used as part of a starter or during a review. Explain that you will ask some multiplication and/or division questions for the 2-, 3-, 4-, 5-, 6- and 10-times tables. For example: *What is 5 multiplied by 4? 10 times 10? 8 multiplied by 6? What is 36 divided by 4? 27 divided by 3? How many 5p sweets can I buy with 45p?* Children must write answers on their whiteboards, revealing them when you say *Show me.* Note which children are confident with table facts and which need more experience. Decide whether to use the self-assessment sheet for the children to note the times tables with which they are confident and those where they need more practice.

Teacher support
Less confident learners: Decide whether to limit the activity to just one table at a time in order to test confidence with these facts.
More confident learners: Include more word problems that use the table facts. Check that the children are able to recall or derive facts quickly.

Common misconceptions
Children do not have rapid recall of the table facts.
Identify which facts the children know. Identify how they recall facts, as some children may count in their heads, or recite the table to themselves to find the relevant fact. While these are useful strategies, by this stage you should expect quicker recall. Provide activities in which the children derive a multiplication fact, such as counting up on a number line and matching the numbers to a fact. Also include chanting of the tables so that the children hear and begin to commit them to memory.

Probing questions
● How many sides do six triangles have? What multiplication fact do you need to work out to answer this problem? What is the answer?
● How can you use the fact 7 × 3 = 21 to find the answer to 7 × 6?
● What tips would you give someone who cannot remember the 4-times table?
● Complete this division fact in as many ways as you can: 20 ÷ □ = □. What multiplication facts did you use to help you do this?

BLOCK E

▷ **Next steps**
Support: Work with one table at a time. Provide starter opportunities. Once one table is secure, move to the next, but include the first table facts so that these are rehearsed and remembered. Refer back to Year 3 Block E Unit 1.
Extension: Provide word problems that utilise the table facts. Ask the children to write their own word problems for others to solve. Refer to Year 3 Block E Unit 3.

Activity ④

Prior learning Children can multiply a number by 10 or 100.	**Framework objective** Multiply one-digit and two-digit numbers by 10 or 100, and describe the effect **Vocabulary** multiply, times, multiplied by, product **Resources** **Worksheet:** Multiplying by 10 or 100 **Resource sheet:** 0-9 numeral cards (two sets per pair of children)

④ Multiplying by 10 or 100

Ask the children to work in pairs with copies of the worksheet 'Multiplying by 10 or 100'. They then take turns to take two numeral cards and make two TU numbers. For example, if 8 and 9 are chosen these make 89 and 98. The 0 cards should be left in so that children can make single-digit numbers – for example, for the cards 0 and 4 they can make 04 (4) and 40. They should both write the ×10 and ×100 number sentences for both of the selected numbers.

Teacher support
Less confident learners: Let the children work with one set of 1-9 cards until they are confident with multiplying a one-digit number by 10 and 100.
More confident learners: Decide whether to add the challenge of using three numeral cards to make three-digit numbers to be multiplied by 10 and 100.

Common misconceptions
Children do not understand that multiplying by 10 is not 'adding a nought'.
Choose a simple multiplication sentence such as 6 × 10. *What is the answer?*
Write down: 6 × 1 = 6. 6 ×10 = 60. Discuss how when multiplying by 10 the units digit moves one place to the left, and when multiplying by 100 it moves two digits to the left. Repeat for other examples with a one-digit number, then two-digit numbers, until the children understand what is happening each time.

Probing questions
● What is the value of the 5 in the number 15? Multiply 15 by 10. What is the value of the 5 in your answer?
● What operation would change 37 into 370? What operation would change 4 into 400? How did you decide on your answers?

Next steps
Support: Extend from multiplying single-digit numbers by 10 or 100 to multiplying a teen number, then any two-digit number. Refer back to Year 3 Block A Unit 2.
Extension: Challenge these children's experience by asking them to divide a three-digit number which has zero in its units place by 10, and a three- or four-digit number that has a zero in both its units and tens places by 100. Refer to Year 4 Block A Unit 1.

Activity ⑤

Prior learning
Children can multiply a multiple of 10 by a one-digit number.

Framework objective
Use practical and informal written methods to multiply and divide two-digit numbers (for example, 13 × 3, 50 ÷ 4); round remainders up or down, depending on the context

Vocabulary
multiply, times, multiplied by, product, multiple of 10

Resources
Display page: Multiplying by tens
Resource sheet: Self-assessment

⑤ Multiplying by tens

Reveal the first screen of the display page 'Multiplying by tens'. Read the problem together. Ask the children to write down a number sentence for the problem and their jottings to find the answer. Invite individuals to explain how they solved the first problem. Repeat this for the next three problems displayed on the following pages. Decide whether to use the self-assessment sheet for the children to record their achievements and what they need to do next.

Teacher support
Less confident learners: Decide whether to ask an adult to work with this group and to discuss how to solve each problem, then for the children to try to solve it themselves.
More confident learners: Invite the children to discuss how they might solve the problem mentally.

Common misconceptions
Children do not see the link between multiplying by 10 and by multiples of 10. Write 10 × 3 and ask for the answer. Now write 20 × 3 and ask: *How can we use 10 × 3 = 30 to help us to solve this?* After discussion, write 20 × 3 = 10 × 2 × 3 = 10 × 6 = 60. Repeat for other examples until the children are confident with this.

Probing questions
● What calculation do you need to do to work this out?
● Rulers are 30cm long. If you place six of them end to end, how long a line will they make? Explain how you solved this problem. Did you write anything down?
● How can you use 4 × 6 = 24 to work out 4 × 60?
● How many threes make 36? How do you know?

Next steps
Support: Provide further examples of problems such as: *Mrs Jones drives 20 miles each day. How far does she drive in 2 ... 3 ... 4 ... 5 ... 6 ... 10 days?* Refer back to Year 3 Block D Unit 3.
Extension: Ask the children to try some problems which use table facts that they do not yet know, such as: *Mariam drives 60 miles each day. How far does she drive in eight days?* Discuss how they could solve this, such as using double ×4 facts. Refer to Year 3 Block E Unit 3.

BLOCK E

Activity ⑥

Prior learning Children can give the multiplication fact that is linked to a division fact.	**Framework objective** Understand that division is the inverse of multiplication and vice versa; use this to derive and record related multiplication and division number sentences **Vocabulary** inverse, multiply, times, multiplied by, product, share, share equally, divide, divided by, divided into **Resources** **Resource sheet:** Self-assessment **Classroom resources:** calculators

⑥ Multiplication and division facts

Ask the children to work in pairs with a calculator. They must take turns to input the multiplication fact that you say, such as 7 × 4, and to say the answer before they press the equals key. Their partner inputs ÷ 4 and says the answer before they press the equals key. Check the answers after each division and ask the children to keep a score of their correct answers. After about ten multiplications, switch around and begin with a division, followed by the children finding the multiplication. Decide whether to use the self-assessment sheet for the children to record their achievements and what they need to do next.

Teacher support
Less confident learners: Decide whether to limit this to the 2- then 3-times tables and so on, until the children are confident enough to work with a mix of table facts.
More confident learners: Challenge the children to use multiples such as 24, 36 and 48, and to find as many multiplications, then the related division facts, as they can.

Common misconceptions
Children do not relate multiplication and division facts.
Draw an array such as 5 × 2 and ask: *What multiplication fact does this show?* Write down 5 × 2 = 10. *What division fact can we find from these numbers?* Write down 10 ÷ 2 = 5. *Is there another multiplication fact that we can find from this array?* If children need help, point out that the array can be read as 2 × 5 = 10 and that the division fact 10 ÷ 5 = 2 can also be found. Repeat for other facts until children are confident with finding the related facts.

Probing questions
● Write the two multiplication and two division facts that are linked to this array.
● Mary keys 27 ÷ 3 into a calculator to get the answer 9. What operation should she key in to turn the 9 back into 27?

Next steps
Support: Provide starter activities that ask children for the related facts, either multiplication or division, so that they have further practice in recalling what they know and deriving from this. Refer back to Year 3 Block D Unit 3.
Extension: Challenge the children to write all the multiplication and related division facts for numbers such as 60, 72, 80… Refer to Year 4 Block A Unit 1.

■ **SCHOLASTIC**

Activity ⑦

Prior learning
Children can find a fraction of a number by using division.

Framework objective
Find unit fractions of numbers and quantities (for example, $^1/_2$, $^1/_3$, $^1/_4$ and $^1/_6$ of 12 litres)

Vocabulary
fraction, part, equal parts, one whole, parts of a whole, number of parts, one half, one third, one quarter, one fifth, one sixth, one tenth, two thirds, three quarters, three fifths, unit fraction

Resources
Worksheet: Fraction problems (parts 1 and 2)
Classroom resources: counters

⑦ Fraction problems

Provide part 1 of the worksheet 'Fraction problems'. Ask the children to write their jottings, a number sentence and the answer for each question. Decide whether to remind them that they can use division to find a fraction of a number.

Teacher support
Less confident learners: Decide whether to simplify the problems, changing the numbers to table facts with which the children are confident. Part 2 of the worksheet is a blank template to allow you to do this.
More confident learners: Encourage the children to work quickly but accurately so that they can demonstrate that they can recall the necessary table facts in order to derive division ones.

Common misconceptions
Children do not see the link between fractions of numbers and using division. Count out 12 counters. Ask the children to share these to find a half. *How many is a half? So half of 12 is 6.* Now ask: *What is 12 divided by 2?* Repeat for other quantities, such as 16 or 20 counters until the children are able to tell you $^1/_2$, $^1/_3$, $^1/_4$, $^1/_5$, $^1/_6$, $^1/_{10}$ of quantities without sharing out the counters.

Probing questions
● Barry has saved 60p. He decided to spend $^1/_3$ of it. How much does he spend? What calculation did you do to find your answer?
● $50 \div 5 = 10$. Now complete: $\frac{1}{\Box}$ of 50 = 10.
● Explain how to find $^1/_4$ of a number. Is there another way to do it?

Next steps
Support: Provide further experience with finding fractions of numbers using division. Build confidence by concentrating on the table facts that the children know well, then move to the other table facts. Refer back to Year 3 Block E Unit 1.
Extension: Extend the range of experience by introducing other table facts, such as 8s (double 4s) in fraction problems. Refer to Year 3 Block E Unit 2.

BLOCK E

Unit 3 ▢ Securing number facts, relationships and calculating

Introduction
In this unit, the children are involved in making decisions about how to calculate, which methods to use and record. They solve one- and two-step problems and discuss the choices they made, giving reasons for this. They develop their skills in partitioning numbers, identify patterns and relationships to help them to calculate. They further develop their skills in addition, subtraction, multiplication and division, and use both informal and formal written methods. They find fractions of shapes and quantities and link this to division. By now they should have rapid recall of all multiplication facts in the 2-, 3-, 4-, 5-, 6- and 10-times tables and derive the related division facts swiftly.

Framework objectives	Assessment focuses		Success criteria for Year 3	Learning outcomes
	Level 3	Level 2		
① Division problems				
Solve one-step and two-step problems involving numbers, money or measures, including time, choosing and carrying out appropriate calculations	• select the mathematics they use in a wider range of classroom activities • use mental recall of addition and subtraction facts to 20 in solving problems involving larger numbers	• select the mathematics they use in some classroom activities • choose the appropriate operation when solving addition and subtraction problems • solve number problems involving money and measures	• Chooses appropriate strategies for the task • Recognises what mathematics the problem needs in order to be solved • In a division problem, recognises that the problem can involve sharing or grouping	*I know that a division problem can involve sharing or grouping.*
① Division problems				
Derive and recall multiplication facts for the 2-, 3-, 4-, 5-, 6- and 10-times tables and the corresponding division facts; recognise multiples of 2, 5 or 10 up to 1000	• recognise a wider range of sequences • derive associated division facts from known multiplication facts • use mental recall of the 2, 3, 4, 5 and 10 multiplication tables	• recognise sequences of numbers, including odd and even numbers, e.g. • recognise numbers from counting in tens or twos • use mental calculation strategies to solve number problems including those involving money and measures	• Has quick recall of multiplication facts for 2-, 3-, 4-, 5-, 6- and 10-times tables • Uses recall of multiplication facts to derive division facts • Can write the related division fact for a multiplication one and vice versa	*I can use my knowledge of multiplication tables to find division facts.*
② Remainders				
Follow a line of enquiry by deciding what information is important; make and use lists, tables and graphs to organise and interpret the information	• begin to organise their work and check results • discuss their mathematical work and begin to explain their thinking • use and interpret mathematical symbols and diagrams	• discuss their work using mathematical language, e.g. with support • describe the strategies and methods they use in their work • listen to others' explanations, try to make sense of them, compare... evaluate... • begin to represent their work using symbols and simple diagrams	• Chooses appropriate information when following a line of enquiry • Tests examples to check the outcomes • Makes decisions based on the outcomes about what to try next	*I can test examples to follow an enquiry about numbers.*

BLOCK E

Unit 3 ⬜ Securing number facts, relationships and calculating

Framework objectives	Assessment focuses		Success criteria for Year 3	Learning outcomes
	Level 3	Level 2		
② Remainders				
Use practical and informal written methods to multiply and divide two-digit numbers (e.g. 13 × 3, 50 ÷ 4); round remainders up or down, depending on the context	● solve whole number problems including those involving multiplication or division that may give rise to remainders, e.g. ● identify appropriate operations to use ● round up or down after simple division, depending on context	● choose the appropriate operation when solving addition and subtraction problems, e.g. ● use repeated addition to solve multiplication problems ● begin to use repeated subtraction or sharing equally to solve division problems	● Has practical or informal written methods for multiplying and dividing a two-digit number by a one-digit number	*I can multiply and divide a two-digit number by a one-digit number.*
③ Number patterns				
Identify patterns and relationships involving numbers or shapes, and use these to solve problems	● understand a general statement by finding particular examples that match it, e.g. ● make a generalisation with the assistance of probing questions and prompts	● predict what comes next in a simple number, shape or spatial pattern or sequence and give reasons for their opinions	● Recognises patterns in numbers ● Continues number patterns	*I can recognise and continue a pattern.*
③ Number patterns				
Partition three-digit numbers into multiples of 100, 10 and 1 in different ways	● understand place value in numbers to 1000, e.g. ● represent/compare numbers using number lines, 100-squares, base 10 materials etc ● recognise that some numbers can be represented as different arrays ● use understanding of place value to multiply/divide whole numbers by 10 (whole number answers)	● begin to understand the place value of each digit; use this to order numbers up to 100	● Demonstrates understanding of place value through partitioning numbers ● Can explain the partition using place value vocabulary	*I can partition numbers in different ways.*
④ Fraction shapes				
Read and write proper fractions (e.g. $^3/_7$, $^9/_{10}$), interpreting the denominator as the parts of a whole and the numerator as the number of parts; identify and estimate fractions of shapes; use diagrams to compare fractions and establish equivalents	● use simple fractions that are several parts of a whole and recognise when two simple fractions are equivalent, e.g. ● recognise and record fractions that are several parts of the whole, such as $^3/_4$, $^2/_5$	● relate the concept of half of a small quantity to the concept of half of a shape, e.g. ● shade one half or one quarter of a given shape including those divided into equal regions	● Recognises what fraction of a shape is shaded ● Says and writes the fraction appropriately ● Can explain when a shape has not been divided into equal parts	*I can recognise what fraction of a shape is shaded, and say and write it.*

BLOCK E

Unit 3 ◻ Securing number facts, relationships and calculating

Framework objectives	Assessment focuses		Success criteria for Year 3	Learning outcomes
	Level 3	Level 2		
⑤ Add and subtract larger numbers				
Develop and use written methods to record, support or explain addition and subtraction of two-digit and three-digit numbers	• add and subtract three-digit numbers using written methods, e.g. ● use written methods that involve bridging 10 or 100 ● add and subtract decimals in the context of money, where bridging is not required	• record their work in writing, e.g. ● record their mental calculations as number sentences	• Has an efficient and effective method of recording addition and subtraction • Can add two-digit and three-digit numbers using an appropriate written method • Can subtract two-digit and three-digit numbers using an appropriate written method	*I can add and subtract two-digit and three-digit numbers by writing them down.*
⑥ Fractions of numbers				
Find unit fractions of numbers and quantities (e.g. $\frac{1}{2}$, $\frac{1}{3}$, $\frac{1}{4}$ and $\frac{1}{6}$ of 12 litres)	• use simple fractions that are several parts of a whole and recognise when two simple fractions are equivalent, e.g. ● understand and use unit fractions such as $\frac{1}{2}$, $\frac{1}{4}$, $\frac{1}{3}$, $\frac{1}{5}$, $\frac{1}{10}$ and find those fractions of shapes and sets of objects	• begin to use halves and quarters, e.g. ● use the concept of a fraction of a number in practical contexts such as sharing sweets between two to get $\frac{1}{2}$ each, among four to get $\frac{1}{4}$ each ● work out halves of numbers up to 20 and begin to recall them	• Recognises that table facts can be used to find unitary fractions of $\frac{1}{2}$, $\frac{1}{3}$, $\frac{1}{4}$, $\frac{1}{5}$, $\frac{1}{6}$ • Uses table facts for the 2-, 3-, 4-, 5-, 6- or 10-times tables and derives the appropriate division fact to find fractions of numbers	*I can find fractions of numbers.*

BLOCK E

Activity

Prior learning
Children know that a division problem can involve sharing or grouping. They can use their knowledge of multiplication tables to find division facts.

Framework objectives
● Solve one-step and two-step problems involving numbers, money or measures, including time, choosing and carrying out appropriate calculations
● Derive and recall multiplication facts for the 2-, 3-, 4-, 5-, 6- and 10-times tables and the corresponding division facts; recognise multiples of 2, 5 or 10 up to 1000

Vocabulary
multiply, times, multiplied by, multiple, product, share, share equally, divide, divided by, divided into, left, left over, remainder, round up, round down, problem, solution, calculate, calculation, inverse, answer, method, explain

Resources
Display page: Division problems
Resource sheet: Self-assessment
Classroom resources: individual whiteboards and pens

Division problems

Reveal the first screen of the display page 'Division problems'. Read the problem with the children, then ask them to work on their own to write a number sentence and the answer. Give the children a few minutes to solve the problem. *How did you solve it? What facts did you find to help you?* Discuss which table fact they used in order to find the related division fact. Repeat this for problems 2 and 3 on the screen. Problem 4 asks children to write four division sentences, each with the answer of 7. Answers include: $14 \div 2 = 7$; $21 \div 3 = 7$; $28 \div 4 = 7$; $35 \div 5 = 7$; $42 \div 6 = 7$; $70 \div 10 = 7$. Discuss the children's methods. Decide whether to provide the self-assessment sheet for the children to record how well they can derive division facts and respond to word problems.

Teacher support
Less confident learners: Decide whether to ask an adult to work with these children to discuss how to solve each problem.
More confident learners: Challenge the children to find further answers to problem 4, such as $63 \div 9 = 7$, and so on.

Common misconceptions
Children do not recognise that they can use multiplication facts to find related division facts to solve a problem.
Check that the children are confident in recalling the multiplication table facts for the 2-, 3-, 4-, 5-, 6- and 10-times tables. Draw an array of 4×6. *Which two multiplication facts does this show?* ($4 \times 6 = 24$ and $6 \times 4 = 24$) *What division facts can you find from these multiplication facts?* Look at the array and agree that there are 24 smaller squares. Discuss how if the array was grouped in fours then there would be six groups; if it was grouped in sixes there would be four groups. Write the two division sentences: $24 \div 4 = 6$ and $24 \div 6 = 4$. Repeat for another example, such as 9×4.

Probing questions
● Fifteen grapes are shared equally onto three plates. How many grapes are there on each plate? What calculation did you do to answer this problem? Draw a picture to represent the problem.
● How many bunches of three grapes can you get from 15 grapes? What calculation would you do to answer this problem? Draw a picture of it.
● What multiplication fact can you use to find the answer to $28 \div 4$?

BLOCK E

● What tips would you give to someone who cannot remember the 6-times table?
● Is 354 a multiple of 10, 5 or 2? Explain how you know.

Next steps

Support: Ensure that the children are confident in recalling their tables and that they can make the link to the relevant division fact. Provide further examples of word problems: *There are 25 eggs in the box. Mum puts the eggs into five bowls. How many eggs are in each bowl?* Refer back to Year 3 Block E Unit 2.
Extension: Challenge the children to write their own word problems involving division for others to solve. Refer to Year 4 Block A Unit 1.

Activity ②

Prior learning

Children can test examples to follow an enquiry about numbers. They can multiply and divide a two-digit number by a one-digit number.

Framework objectives

● Follow a line of enquiry by deciding what information is important; make and use lists, tables and graphs to organise and interpret the information
● Use practical and informal written methods to multiply and divide two-digit numbers (for example, 13 × 3, 50 ÷ 4); round remainders up or down, depending on the context

Vocabulary

problem, solution, calculate, calculation, inverse, answer, method, explain, predict, estimate, reason, pattern, relationship, compare, order, information, test, list, table, diagram, calculation, written calculation, informal method, jottings, number line, count on, count back, double, halve, inverse, multiply, times, multiplied by, product, share, share equally, divide, divided by, divided into, left, left over, remainder, round up, round down

Resources

Resource sheet: Self-assessment

② Remainders

Set the task: *What are the possible remainders when dividing a two- or three-digit number by 6? Work with a partner. Keep careful records of what you decide to do. Set out your calculations. Record your findings.* Give the children plenty of time to carry out this task. When they have finished, invite pairs to present their findings. Discuss how they carried out the task, recorded their calculations and their results. Decide whether to provide the self-assessment sheet for the children to record their achievements.

Teacher support

Less confident learners: Decide whether to simplify the task to dividing a two-digit number by 6, or another times table where the children are more confident of their multiplication facts.
More confident learners: Ask the children to explain why the remainders when dividing by 6 will always be 1, 2, 3, 4 or 5.

Common misconceptions

Children do not understand the significance of a remainder and ignore it in an answer.
Work together to solve divisions such as 34 ÷ 5. *Will 5 divide into 34 exactly? How do you know?* Agree that all ×5 facts have a zero or 5 in their answers, so any number that will divide exactly by 5 will have a unit number of 5 or 0. Discuss the remainder in this case. *Can we just forget about the 4 left over?*

 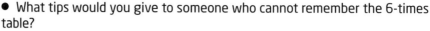

Say, for example: *If I give you 34 sweets to divide into five groups and tell you that you can have what is left over, how many will you get?* Repeat this for other divisions with and without remainders.

Probing questions
● What is the largest remainder when you divide a number by 3? How did you collect information to answer this question? How did you record your findings?
● How many 3p lollies can you buy with 45p? Show me your working out.
● Harry saves 20p coins. He has saved £3.20. How many coins has he saved? Show how you work it out.

Next steps
Support: Provide further opportunities for children to use their knowledge of multiplication and division through investigations, such as finding the first common multiple of 2, 3 and 5 (30). Refer back to Year 3 Block E Units 1 and 2.
Extension: Encourage the children to try further investigations that involve multiplication and division, such as: *There is £6 in my pocket. I need to divide the money between four people. What coins will I give each person? Try to find at least five different ways to solve this.* Refer to Year 4 Block B Unit 1.

Activity ③

Prior learning
Children can recognise and continue a pattern. They can partition numbers in different ways.

Framework objectives
● Identify patterns and relationships involving numbers or shapes, and use these to solve problems
● **Partition three-digit numbers into multiples of 100, 10 and 1 in different ways**

Vocabulary
method, explain, predict, reason, pattern, relationship, compare, order, information, test, list, table, diagram, place value, partition, ones, tens, hundreds, one-digit number, two-digit number, three-digit number

Resources
Worksheet: Number patterns

③ Number patterns

Provide each child with the worksheet 'Number patterns', which asks the children to continue partitioning patterns of three-digit numbers and describe any patterns. When they have finished, invite children to describe the patterns that they have found. The final question asks them to make their own partitioning pattern for 612. Encourage children to explain their patterns to others.

Teacher support
Less confident learners: Limit this work to two-digit numbers at first.
More confident learners: Ask the children to write their own number patterns and to explain their patterns to others.

Common misconceptions
Children have poor understanding of place value and so cannot make a partitioning pattern.
Write down 546. What does the 5... 4... 6 stand for? Now write 500 + 46 and ask the children to explain how this totals 546. Write 400 + 156 and ask how this still totals 546. Continue the pattern. Repeat for other numbers until the children understand how the pattern is formed.

Probing questions

● What is the next calculation in this pattern? Explain how you know.
853 = 800 + 53;   853 = 700 + 153;   853 = 600 + 253
● How many £1 coins do you need to make £2? How many 10p coins? What is the relationship between the answers?
● What number is equal to 200 + 110 + 7? Partition the number in a different way.
● To work out half of 34, Winston partitions it into 20 and 14 then halves each part. What answer does he get? Why do you think he partitioned 34 like this?

Next steps

Support: Provide further opportunities for children to explore place value and partitioning of numbers. Refer back to Year 3 Block A Unit 2 and Block B Unit 3.
Extension: Decide whether to extend this work to include four-digit numbers. Refer to Year 4 Block A Unit 1.

Activity ④

Prior learning
Children can recognise what fraction of a shape is shaded and say and write it.

Framework objective
Read and write proper fractions (for example, $3/7$, $9/10$), interpreting the denominator as the parts of a whole and the numerator as the number of parts; identify and estimate fractions of shapes; use diagrams to compare fractions and establish equivalents

Vocabulary
fraction, part, equal parts, one whole, parts of a whole, number of parts, one half, one third, one quarter, one fifth, one sixth, one tenth, two thirds, three quarters, three fifths, unit fraction, equivalent fraction

Resources
Worksheet: Fraction shapes

④ Fraction shapes

Provide the worksheet 'Fraction shapes'. Explain that the sheet asks the children to calculate and write down the fraction of each shape that is shaded. The second part gives the fraction for the children to shade. Check those children that you are targeting for assessment. Ask them to say the fractions that they have written and to explain how they worked out each fraction.

Teacher support

Less confident learners: Decide whether to provide simpler fractions, such as $1/4$, $1/2$ and so on.
More confident learners: Ask the children to write, where possible, an equivalent fraction.

Common misconceptions

Children do not recognise equivalent fractions.
Draw a 2 × 2 square, divided into the smaller squares. *How many squares are there here? So how many equal parts does this shape have?* Shade one square and ask: *What fraction has been shaded? Does it matter which square I shade? Why not?* Now shade another square and ask: *What fraction is shaded now?* Accept $2/4$ and ask for an equivalent fraction. Write down $2/4$ and $1/2$ and explain that these are equivalent. Repeat with other fractions until the children are confident with finding fractions and recognising equivalent fractions.

Unit 3 ⬛ Securing number facts, relationships and calculating

Probing questions
● Complete the shading on this diagram so that ¹/₂ is shaded. Describe the shaded part in another way.

● Leah says that this rectangle is divided into thirds because it is divided into three parts. Is she right? Explain your answer.

● What fraction of this shape is shaded?

● Use a fraction wall to find a fraction that is the same as ³/₄.

Next steps
Support: Provide further opportunities for the children to find fractions of shapes, and equivalent fractions. Refer back to Year 3 Block B Unit 3.
Extension: Ask children to investigate fractions of shapes. Show them a 6 × 6 square with six squares shaded. They must find as many equivalent fractions for the shaded part as they can (⁶/₃₆, ²/₁₂, ¹/₆). Refer to Year 4 Block E Unit 1.

Activity ⑤

Prior learning
Children can add and subtract two-digit and three-digit numbers by writing them down.

Framework objective
Develop and use written methods to record, support or explain addition and subtraction of two-digit and three-digit numbers

Vocabulary
sign, equals (=), operation, symbol, number sentence, equation, mental calculation, written calculation, informal method, jottings, number line, count on, count back, add, plus, sum, total

Resources
Resource sheet: Self-assessment

⑤ Add and subtract larger numbers

Explain that you will say a word problem and the children must decide how to solve it, then to show their workings out. *Mia has 56 cuddly toys. Her sister Sabine has 78. How many cuddly toys do they have in total?* (134) Ask the children to give their answer and to say what method they chose to calculate. *Janak and Marek have 346 marbles between them. Janak has 129 marbles. How many does Marek have?* (217) Again, ask for answers and methods. Now try these two problems in the same way: *Jodi has saved £3.45. She buys a magazine for £2.49. How much money does she have left?* (96p) *Olga has £5.67. Her brother Igor borrows £2.86. How much does Olga have left?* (£2.81) Decide whether to use the self-assessment sheet for the children to record their achievements and what they need to do next.

Teacher support
Less confident learners: Decide whether to simplify the numbers, using just two-digit numbers.

More confident learners: Ask the children to write similar word problems for their partner to try.

Common misconceptions
Children do not have an efficient written method for addition and/or subtraction.
Begin with addition of two two-digit numbers, such as 56 + 87. Ask the children to demonstrate how they would tackle the question. Teach a written method and give further questions for the children to tackle. When they are confident, extend this to include three-digit numbers. Tackle subtraction in the same way, beginning with two two-digit numbers, such as 97 − 49. Check the children's method and, where necessary, teach the written method. When children are confident, extend this to include three-digit numbers.

Probing questions
● Find the sum and the difference of 164 and 136 using written calculations. Explain each step.
● Molly drew a number line to find the answer to 43 + 32.

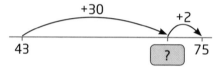

● What number is hidden under the card?

Next steps
Support: Provide further opportunities for using addition or subtraction of two- and three-digit numbers until the children are confident. Ensure that they have an efficient written method. Refer back to Year 3 Block D Unit 3.
Extension: Set further word problems such as: *There are 587 children in Plane Tree Primary School. If 289 are in Key Stage 1, how many children are in Key Stage 2?* Refer to Year 4 Block A Unit 2.

Activity ⑥

Prior learning Children can find fractions of numbers.	**Framework objective** Find unit fractions of numbers and quantities (for example, $1/2$, $1/3$, $1/4$ and $1/6$ of 12 litres)
	Vocabulary fraction, part, equal parts, one whole, parts of a whole, number of parts, one half, one third, one quarter, one fifth, one sixth, one tenth, two thirds, three quarters, three fifths, unit fraction, share, share equally, divide, divided by, divided into
	Resources **Worksheet:** Fractions of numbers **Classroom resources:** counters

BLOCK E

⑥ Fractions of numbers

Explain to the children that they will be finding fractions of numbers. Provide the worksheet 'Fractions of numbers'. Ask them to show their working out. Discuss how they found the answers; what table facts did they need? Check that the children understand that in order to find fractions of numbers they must use division.

Teacher support

Less confident learners: Decide whether to simplify the numbers and fractions so that children can use the table facts with which they are confident.

More confident learners: Ask the children to write their own word problems involving fractions to swap with a partner.

Common misconceptions

Children do not recognise the link between unit fractions and division.

Put out 12 counters. Ask the children to find $1/4$ of the counters. *How will you do that?* Discuss how sharing out the counters into four piles is the same as dividing by 4, and that both approaches achieve the answer of 3. Repeat for other unit fractions such as finding $1/2$ of 10, $1/3$ of 15 and so on. Make sure that the children understand that they can use division to solve unit fraction problems.

Probing questions

● Would you rather have $1/3$ of 30 sweets or $1/5$ of 40 sweets? Why?
● Fifteen grapes are shared equally onto five plates. What fraction of the grapes is on each plate?

Next steps

Support: Provide further fraction problems. Over time extend this to table facts where the children may not be so confident. Refer back to Year 3 Block E Unit 2.

Extension: Provide more challenging problems for the children to solve, such as: *Find as many unit fractions as you can of 48.* Answers might include finding $1/2$, $1/4$, $1/3$, $1/8$, $1/6$ or $1/12$. Refer to Year 4 Block E Unit 1.

These activities can be used at any time during the teaching of this block to assess those children that you think have achieved the objective. A grid highlighting the related assessment focuses and expected learning outcomes for each activity can be found on the CD-ROM.

Addition and subtraction

Framework objective

Derive and recall all addition and subtraction facts for each number to 20, sums and differences of multiples of 10 and number pairs that total 100

Learning outcomes
- I know addition and subtraction facts for numbers to 20.
- I can add and subtract multiples of 10.

Ask the children to write the answers to the addition or subtraction sentences that you say on their whiteboards, holding them up when you say *Show me*. For each correct answer they should record a tally mark in the corner of their whiteboards. Ask questions such as: *What is 15 add 17? 19 subtract 13? 20 minus 3? What is the total of 16 and 18? What is the difference between 17 and 8? What is 70 add 60? 90 subtract 50? What is the difference between 80 and 40? 50 and 80?* Keep the pace sharp and note, as the children hold up their boards, who has answered correctly and who will need further support.

Now ask the children to answer the word problems on the worksheet 'Addition and subtraction (2)', which contains problems that can be solved by addition and subtraction of numbers to 20 and multiples of 10.

Partitioning

Framework objective

Partition three-digit numbers into multiples of 100, 10 and 1 in different ways

Learning outcome
- I can partition numbers in different ways.

Ask the children to work in pairs, each with a copy of the worksheet 'Partitioning (2)'. They must shuffle the 0-9 numeral cards and place them in a stack, then take turns to take the top three cards. They should each make a number from the cards and write it on their worksheet, partitioning it in three different ways. They then compare the numbers that they have made and check each other's partitioning. They should repeat this three more times.

Table facts

Framework objective

Derive and recall multiplication facts for the 2-, 3-, 4-, 5-, 6- and 10-times tables and the corresponding division facts; recognise multiples of 2, 5 or 10 up to 1000

Learning outcomes
- I know the 2-, 3-, 4-, 5-, 6- and 10-times tables.
- I can use knowledge of multiplication tables to find division facts.

Ask the children to write the answers to the multiplication table questions that you ask. Ask, for example: *What is 6 multiplied by 2? By 3? By 4? By 5? By 6? By 10? What is 9 multiplied by 6? What is the product of 5 and 4?* Keep the pace sharp, and note, as the children hold up their boards, who has answered correctly and who will need further support. Repeat this on another occasion, this time asking division questions, such as: *What is 35 divided by 5? How did you work that out? What is 48 divided by 6?* On another occasion ask a mix of multiplication and division questions in the same way.

Now ask the children to complete the worksheet 'Table facts'. This contains word problems for which children will need to use their table facts.

BLOCK E

Name   Date

Addition and subtraction (2)

Work mentally to solve these word problems.

◼ Write your answers.

1. There are 18 marbles in Jack's pocket.
Sam has another 16 marbles.
How many marbles is that in total?...

2. Sunil has a packet of 20 toffees.
On Monday he eats six toffees.
On Tuesday he eats eight toffees.
How many toffees does Sunil have left?.....................................

3. There are 30 cars in the supermarket's car park.
Another 40 cars park in the car park.
How many cars are there altogether?...

4. Ella has 90p.
She buys a comic for 60p and a lolly for 20p.
How much money does she have left?...

5. Alesha spends 30p on a pencil.
She buys an eraser for 20p and a pencil sharpener for 40p.
How much change does Alesha have from £1?.........................

6. Carl counts how many books there are on his two bookshelves.
He has 90 in total.
On the top shelf there are 50 books.
How many are there on the second shelf?.................................

How easy?

Red
Amber
Green

How do you think you have done?
_____

_____

Name Date

Partitioning (2)

Work with a partner.

- You need three sets of 0–9 numeral cards.
- Shuffle the cards and place them in a stack.
- Take turns to choose three cards.
- You should each make a HTU number from the cards.
- Write the number that you made in the table below.
- Partition the number in three different ways.
- Repeat this five more times.

Your number	Partition 1	Partition 2	Partition 3

How easy?

Red
Amber
Green

How do you think you have done?

Name   Date

Table facts

Work mentally to find the answers to these questions.

1. Polly has three times as many hair ties as does Molly.
Molly has six hair ties. How many hair ties does Polly have?............. ☐

2. Aidan buys five sweets at 6p each.
How much does he spend?... ☐

3. There are four plates of cakes. Each plate has eight cakes
on it. How many cakes are there altogether?................................ ☐

4. Seven children buy six felt pens each.
How many felt pens are bought?... ☐

5. There are six fruit bowls. Nine oranges are placed in
each fruit bowl. How many oranges is that in total? .... ☐

6. There are eight chickens in the coop. Each chicken lays five eggs
each week. How many eggs do the chickens lay in one week? .... ☐

7. There are 24 bulbs to be planted in four pots.
How many bulbs will go into each pot? .... ☐

8. There are 24 flowers to be shared between three vases.
How many flowers will go into each vase?................................... ☐

9. The farmer packs eggs in boxes of 6. There are 42 eggs in
total. How many boxes does the farmer fill? .... ☐

10. There are 90 sheep at the farming fair. Ten sheep will fit
into one pen. How many pens are needed for the sheep?................. ☐

11. There are 36 rulers in Class 3. The monitor puts four rulers
on each table. How many tables are there in Class 3? .... ☐

12. All of the children in Class 3 like orange juice. The teacher
has six bottles of juice. She pours each bottle into five beakers.
Everybody has a beaker of juice. How many children are there
in Class 3?.. ☐

How easy?

Red
Amber
Green

How do you think you have done?

_____

_____

Transitional assessment

Activity	Type	Level	Description
2.1	Single-level written assessment	2	30-minute formal test paper covering objectives from all Strands of the Framework at Level 2
2.2	Single-level written assessment	2	30-minute formal test paper covering objectives from all Strands of the Framework at Level 2
2.3	Single-level written assessment	2	30-minute formal test paper covering objectives from all Strands of the Framework at Level 2
2.4	Single-level oral assessment	2	Approximately 5-minute oral paper covering objectives from all Strands of the Framework at Level 2
2.5	Single-level oral assessment	2	Approximately 5-minute oral paper covering objectives from all Strands of the Framework at Level 2
3.1a 3.1b	Single-level written assessments	3	Two 20-minute formal test papers covering objectives from all Strands of the Framework at Level 3 (one calculator, one non-calculator)
3.2a 3.2b	Single-level written assessment	3	Two 20-minute formal test papers covering objectives from all Strands of the Framework at Level 3 (one calculator, one non-calculator)
3.3a 3.3b	Single-level written assessment	3	Two 20-minute formal test papers covering objectives from all Strands of the Framework at Level 3 (one calculator, one non-calculator)
3.4	Single-level oral assessment	3	Approximately 5-minute oral paper covering objectives from all Strands of the Framework at Level 3
3.5	Single-level oral assessment	3	Approximately 5-minute oral paper covering objectives from all Strands of the Framework at Level 3

Written test instructions

Allow 30 minutes for each paper at Level 2 and 20 minutes for each paper at Level 3.

Children should work so that they cannot see each other's work.

Do not explain questions or read numbers to the children.

Teachers may choose to read the questions aloud to children, if they feel it is appropriate.

The test may be administered to groups of children or to the whole class.

The total marks available for each paper is given in the mark scheme.

Say to the children:

Here are some questions (I am going to read some questions) for you to answer.
For some questions you will write your answer in a box. [Show example.]
For some questions you may need to draw lines or rings to show your answer. [Show example.]
If you make a mistake, you should cross it out (or rub it out neatly) and write your answer clearly.
You may use spaces on the paper to do any working out that may help you.
Try to work out the answer to each question before going on to the next one.
If you can't answer a question, move on to the next one – it may be easier.

Equipment for each child

pencil, eraser (or children may cross out mistakes), a 30cm ruler (marked in millimetres), structured apparatus consisting of tens and units (for example, base 10 equipment, interlocking cubes), mirror, tracing paper

Oral test instructions

Read questions to the children no more than twice.
Allow five seconds for each answer.
Children record their answers on paper.
1 mark per question: 15 marks total

Equipment for each child

pencil, eraser (or children may cross out mistakes), a 30cm ruler
Separate teacher resources are listed for each paper.

Levelling the children

Add together the marks from an oral test and a written test (both A and B at Level 3).

Level 2		Level 3	
Below Level 2	0 – 15 marks	Below level 3	0 – 21 marks
Low Level 2	16 – 22 marks	Low level 3	22 – 31 marks
Secure Level 2	22 – 28 marks	Secure Level 3	32 – 40 marks
High Level 2	28 – 36 marks	High Level 3	40 – 50 marks

When awarding an end-of-year Teacher Assessment Level, teachers also need to consider a child's performance on Periodic and Day-to-Day Assessments.

Mathematics: making a level judgement

Use these steps to formalise your assessments of pupils' mathematics into level judgements.

You will need
- evidence of the pupil's mathematics that shows most independence, for example from work in other subjects as well as in mathematics lessons
- other evidence about the pupil as a mathematician, for example notes on plans, the pupil's own reflections, your own recollections of classroom interactions, oral answers given during mental starters
- a copy of the assessment guidelines for the level borderline that is your starting point.

Step 1: Making best-fit judgements
Within each assessment focus, draw on the pupil's work and other evidence including what you know about the pupil's mathematics. Use the criteria in the assessment guidelines to decide which level provides the best fit.

Step 2: Work through Ma2 Number
Begin with the assessment guidelines for Ma2 Number.

Look at the criteria within each AF. Decide which level describes the pupil best.

Record the level for each AF in the appropriate box.

Record 'insufficient evidence' (IE) if you do not know enough about this aspect of the pupil's mathematics to make a judgement. This has implications for planning.

If you feel the pupil is operating below the level, check the criteria on the assessment guidelines for the level below.

Step 3: Making an overall level judgement for Ma2 Number
Now make your level decision for Ma2 Number.

- Your AF judgements give an impression of the best-fit level for Ma2.
- Read the complete level descriptions for both levels to confirm your impression of the best-fit level for Ma2

Decide whether the level is Low, Secure or High. Do this by thinking about what the pupil demonstrates:
- how much of the level
- how consistently
- how independently
- in what range of contexts.

Tick the relevant Low, Secure or High box for the level.

Step 4: Repeat the process for Ma3, Ma4 and then Ma1
For the Ma1 judgement, consider how the pupil uses and applies the mathematics of Ma2, Ma3 and Ma4.

Name	Date

Activity name _____

Objective:
Learning outcome:
Comments:

Self-assessment

How well did you do this? _____

_____

_____

_____

What do you still need to do? _____

_____

_____

_____

How easy?

Red ◯

Amber ◯

Green ◯

How do you think you have done?

_____

_____